For Microsoft® Windows® and Macintosh®
Operating Systems

GW00703083

Official
Microsoft®
Internet
Explorer
Book

Bryan Pfaffenberger

PUBLISHED BY
Microsoft Press
A Division of Microsoft Corporation
One Microsoft Way
Redmond, Washington 98052-6399

Copyright © 1996 by Microsoft Corporation

Library of Congress Cataloging-in-Publication Data pending.

Printed and bound in the United States of America.

1 2 3 4 5 6 7 8 9   MLML   1 0 9 8 7 6

Distributed to the book trade in Canada by Macmillan of Canada, a division of Canada Publishing Corporation.

A CIP catalogue record for this book is available from the British Library.

Microsoft Press books are available through booksellers and distributors worldwide. For further information about international editions, contact your local Microsoft Corporation office. Or contact Microsoft Press International directly at fax (206) 936-7329.

AT&T is a registered trademark of American Telephone and Telegraph Company. America Online is a registered trademark of America Online, Inc. Apple, Macintosh, Quick-Time, and TrueType are registered trademarks of Apple Computer, Inc. CompuServe is a registered trademark of Compu-Serve, Inc. Intel is a registered trademark of Intel Corporation. IBM is a registered trademark of International Business Machines Corporation. Macromedia is a registered trademark of Macromedia, Inc. Cinemania, Microsoft, MS-DOS, PowerPoint, and Windows are registered trademarks and Active-Movie, ActiveX, MSN and NetMeeting, are trademarks of Microsoft Corporation. Netscape is a trademark of Netscape Communications Corporation. Silicon Graphics is a registered trademark of Silicon Graphics, Inc. Sun is a registered trademark of Sun Microsystems, Inc. UNIX is a registered trademark in the United States and other countries, licensed exclusively through X/Open Company, Ltd. All other trademarks and service marks are the property of their respective owners.

Acquisitions Editor: David Clark
Project Editor: Ron Lamb
Technical Editor: Rosyln Lutsch

For Suzanne, always

Acknowledgments

Writing a book such as this one isn't a solitary effort. On this project, I've been very fortunate to work with some of the best editorial and production people in the business. I'd like to thank everyone who played a role in bringing this book to you. Special thanks are due to the following: my literary agent, Carole McClendon; acquisitions editor David Clark; managing editors Richard Gold and Kim Field; project editor Ron Lamb; technical editor Roslyn Lutsch; designer Kim Eggleston; composition supervisor Laurie Dawson; supervising composition technician Jim Kramer; compositors Barbara Remmele, Barbara Runyan, Abby Hall, Linda Robinson, Jeff Brendecke, Sandra Haynes, Sue Prettyman, Paul Vautier, and Candace Gearhart; graphic artist Travis Beaven; proofreaders/copy editors Devon Musgrave, Richard Carey, Ronald Drummond, Paula Thurman, Patrick Forgette, Cheryl Penner, and Roger LeBlanc; proofreader/copy editor manager Brenda Morris; traffic coordinator Wendy Zucker; and traffic assistant Wendy Sharp. Just because book cover designers are often unsung heroes, I'd like to give special thanks to Greg Erickson for this book's cool cover. Very, very special thanks are due to the Internet Explorer team.

Table of Contents

PART

1

Getting Started with the Internet

PART

II

Using Internet Explorer

PART III

Surfing the World Wide Web

PART IV

Exploring the Internet

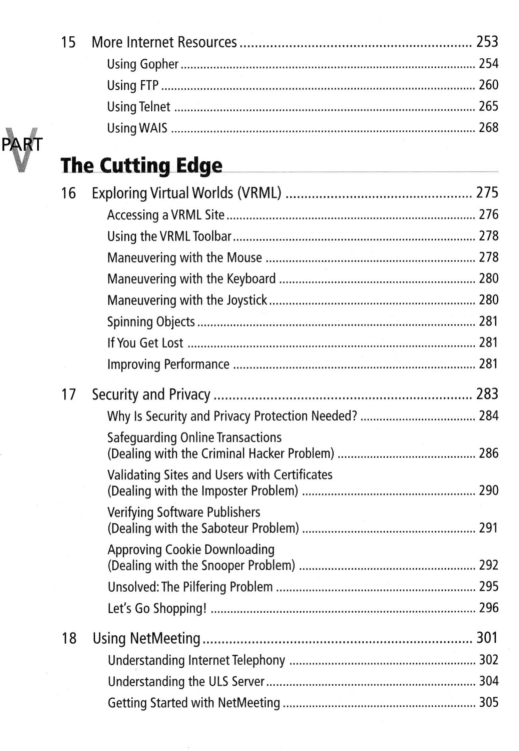

PART V

The Cutting Edge

Introduction

The Internet. It's the latest communication medium to join the telephone, the radio, and the television as a near necessity in homes and offices. It's growing and developing at an amazing rate. (A prominent sign at one of Silicon Valley's leading World Wide Web design studios says, "One Web year = 2.5 calendrical months.") Around the world, millions of people are concluding that the Internet and its tools—including the World Wide Web, Internet electronic mail (e-mail), Usenet discussion groups, and more—are close to indispensable for career and professional development, lifelong learning, and just plain fun. The question now isn't whether it's worthwhile, but whether you'll be left behind.

If you're planning to join the swelling ranks of Internet users right now, or if you're looking for the best Internet software you can find, you're in luck. As part of a major push to include the Internet in its overall business strategy, Microsoft Corporation has released what is currently the most technically advanced package of Internet software—Internet Explorer version 3 and its add-in programs, including Internet Mail and News, Microsoft Comic Chat, and Microsoft NetMeeting.

Don't let the "technically advanced" part scare you off; truly advanced technology not only does amazing things, but it's easy to use. With Internet Explorer, you can quickly learn how to browse the exciting resources of the World Wide Web—and what's more, the entire Internet lies at your fingertips. Remember: Internet Explorer and its add-in programs (Internet Mail and News, Microsoft Comic Chat, and Microsoft NetMeeting) are very easy to use, but their ease of use deceptively masks their stunning, underlying power. After you've learned to use these programs, you'll possess skills and knowledge that put you at the cutting edge of Internet mastery. You'll explore three-dimensional worlds, share applications with other Internet users in real-time conferencing, engage in real-time chats with people from all over the world, and much more. Learning how to use this remarkable software propels you to the highest ranks of Internet mastery.

That's the aim of this book: to make you an absolute, flat-out master of Internet Explorer and the Internet, and to do so with the minimum investment of your time. The *Official Microsoft Internet Explorer Book* is based on a simple premise: With these powerful new Internet tools, anyone who can use a computer can quickly join the ranks of seasoned, virtuoso Internet users.

In concise, clear language, this book shows you how to develop these skills by taking one step at a time, building your skills as you go. Along the way, you'll learn the tips, tricks, and strategies that enable experienced Internet users to transform the Internet from a plaything into a tool of immense personal and professional value.

The Internet Explorer Family

Key ingredients of the Internet's success: You can access the Internet using almost any kind of computer, and you can exchange data (*sans* hassles) with people who use a type of computer that differs from yours. To provide a comprehensive solution for personal and professional Internet usage, Microsoft offers versions of Internet Explorer for computers running Macintosh System 7.0.1, Microsoft Windows 95, Microsoft Windows NT 4.0, and Microsoft Windows 3.1 operating systems.

🌐 **Internet Explorer version 3 for Windows 95 and Windows NT.** This is the flagship version of Internet Explorer, the most technically advanced browser available today. Building on the features of Internet Explorer version 2 for Windows 95, version 3 introduces features that give Web designers the ability to create a new generation of beautifully designed Web documents that use fonts, borderless frames, and colorful tables. In addition, version 3's ActiveX technology enables designers to incorporate active content into Web presentations, including movies and animations that appear alongside the text you're reading. With Internet Explorer version 3, the Web comes alive with professional design and engaging multimedia. And you won't be shut out when you encounter Web content developed for Netscape Navigator: version 3 includes the most technically advanced and efficient support for

Java programs, as well as support for Netscape plug-in programs (programs that extend Netscape Navigator's ability to deal with multimedia data).

🌐 **Internet Explorer version 2 for the Macintosh.** Incorporating all the features of Internet Explorer version 2 for Windows 95, the Mac OS version of Internet Explorer adds support for Netscape plug-ins and can deal with most of the video and sound formats you'll encounter while browsing the Web.

🌐 **Internet Explorer version 2 for Windows 3.1.** Like the Mac OS version of Internet Explorer, the Windows 3.1 version incorporates all the features of Internet Explorer version 2 for Windows 95.

This book features Internet Explorer version 3 for Windows 95 and Windows NT and fully covers the programs developed to work with Internet Explorer, including Internet Mail and News, Microsoft Comic Chat, and Microsoft NetMeeting. In addition, you'll find coverage of Internet Explorer version 3's advanced support for Web multimedia (thanks to ActiveMovie, Microsoft's new generation of video and audio support), three-dimensional Web presentations with VRML, Java programs and the use of Netscape plug-ins, and much more. Macintosh and Windows 3.1 versions of Internet Explorer are covered briefly in Appendix B.

How This Book Is Organized

This book is designed to transform you from a total Internet beginner into a master of all that you wish to take from the Internet's many riches. You'll learn how to comb the Web for valuable information, how to send and receive electronic mail, how to meet people on the Internet, and even how to work collaboratively using real-time audio teleconferencing. Just how far you go is up to you, and you can take it one step at a time. This book assumes only that you've installed Windows 95 or Windows NT on your computer and that you've learned the basics of using Windows.

Part I: Getting Started with the Internet

Part I of the *Official Microsoft Internet Explorer Book* is designed to get you started with the Internet, and with Internet Explorer, as quickly as possible.

🌐 You'll find a plain-English introduction to the Internet in Chapter 1.

- If you've installed Internet Explorer, you can get started quickly in Chapter 2. This chapter concisely introduces the most important features of Internet Explorer.

- Chapter 3 serves as your guide to the riches of the World Wide Web. If you've never surfed the Web before, this chapter will show you why the Web is described as the most important innovation in mass media since the invention of television.

Part II: Using Internet Explorer

In Part II, this book focuses on Internet Explorer itself. Its aim: to give you complete mastery of this program's exciting and useful features.

- In Chapter 4, you'll take a closer look at Internet Explorer's screen and learn what all the little icons and buttons do. Along the way, you'll learn lots of tricks that will enable you to increase your enjoyment and practical use of the Internet.

- Chapter 5 fully covers Internet Explorer's advanced multimedia capabilities, including ActiveMovie. You'll learn how easy it is to listen to sounds, view movies and animations, explore the new world of ActiveX content, run Java programs, and use Netscape plug-ins.

- Run across something you'd like to see again? Chapter 6 shows you how to find and download shareware and freeware programs, how to create shortcuts, and how to organize all those favorite sites you've been saving. Plus, you'll learn how to save and print Web documents and graphics.

- Chapter 7 reveals the tricks you can use to squeeze the maximum performance from Internet Explorer.

- In Chapter 8, you'll learn all the nifty ways you can personalize and customize Internet Explorer. An example: Customize the start page so that you see your favorite news, stock prices, and comic strips (including Dilbert) every time you start the program.

Part III: Surfing the World Wide Web

By now, you've learned the basics of Internet exploration and you've mastered Internet Explorer. With this knowledge under your belt, you're ready to master the World Wide Web.

Web browsers such as Internet Explorer are easy to use. Even so, experienced Web surfers have learned tricks that make Web surfing more enjoyable and more productive. You'll learn them in Chapter 9.

With more than 55 million resources on the Web, finding the information you want can be challenging. In Chapter 10, you'll learn the same strategies professional information specialists use when they're hunting for information on the Web.

In Chapter 11, you'll learn what to do when something goes wrong during your Web explorations, such as encountering a "404—Document Not Found" or "403—Forbidden" error message.

Part IV: Exploring the Internet

Internet Explorer and its add-in programs provide access to all the Internet's riches. Now that you've mastered the Web, it's time to turn your attention to additional ways you can use the Internet.

Many Internet users believe electronic mail to be the most useful and valuable of all Internet tools. In Chapter 12, you'll learn how to use Internet Mail, an elegant and superfast Internet e-mail application that's part of the Internet Explorer package.

Usenet spans the gamut from invaluable to ridiculous, but there's no denying its vitality. Every day, hundreds of thousands of people contribute the equivalent of more than 80,000 pages of text to more than 15,000 topically named discussion groups. In Chapter 13, you'll learn how you can join the hue and cry—and what's more, how you can make practical use of it.

The Internet doesn't have to be deadly serious, and there's no better example of this than Microsoft Comic Chat, the subject of Chapter 14. This deliciously fun program formats an Internet Relay Chat (IRC) session as an ongoing comic strip in which you can choose your own character and its emotion.

In Chapter 15, you'll learn how you can use Internet Explorer to harvest the still-impressive resources of the "old" Internet (pre-1995), including Gopher menus, Veronica searches, Telnet sessions on mainframe computers, FTP file archives, Archie software searches, and WAIS database searches.

Part V: The Cutting Edge

Where's the Web headed? New technologies are pushing the envelope, showing us where the Web's going to be a couple of years down the road—and not coincidentally, what the mass information systems of the 21st century might look like. One of the compelling attractions of Internet Explorer is that you can get a taste of these technologies right now.

🌐   In Chapter 16, you'll learn how to use Internet Explorer's VRML Support to explore three-dimensional worlds created with the Virtual Reality Modeling Language (VRML).

🌐   Chapter 17 fully introduces secure online shopping, which might be poised for a takeoff. In plain English, you'll learn just what's at risk when you shop on line, and you'll also learn why the Web will soon become a much safer way to shop than ordering by mail or telephone. In addition, you'll find a full discussion of the Internet Explorer features that can protect your privacy while you're on line.

🌐   Chapter 18 discusses the most advanced software included with Internet Explorer—Microsoft NetMeeting. With NetMeeting, you can place free long-distance audio calls to other Internet users, but NetMeeting is much more than a tool for Internet telephony. NetMeeting enables you to start a Windows application and share its control with multiple conferees, even if they're separated by transcontinental or intercontinental distances. In a shared application workspace, you can collaboratively create documents, run presentations, play with spreadsheet numbers—whatever you'd like.

The Appendixes

Appendix A shows you how to connect to the Internet with Get On The Internet, the new Internet connection wizard that comes preconfigured with some great connectivity deals. Appendix A also shows you how to install Internet Explorer and all the software you'll find on this book's CD-ROM disc, including a bevy of ActiveX controls that will make Explorer come alive.

In Appendix B, you'll find an explanation of how the Windows 3.1 and Mac OS versions of Internet Explorer differ from the flagship version discussed in this book, Internet Explorer version 3 for Windows 95 and Windows NT.

From Here

- 🌐 To learn how to get connected to the Internet or to install Internet Explorer, begin with Appendix A.

- 🌐 Does it sound like classical Greek when people start talking about the Internet? Flip to Chapter 1 for some plain English.

- 🌐 Ready for your first surf? Test the waters in Chapter 2.

- 🌐 If you've already surfed a bit, Chapter 3 provides a guide to the Web that unlocks its sometimes hidden treasures and practical uses.

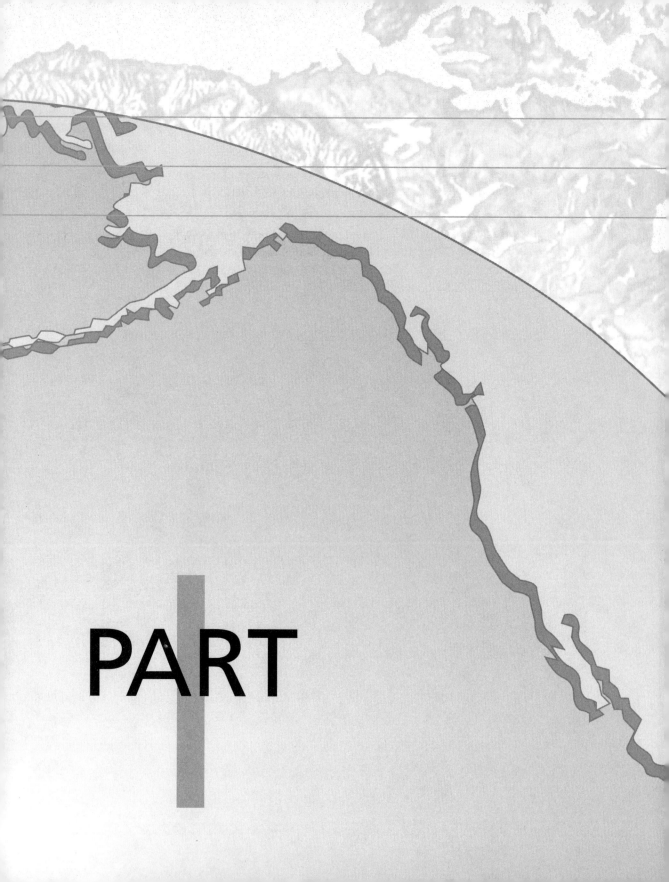

PART

Getting Started with the Internet

CHAPTER 1

Introducing
the Internet

The Internet is a wide-area network (WAN) that's capable of linking millions—potentially billions—of computers. It spans the globe, with servers on every continent.

You can think of the Internet as something like the international telephone system, except that it connects computers instead of phones. No one country or organization owns the whole thing, but there's a set of international standards that enables all of its pieces to hook up and work as if it were one *huge* network. When you connect to the Internet, your computer becomes capable of establishing contact with any of more than ten million Internet-connected computers worldwide—and by the time you read this, the number of linked computers may well have doubled.

Why is the Internet growing so fast? Because people find it so useful and fun. After connecting to the Internet and learning how to use it, you experience an almost unbelievable expansion of your computer system's capabilities. You're able to access the resources on other computers (including more than 150,000 free or shareware computer programs, 30 million documents covering every conceivable field of knowledge and artistic expression, the full text of major national newspapers, and more—much more). You'll be in touch with more than 50 million people worldwide who have electronic mail addresses, including old friends, professional colleagues, and pen pals far and wide. Few people who have worked with the Internet would willingly surrender their connection.

If you're new to the Internet, you're naturally wondering what it's all about—and how it differs from online services such as CompuServe and the Microsoft Network (MSN). This chapter provides a nontechnical introduction to the Internet, so it's a good place to start if you need these questions answered. If you're the plunge-right-in type and you prefer to get started right away with Internet Explorer, turn to Chapter 2.

The Internet: Useful and Fun

Is the Internet *really* useful? The answers may be as varied as the people who use it:

- 🌐 Adam, 24, tracks his mutual fund portfolio using NETworth, a Web site specializing in mutual funds (http://networth.galt.com/). Using NETworth's Mutual Funds Market Manager, shown in Figure 1-1, Adam can quickly determine which funds have performed the best over the past three years. He tracks his holdings' performance using NETworth's online portfolio manager.

- 🌐 Claire, 57, used the Internet to price her used car when she sold it. She also used the Internet to research new cars, new car prices, and owner satisfaction. She found an Internet-based buying service that enabled her to buy her new car at 3 percent above invoice from a local dealer, with none of the idiotic games or haggling that normally go along with such transactions. You'll find this kind of information, and more, at Edmund's Automotive Buyer's Guides on the World Wide Web (http://www.edmunds.com/).

Julia, 15, wouldn't think of writing an English or history paper without researching it on the Internet. A recent assignment concerned the Battle of Britain, in which the Royal Air Force fended off a full frontal attack by the Luftwaffe in the opening years of World War II. Julia located a fascinating Web document that casts light on the British victory: Unlike the Germans, the British fully understood the strategic importance of radar. Their coastal radar defense shield enabled the RAF, outnumbered two to one, to mobilize their aircraft efficiently.

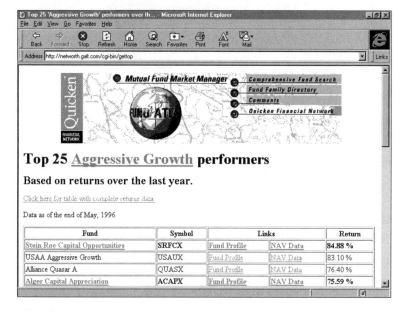

Figure 1-1
Looking for the best-performing mutual funds with NETworth.

And now for the fun part!

Internet Underground Music Archive (IUMA). Imagine being able to download and listen to near-CD-quality recordings from hundreds of the world's weirdest, wildest, and most wonderful bands, spanning the gamut from garage ensembles to some of the recording world's hottest acts. You'll hear industrial,

trance/rave music, reggae, African pop, grunge, and more. See
Figure 1-2 for a taste of the site's great graphics.

Figure 1-2

The Internet Underground Music Archive (IUMA).

- **The Useless Web Pages.** The Web enables just about anyone
  to publish just about anything they want on the Internet, a free-
  dom that seems to have pushed some individuals over the edge
  into high ridiculousness. A few samples: Find Your Name In
  Hawaiian, Give Ben Money, and my favorite, the refreshingly
  unrepentant Terri's Shoe Page.

- **The Internet Anagram Server.** You type letters, click the Send
  button, and moments later you see all the words (*anagrams*) that
  can be made from the letters you typed. Anagrams can be very
  diverting, and sometimes they seem, astonishingly, to contain deep
  truths. Here are some words and the results from The Internet Anagram Server (http://www.wordsmith.org/awad-cgibin/anagram/):

Microsoft	= Comfort Is *or* Cost From I
Macintosh	= Isn't Macho *or* Cash I'm Not
World Wide Web	= We Do Wild Brew

A Parent's Guide to the Internet

Is there pornography on the World Wide Web? Yes, and it isn't going to go away, despite recent attempts by the U.S. Congress to criminalize indecent speech on the Internet. Much of this material originates from outside the U.S., where U.S. laws don't apply. Although the press has greatly exaggerated the amount of porn on the Net, parents should be aware that kids might discover objectionable pictures and stories while surfing the Net.

The best remedy lies in parental supervision. Sit down with your kids and show them the good things the Net has to offer. Teach them how to research a homework assignment using tools such as Lycos, and show them sites loaded with fun, educational content (such as The Discovery Channel's award-winning Web presentation). Along the way, they'll learn not only how to use Internet Explorer but they'll also learn from you—specifically, how you acquire and analyze information. These are indispensable skills in today's society.

New In Version 3: Thanks to Internet Explorer's new Ratings options, you can set up the program so that it won't access sites containing offensive language, nudity, sex, or violence. A supervisor password enables you to adjust these settings the way you want; your kids can't change them. For sites that aren't rated, Internet Explorer can consult an independent rating bureau before allowing access to them. Optionally, you can prevent Internet Explorer from accessing unrated sites, enabling you to let your kids surf without supervision. You'll find full coverage of this important new feature in Chapter 9, "Surfing Tips and Tricks."

Understanding the Internet

You've been hearing plenty about the Internet—in newspapers and even on talk shows. But what is it?

It's About Connectivity

Chances are you think of the Internet as a physical network—big cables carrying tons of computer data. That's part of the Internet, but it's not the essence. At its heart, the Internet isn't a physical thing (wires, cables, and computers) like the *local area networks* (*LANs*) you may have seen at work. Rather, it's a set of standards (called *protocols*) that allows computers of any

CHAPTER 1

brand or model to connect with each other and to exchange data over just about any kind of wiring, and even wireless connections such as satellite uplinks and microwave relays.

These standards are called the *Internet protocols.* (In computer-speak, a *protocol* is simply an accepted standard that enables two or more computers to communicate.) They're also called the *TCP/IP protocols,* after the two most important standards—the Transmission Control Protocol (TCP) and the Internet Protocol (IP).

The most amazing characteristic of the Internet is that the Internet protocols enable all kinds of computers to link and exchange data and even control each other. After you connect your computer to the Internet, you'll be able to access and use computer resources—including documents, sounds, videos, animations, and graphics—that might be stored on virtually any kind of computer system. You'll exchange e-mail with Macintosh users, download files from UNIX systems, and even search databases on cranky old IBM mainframes dating from the lower Paleolithic of the computer age. Actually, you won't even know, most of the time, what kind of computer you're accessing. It might seem to you as if your computer desktop expands in all directions, almost infinitely.

At the top end of the pyramid, the national and international service providers—the AT&Ts, MCIs, and Sprints of the world—are adding data transmission capacity like crazy, trying to keep up with the deluge of new data. With each passing day, the Internet's infrastructure expands and is paid for—and the bigger it gets, the more valuable it becomes.

Don't look for Internet Central, an organization or a big computer that ties the whole Internet together. It doesn't exist, any more than there's a center of the world telephone system. Nobody has to get permission to expand the Internet—they just pay a connection fee, which the existing service uses to back up capacity. In this sense, the Internet's like a chain letter. You could extend the Internet yourself by running a 56,000 bit-per-second conditioned phone line out to your hometown, selling a bunch of subscriptions, getting a registered address ($50), and purchasing a connection from a regional service provider downtown.

Decentralization is the downside of the Internet—there's no central agency (beyond the not-for-profit organization that registers Internet addresses). Such an agency could organize all the available content so that information is easier to find. As it is right now, getting on the Internet is somewhat like getting onto the L.A. freeway system without a map: Roads extend like spaghetti in all directions, and it's easy to get lost. In this area, online services, such as The Microsoft Network and CompuServe, have the edge. (That's why accessing the Internet through an online service is a popular option—you get a well-organized home base, so to speak, from which you can begin to explore the wild reaches of the Net.)

But decentralization has its plusses, too. On the Internet, you don't need to get permission from anyone to publish content—and you don't have to pay fees, either, beyond basic connection and disk storage fees. You can have your say on electronic mail, mailing lists, and Usenet right away. With the requisite technical knowledge and access to a server, just about anyone can make content available on the Web, too. In this sense, the Internet is the most democratic mass medium ever devised. In the words of a U.S. judge who recently overturned a Congressional measure that would have sharply restricted free speech on the Internet, it's a "never-ending world conversation."

How the Internet Protocols Work

If you're interested in the technical side of how the Internet protocols work, here's a quick and relatively painless explanation. The first thing you need to know is that every Internet-connected computer has a unique address (called *Internet address, IP address,* or just *address),* just as every house and apartment on your street does. Everything that happens on the Internet boils down to one computer flinging data out that's addressed to another Internet-connected computer.

To send data over the Internet, an Internet computer chops up the data into segments, called *packets.* Each packet has a *header,* which is like the address on an envelope—it indicates where the packet is supposed to be sent. Along the way, computer devices called *routers* examine each packet and send it along a pathway, called a *route,* to the next router. If one route is down, the router chooses another. Eventually, the packet reaches its destination. The receiving computer reassembles the packets into data. If any packets are missing, the receiving computer requests a retransmission.

You'll see the Internet working when you use Internet Explorer. As you'll learn later in this chapter, you access Web documents by clicking an underlined word or phrase on your screen. At the bottom of the screen, you'll see a status bar that tells you what's going on. First, you'll see a message that your computer is trying to contact the distant computer that contains the Web document. Once the connection is made, the distant computer begins sending the packets. As they are received, your computer transforms the packets into a file, which is temporarily stored on your hard disk, and you see the document emerge on your screen.

CHAPTER 1

Where Did the Internet Come From?

The Internet is a spin-off of U.S. defense research. In the late 1960s, computer networks depended on a vulnerable central computer system. The U.S. Department of Defense Advanced Research Projects Agency (ARPA) funded early development of a decentralized computer network, one that could keep on transferring data even if some parts of it were knocked out. The early-to mid-1970s test bed network, ARPANET, enabled researchers to develop the TCP/IP protocols.

Initially, ARPANET linked researchers at a few universities and defense research institutes. They found it enormously valuable as a means for professional collaboration and data exchange. As more universities clamored for ARPANET connections, ARPANET was split into two sections, NSFNET (a civilian network) and MILNET (a military network). Under the administration of the U.S. National Science Foundation, its namesake, NSFNET grew steadily throughout the 1980s, sending branches into Europe and Asia. Although NSFNET was not the only network that used TCP/IP protocols, it soon became known as *the* Internet because it was the biggest and most impressive of them all. Still, it was mainly a college and university network in those days. (The Internet still has something of an academic air about it, but it's not as pronounced as it used to be.) Pushing the Internet's growth out from the NSFNET's continent-spanning cables were a host of regional service providers, who extended Internet connectivity throughout the U.S. and much of Europe and Asia.

The big news in the 1990s? The Internet's commercialization and explosive growth. Correctly predicting that the Internet was on the way to becoming a valuable public medium, regional service providers created nation-spanning transmission lines free of NSF's restrictions. The Internet spread beyond colleges and universities, and it caught the public's imagination. In 1994, the National Center for Supercomputing Applications (NCSA), an Illinois-based computer science think tank, released Mosaic, a program that hid all the complexity of the Internet and made it easy to access rich, multimedia data. Since then, it's been Katy by the gate. Predicted to reach 35 percent of U.S. households by the year 2000, the Internet is well on its way to becoming a new mass communications medium, joining the ranks of the telephone, radio, broadcast TV, and cable television.

How Does the Internet Differ from Online Services?

An online service, such as The Microsoft Network (MSN), America Online, or CompuServe, enables computer users to subscribe to a centralized service. Each service distributes proprietary software (programs that work only with that service and no other), which enables users to connect easily. This software also organizes all the services' content in a logical way. Available on these services, typically, are thousands of downloadable computer programs, stock quotes, discussion groups, the full text of major national newspapers, and much more.

The problem with online services is that they're costly. Unless you choose a pricey, flat rate plan for unlimited access, the clock is ticking away, and you pay by the minute after you've used up your monthly allotment of free hours. When you access premium services, such as real-time stock quotes, there are additional charges. Content providers have to pay fees, too, and they have to convert their data into the service's proprietary format.

The Internet does not offer up-front, centralized organization as online services do, but it's pretty easy to find an *Internet service provider* (*ISP*) who will give you *unlimited* access to the Internet for as little as $19.95 per month. You don't have to worry about completing your work quickly to keep costs down, and you're free to explore without running up a huge monthly bill.

Content providers are moving to the Internet, too. Rather than paying big fees to online services, they often find that it is cheaper to make content available on the Internet. To attract visitors, they typically make a considerable amount of valuable content available for free, in the hope that they can entice some users to subscribe to fee-based services. Also, they sell advertising, often carried in an inch-high horizontal panel, as shown in Figure 1-2 on page 8. In part, this explains why there is so much valuable information available on the Internet at no charge.

But don't count online services out. Right now, they're reconfiguring themselves as value-added Internet service providers. They still offer all their proven advantages: easy first-time connection, the best online chat services around, and a well-planned, central gateway to all the content they offer. And now they've thrown in free access to all the Internet goodies. Best of all, you can use Internet Explorer as your default browser with most of these services.

What Do You Need to Connect to the Internet?

To connect to the Internet, you need the following:

- **A computer running Microsoft Windows NT, Microsoft Windows 95, or the Macintosh operating system.** Windows NT and Windows 95 include all the software you need in order to access the Internet. You can still access the Internet with Windows 3.1, but it's a more challenging proposition: you must obtain, install, and configure the basic Internet software. If you're using

13

CHAPTER

Windows 3.1, you might want to consider upgrading to Windows 95. Some of the software you need to access the Internet is included in the Mac OS version 7.5; you'll find the rest in the Apple Internet connection kit, available from Apple.

- **A 14.4 or 28.8 Kbps modem.** A *modem* enables your computer to send and receive data via a telephone line. Modems are rated by the amount of data they can transmit per second. A 14.4 Kbps modem can transmit 14,400 bits of data per second. That might sound like a lot, but consider that a typical Web page contains about 150,000 bits' worth of pictures and text. You'll be happier with a 28.8 Kbps modem. Available in some areas are ISDN (Integrated Service Digital Network) connections, offering speeds up 64 Kbps, but special hardware is required. Cable companies are gearing up to offer Internet services, too, and they're talking about speeds in the 10 to 40 *million* bit-per-second range.

- **Internet Explorer.** As you'll see in the next section of this chapter, "Tools for Internet Communication," Internet Explorer is the only program you need to access the Internet. It includes access to the World Wide Web, electronic mail, Usenet discussion groups, and much more.

- **A subscription with an Internet service provider (ISP) or an online service that provides Internet access.** The choice is yours: Pay extra for the convenience of easy installation and a well-organized, central gateway (online services), or get an unlimited-access subscription from an Internet service provider. For more information, see Appendix A.

TIP

In many households with new Internet connections, TV usage goes down as Internet usage goes up. This is good news for national literacy levels but bad news for people trying to reach you on the family phone—it's going to be tied up for hours. Many homes are already wired for two phone lines, so you might think about getting a second line so that only one of them's tied up by the computer.

Tools for Internet Communication

The Internet protocols establish the general basis for sending and receiving data across the Internet. Additional standards define just how specific types of data should be sent and received. Here's a quick overview of the most popular standards and the type of data they handle:

- **World Wide Web.** This is the tool that makes the Internet easy to use. Hiding all the complexity of locating and connecting to distant Internet computers, the Web makes using the Internet as simple as clicking an underlined word or phrase.

- **Electronic Mail.** By far the most popular of all Internet tools, electronic mail (e-mail for short) enables you to send messages to and receive messages from other people with Internet connections (or links to the Internet through other services). An estimated 50 million people worldwide have e-mail addresses. E-mail is proving invaluable for everything from keeping in touch with friends and family to networking for career success. With Internet Mail, you can quickly learn to send and receive electronic mail via the Internet. You learn how to use Internet Mail in Chapter 12.

- **Mailing Lists.** After you subscribe to a mailing list, your e-mail messages to the list are automatically duplicated and sent to everyone on the list. For people who share an interest, mailing lists provide a valuable way to share perspectives, information, and resources. There are thousands of publicly accessible mailing lists, and subscribing to them is easy. For information on accessing Internet mailing lists with Internet Mail, see Chapter 12.

- **Usenet.** Offering more than 20,000 topically named discussion groups, Usenet participants contribute more than 80,000 pages of text per day, touching on every conceivable subject. You can read others' contributions and contribute your own two cents worth. Search services comb through the estimated three million current articles to pinpoint the ones containing information of special interest to you. In Chapter 13, you learn how to use Internet News to access Usenet newsgroups.

- **Internet Relay Chat (IRC).** With IRC, you can carry on real-time text-based conversations with other Internet users concerning thousands of subjects. IRC servers typically offer hundreds of user-created channels, which resemble the chat rooms that are so popular among users of online services. In Chapter 14, you learn how to use Microsoft Comic Chat, an IRC program that formats your ongoing IRC conversations as a comic strip.

CHAPTER 1

- ❂ **Gopher.** Developed from university campus information systems, Gopher enables organizations to make information available via easy-to-use menus. The only Internet tool to suffer decreased usage of late, Gopher is still around, but the World Wide Web provides a much better way to make information publicly available. For more information on Gopher, including how to access Gopher menus with Internet Explorer, see Chapter 15.

- ❂ **Telnet.** Some computers are designed in a way that does not permit them to connect to the Internet directly, but they still contain valuable resources. Telnet enables you to access these resources using a text-based interface. A major Telnet goodie: a free Colorado-based service that enables you to search an enormous database of over 17,000 periodicals. For more information on Telnet, see Chapter 15.

- ❂ **File Transfer.** You can transfer computer files (programs or documents) between Internet-linked computers. Error-checking software makes sure the files arrive intact. Companies that formerly had to send computer disks and data via pricey express services or via fee-based private networks can now send them almost instantly via the Internet, for no more than the basic cost of their Internet connectivity. Using a service called *anonymous FTP,* you can access publicly accessible file archives containing upwards of 150,000 free or shareware computer programs. For more information on FTP, including how to access anonymous FTP servers with Internet Explorer, see Chapter 15.

- ❂ **Databases.** A search service called WAIS (short for Wide Area Information Server) enables companies and organizations to make huge amounts of information available to searchers using the Internet. Like Gopher, this service is declining in popularity thanks to the World Wide Web, which provides an easier interface for searching purposes, but it still contains some valuable information. Chapter 15 shows how you can use Internet Explorer to access WAIS resources.

- ❂ **Internet Telephony.** The newest tool on the Internet scene, Internet telephony, involves the use of the Internet for making telephone calls—and the only charge is what you're paying for your Internet connection. In Chapter 18, you learn how to place calls on the Internet using Microsoft NetMeeting, an Internet telephony tool that also offers advanced teleconferencing capabilities.

PART

There's just one other thing you should know about Internet tools. They're all based on what computer people call a *client-server architecture*. In computing, the term *client* means something different than it does in everyday life. An Internet client is a software tool—a program—that knows how to go out on the Internet in search of a certain type of data. *Servers* are programs that make data available. Servers wait patiently until a client contacts them, requesting some specific information. The server provides this information, and the client makes it available to the user. On the World Wide Web, clients are called *browsers,* because they enable you to browse Internet resources by clicking underlined words or phrases.

Internet Explorer May Be the Only Internet Tool You'll Need

Just a year or two ago, most Internet users had to learn several client programs to use the Internet: an electronic mail program, a Usenet newsreader, a file transfer program, a Gopher newsreader, and a Web browser. Now there's a trend to make all these tools available in one program, such as Internet Explorer.

Internet Explorer is much more than a Web browser. When used with Internet Mail and News, Comic Chat, and NetMeeting, it's a complete tool for accessing all the riches of the Internet. With Internet Explorer, you can send and receive electronic mail, join mailing lists, participate in Usenet newsgroups, download files from file archives, access Telnet sessions, browse Gopher resources, join Internet Relay Chat conversations, and use the Internet as a long-distance teleconferencing tool.

From Here

This is how each chapter of this book ends—with suggestions for where to turn from here.

- 🌐 If you haven't already installed Internet Explorer, flip to Appendix A.
- 🌐 Is Internet Explorer already installed? Flip to Chapter 2 for a Quick Start!

CHAPTER 1

Internet Explorer Quick Start

With most computer programs, about 20 percent of the features enable you to do about 80 percent of what you want to accomplish. By learning the most useful 20 percent of the program, you know enough to use it profitably day-to-day. You can put off learning the rest until the need arises.

CHAPTER 2

This chapter teaches enough basics so that, after reading it, you'll be able to make good use of the Web. You'll explore The Microsoft Network's Internet Start Page, which you'll see every time you start Internet Explorer. From this page, you'll learn how you can take a quick Internet tutorial and how to begin your first Web "surfing" session. ("Surfing" is a term coined to describe the fun experience of exploring the World Wide Web.) Along the way, you'll learn the most important Internet Explorer commands and techniques. Do you see lots of ads on TV (as well as in magazines and newspapers) listing those odd-looking Web addresses? This chapter shows you how to access Web sites by typing their addresses. If you encounter something cool on your journey, you'll learn how to make it a favorite so that you can return to it quickly, anytime you want. And if you're having trouble finding the information you're after, you'll learn how to search the Web using easy-to-use search services.

NOTE This chapter assumes that you've installed Internet Explorer and subscribed to the Internet via The Microsoft Network, some other online service, or an independent Internet service provider. See Appendix A if you still need to perform these tasks.

Welcome to the MSN Start Page

When you start Internet Explorer for the first time from MSN, the program automatically displays the Microsoft Network (MSN) Start Page, shown in Figure 2-1. Just what you'll see when you start Internet Explorer depends on how the program has been set up. If you're using the version of Internet Explorer from the companion disc for this book, you'll see the default Internet Explorer home page. If you see something else, type *home.microsoft.com* in the Address box, and press Enter. The program's *start page* is the page that the program automatically displays every time you start it. You also see the MSN Start Page when you click the Home button on Internet Explorer's toolbar.

TIP If you would prefer to view a different page when you start the program, you can set the program to display *any* page on the Web at startup, as explained in Chapter 8, "Personalizing Internet Explorer." But your best bet, also described in Chapter 8, is to customize the MSN Start Page, which is easy to do—and the results are spectacular.

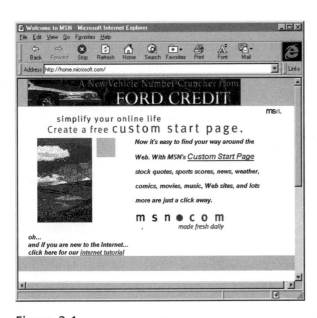

Figure 2-1
The MSN Start Page.

MSN's Start Page doesn't try to organize the whole Internet for you—that's an impossibly big task—but it does provide some useful starting points, including a tutorial. Try it!

Web Sites Are Subject to Change

Web sites grow and evolve constantly. In fact, as you'll learn in Chapter 3, one of the marks of a quality site is that it always has fresh content, drawing you to visit the site over and over. The Web pages shown and described throughout this book may not perfectly match what you see when you visit them, but home pages in particular tend to maintain hyperlinks that serve a constant purpose, even if the surrounding graphics and text look different.

Taking the Internet Tutorial

The Internet Tutorial, accessible from the MSN Start Page, takes only a few minutes. After completing it, you'll know how to move from one document to another on the Web.

To start the tutorial, move your mouse pointer over the words *Internet Tutorial*. You'll notice that the pointer changes to a hand shape.

When the pointer changes to a hand shape, you've positioned it over a *hyperlink*. A hyperlink enables you to jump to another Web document. Also, look at the status bar, way down at the bottom left of the window. You'll see a message: "Shortcut to default.html." The status bar tells you the name of the document to which you're about to jump.

TIP

Remember, if you click something by accident and get lost, you can return to the Start Page quickly by clicking Home. For example, there's a link hidden in the picture on the Start Page. If you click this, you'll see a page explaining how to customize the Start Page. To return to the Start Page, just click Home.

To jump to the Tutorial, click the *left* mouse button. (The right mouse button does lots of important things in Internet Explorer, but you'll learn about that later.) Briefly, the background of the Internet Explorer icon (near the upper right corner of the screen) animates, indicating that the program is looking for the document you requested. Soon you see the first Tutorial page, which provides a roadmap to the whole tutorial, as shown in Figure 2-2. To go to any of the pages in the tutorial, click one of the graphics. To go to the Introduction, for example, click the graphic next to *Introduction*. Try clicking *Introduction*.

When you see the Introduction page, chances are that your screen doesn't have enough space to display the whole page. If it doesn't have enough space, scroll bars appear. You can use the mouse to scroll down to bring additional parts of the document into view. You can do this by clicking the down arrow at the bottom of the scroll bar, dragging the slider, or clicking the scroll bar under the slider. If you prefer to use the keyboard, you can press the PgDn and PgUp keys to scroll the page you're viewing.

At the bottom of the page, you'll notice a button that enables you to go forward. Click this now, and you'll see the next page in the tutorial.

Notice that the text appears before the pictures do. The pictures download separately, and they take a little more time. Until they appear, you see *placeholders*. These show where the pictures will go. In a moment, the pictures appear.

Take a look at the bottom of this page. You'll see two buttons now—a Back button and a Forward button. If you click Back, you'll see the previous page in this presentation. If you click Forward, you'll go to the next page in this presentation.

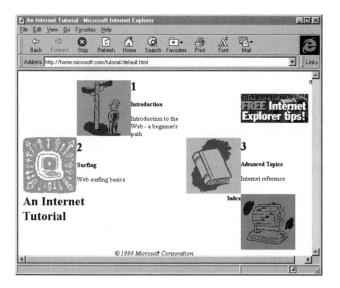

Figure 2-2

First page of the Internet Tutorial.

TIP

When you're viewing a Web presentation that includes navigation aids such as the one at the bottom of the Tutorial page, use these aids instead of the Back or Forward button on the toolbar. The toolbar buttons work in a slightly different way, as you'll see later in this chapter.

Continue working through the Tutorial, if you want. To return to the MSN Start Page at any time, just click Home on the toolbar.

A Few Basic Terms

You'll hear people talking about "Web sites," "Web pages," and "URLs." Here's a quick guide to these basic terms:

 Web site. This is an Internet-connected computer that's running a program called a *Web server*. A Web server makes documents

CHAPTER 2

available to people browsing the Web. A Web site has a unique Internet address that unambiguously identifies its location. Most Web sites contain dozens, hundreds, or perhaps even thousands of Web pages.

- **Web page.** A Web page is a single Web document. In actual length, some are shorter than a page and some are longer—lots longer. Most Web pages average about two screenfuls.

- **URL.** Short for "Uniform Resource Locator," this abbreviation— pronounced "Earl" in some quarters—refers to the unique address that every Web page must have. For simplicity, this book uses the term *address*. Web addresses begin with *http://*. The rest of the address tells the exact location of the document, including the address of the computer where it's stored.

- **Surfing.** Going from Web page to Web page in an exploratory, serendipitous frame of mind. Who knows where you'll wind up? (Hint: If you get lost—and you will—click Home to return to Reason, Light, and the MSN Start Page.)

- **Home page.** People use this phrase in different ways. Basically, it means "home base." In Internet Explorer, you click Home (on the toolbar) to go to the MSN Start Page. This phrase also refers to the welcome page of a Web presentation that includes many linked pages, so you might see a Home icon on somebody's pages. If you click this icon, you see the welcome page, not the MSN Start Page. When somebody says, "I can't wait to put my home page on the Web," what they're talking about is a personal page, which is likely to contain their resume, picture, favorite hobbies and pets, and a few favorite links.

Is It a "Site" or a "Page"?

As you'll quickly discover, people use the terms "site" and "page" more or less synonymously: When somebody says, "Hey, check out this *awesome* site," they're usually referring to a specific Web page or document, not the entire collection of documents that's available on one server. This isn't done just by *newbies*, people new to the Internet, but by seasoned vets, too—and I suspect because "site" sounds more high-tech than "page" or "document." Still, you'll have a better grasp of the Web if you keep the distinction in mind.

Navigation Basics

The easiest way to move around the Web is to click hyperlinks. However, you will sometimes want to use the Back and Forward tools. They're tricky to use, though, until you grasp what they do.

Try this. Click Home, if necessary, to display the MSN Start Page. Click Internet Tutorial to display the first page of the tutorial. Now click Back. You'll see the page you just jumped from—the MSN Start Page. Also, notice that the Forward button is no longer dimmed. If you click Forward now, you'll go the page that you just jumped back from.

A little confusing? It is, at first. It's sort of like trying to ride a bicycle for the first time. After a little practice, it will come naturally. Again, here's what these tools do:

- **Back.** Click Back to see the document from which you just jumped via a hyperlink. If you keep clicking Back, you keep going back in the series of jumps you made in this session. When the Back button dims and becomes unavailable, you're looking at the first document you saw in this session—the Start Page.

- **Forward.** Click Forward to redisplay documents you've gone Back from. If you haven't clicked Back, Forward is dimmed.

Did you notice that, when you clicked Back, pages redisplayed a lot quicker than they did when you first accessed them? That's because Internet Explorer stores recently accessed Web documents on your hard disk. They're stored in a folder called Internet Temporary Documents, which you'll find in the Windows folder. When you return to a recently accessed document, Internet Explorer retrieves the document from your hard disk rather than downloading it from the Internet, which would take more time. For more information on temporary documents, including choosing options for storing them, see Chapter 8, "Personalizing Internet Explorer."

TIP

As noted earlier, the Back and Forward buttons do different things than the navigation aids Web authors often provide to help you navigate through their presentations. You can see this yourself by trying a little experiment. From the contents (opening) page of the Tutorial, click the third lesson—not the second. You'll see the third lesson page. Now click Back on the toolbar. As you can see, Internet Explorer redisplays the Tutorial's opening page, the one you just jumped from. Click Forward, and you see the third lesson again. In sum, the Back and Forward buttons work differently from the navigation aids that are often included in Web presentations.

CHAPTER 2

More Ways to Navigate

If you would like to redisplay a Web page you viewed some time ago, you don't have to click the Back button like mad to get back to it. Try the following:

🌐 From the menu bar, choose Go. On the Go menu, you'll see the last several documents you accessed, as shown in Figure 2-3. You can return to any of these documents by choosing it from the menu or by pressing the number next to the document's name.

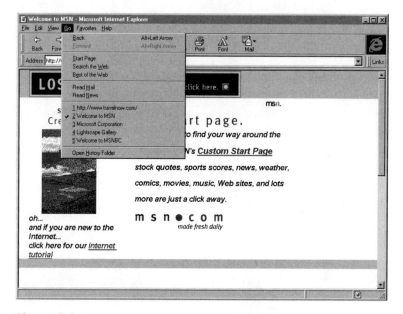

Figure 2-3

Go menu with recently accessed pages.

🌐 If you don't see the document on the Go menu, choose Open History Folder. Internet Explorer displays a new Web page showing all the Web pages you've recently visited, as shown in Figure 2-4. This is a fantastic feature of Internet Explorer, one that isn't as well implemented on any competing product. From this page, you can quickly display any recently visited page just by double-clicking it.

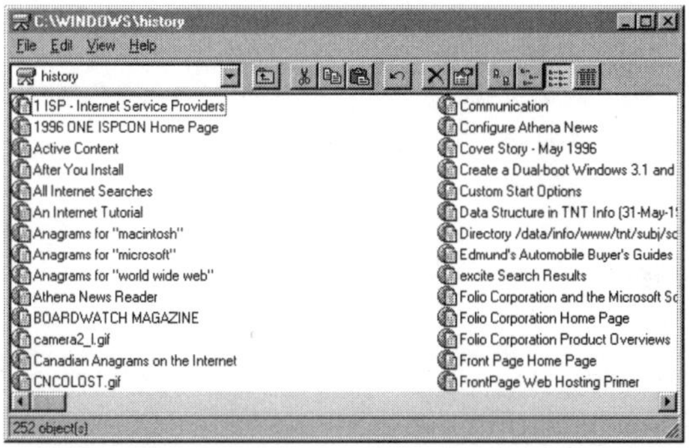

Figure 2-4

Contents of the History folder.

Going to a Web Page
by Typing Its Address

Once word gets around that you're using the Internet, somebody will rattle off a Web address and say, "You've *got* to see this!" To view the page, choose the File Open command, or use the Ctrl + O keyboard shortcut. You'll see the Open dialog box. Note that you don't have to type the *http://* part; Internet Explorer supplies that automatically. Type the address carefully, and click OK.

Try accessing http://www.microsoft.com. In the Open dialog box, you just need to type *www.microsoft.com*. You should see Microsoft's home page, the current version of which is shown in Figure 2-5 on the next page. Note that this page changes practically every day so that Microsoft can bring you the latest.

HELP

It Didn't Work!

You typed the address and pressed OK, but nothing happens. The animation just runs and runs, and nothing happens—until you see an alert box informing you that Internet Explorer couldn't open the site or the document. Chances are you didn't type the address correctly. (If you did type the address correctly, another possibility is that the site is too busy to respond. Try again later.) See the sidebar, "Typing Web Addresses Correctly," on the next page.

CHAPTER 2

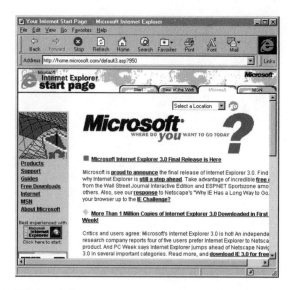

Figure 2-5

Microsoft home page.

Typing Web Addresses Correctly

To avoid errors when you type Web addresses, note the following:

🌐 URLs are case-sensitive, so be sure to copy the capitalization pattern exactly.

🌐 Don't place any spaces within the address.

🌐 Check to make sure you've placed periods and slash marks (/) in the correct places.

🌐 If you grew up with MS-DOS (you poor thing), remember that the slash marks are forward slashes (/), not backward slashes (\).

🌐 Check your typing. You have probably made some tiny, human-forgivable typing mistake that's hardly noticeable— except to computers.

If all else fails, try searching for the site using the search services described in Chapter 10, "Tracking Down Information on the Web."

Branching Off from Today's Links

You know enough now to do some surfing on your own. On the toolbar, click Home to display the start page, and click Links, then click Today's Links. You'll see the nicely done Today's Picks page. Click Best Of The Web on the Links toolbar. You'll find lots of cool links right on this page. If you'd like to see more, just click one of the subjects, such as "Travel and Entertainment" or "Living," as shown in Figure 2-6. (Remember, this page might look different when you visit it.)

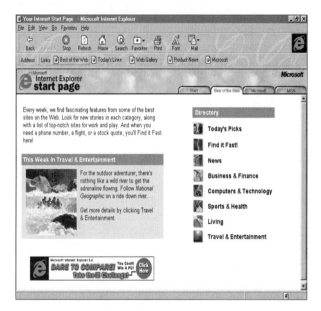

Figure 2-6
Best Of The Web.

Here are some points to keep in mind when you're connecting to a site:

🌐 Most of the Web pages you'll access will start downloading within a few seconds, but it might take a minute or so for all the graphics to download. Because Internet Explorer downloads text first, you can read while the graphics are transferred.

🌐 If you try to access a document and nothing happens for a long time, click the Stop tool and try again later.

CHAPTER 2

⊕ You can get back to Best Of The Web by clicking Back or by choosing Best Of The Web from the Go menu. If you've accessed lots of pages since leaving Best Of The Web, you can get back by choosing Best Of The Web from the History window.

⊕ You don't have to wait until the page downloads completely before you click the next hyperlink. When you click a hyperlink, Internet Explorer stops downloading the current page and begins downloading the one you requested.

What's in a (Domain) Name?

Part of every page's address is a *domain name,* the Internet's name for the computer that houses the document. This name can tell you something about where the document is located. The domain name comes right after the *http://* part, as in http://www.microsoft.com/. The *www.microsoft.com* part is Microsoft's domain name.

It's the last part of the domain name, called the *top-level domain,* that gives you the telltale clues. Here's a list of some of the more common top-level domains you'll encounter:

au	Australia
ca	Canada
com	A U.S. company
de	Germany
edu	A U.S. college or university
fi	Finland
fr	France
gov	A U.S. government agency
org	A U.S. nonprofit organization
se	Sweden
uk	United Kingdom

It's fun to look at top-level domains. In a surfing session, you might have electronically traversed a good part of the globe.

Saving a Favorite

Suppose you've found the ultimate cool Web page, but you don't have the vaguest idea how you got there. Will you be able to return in a subsequent session?

One way to return to a site is to choose it from the History folder, as you've already learned. For those special pages to which you'll return time and again, though, there's a better way: Make it a favorite. After making the page a favorite, you can return to it quickly just by choosing it from the Favorites menu.

To create a favorite, do the following:

1. Display the document.

2. Choose the Favorites Add To Favorites command. You'll see the Add To Favorites dialog box. Internet Explorer proposes the page's title in the Name area.

3. Click the OK button to save the favorite. Internet Explorer creates a shortcut in the Favorites folder, using the document's title as the name. Internet Explorer also adds the document's name to the Favorites menu.

HELP

My Favorites List Is Getting Too Long!

Been adding lots of favorites? Time to organize your Favorites list. You can create categories of favorites, such as "Fun Stuff," "Research-Related Stuff," "Art Sites," or whatever you like, and create submenus that pop up when you click one of these. For the lowdown, see Chapter 8, "Personalizing Internet Explorer."

Adding a Shortcut to the Desktop

Now that you've found the Web site that you'll want to access just about every time you surf the Web, you can create a shortcut to it that will appear on your desktop.

To create a shortcut to a particularly useful Web page:

1. Choose the File Create Shortcut command. If you prefer, click the right mouse button and choose the Create Shortcut command.

You'll see a dialog box informing you that a shortcut to this site will be created on your desktop.

2. Click the OK button.

To access the site in the future, double-click the shortcut icon. If Internet Explorer is running, just drag the shortcut to Internet Explorer's window, and release the mouse button.

To create a shortcut to a link, just drag the link to the desktop.

Looking for Information on a Subject

You've done some serious surfing, and you've seen some cool stuff. What you're wondering right now is whether the Web is anything more than a disconnected set of chance discoveries. You've found that surfing may be fun, but isn't a very efficient way to hunt down information.

Happily, the Web features two kinds of tools that can help you locate information in a particular area. They're called *subject trees* and *search engines*. Chapter 10 returns to subject trees and search engines in more detail. For now, take a quick look and try searching for some information in an area that interests you.

Subject Trees

A subject tree is like the subject catalog in a library. It's called a "tree" because it's organized with "trunks" (categories) and "branches" (subcategories). For example, a major category is "Art," and a subcategory—a branch—is "Impressionism." Within each subcategory there may be additional subcategories, such as Art/Impressionism/Painting.

Subject trees contain only a small fraction of the total number of documents on the Web. For example, Yahoo, one of the most popular subject trees, lists only about 80,000 of the 30 million documents now on the Web. For the most part, these are high-quality pages. Yahoo indexes only those pages that meet its criteria for high-quality content.

You can navigate Yahoo's subject tree manually, but it's quicker to use the site's search tools. The result of a Yahoo search, assuming any matches are found, is a new page that lists the following:

🌐 **Matching Yahoo Categories.** Yahoo subject classifications that match the terms you typed. You can click the classification to see lots of Web pages in this area.

🌐 **Matching Yahoo Sites.** This section lists individual Web pages that match the terms you typed.

To use Yahoo, follow these steps:

1. On the Internet Explorer toolbar, click Search. You'll see the Internet Searches page, shown in Figure 2-7.

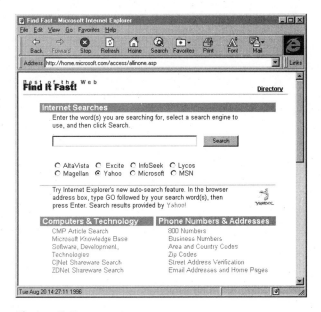

Figure 2-7
Internet Searches page.

2. Underneath the word *Yahoo,* type one or more words that describe what you're looking for. To search for information on mutual funds, for example, type *mutual funds*. With Yahoo, it pays to type fairly general subjects. If you're lucky, Yahoo will have a subject classification that matches what you've typed and you'll find lots of high-quality documents indexed there.

3. Click Search. Internet Explorer sends what you've typed to Yahoo, and in moments you'll see a Yahoo search results page, such as the one shown in Figure 2-8 on the next page.

CHAPTER 2

Figure 2-8
Yahoo search results page.

Note that this page contains hyperlinks. You can jump to any of these documents merely by clicking them. If a document doesn't seem interesting, click the Back button to redisplay the Yahoo search results page. It will stick around for the rest of your session.

Search Engines

Because subject trees index only a small fraction of the total number of available Web documents, you might not find what you're looking for in a subject tree. For this reason, search engines have been created.

Search engines rely on *spiders,* programs that rove the Web hunting for new documents. When one of these programs finds a new document, it reports the document's address (and a little about its content). This information is placed in a database, which you can search.

One of the best search engines is Lycos, which you can access from the Internet Searches page. Currently, Lycos indexes about 30 million Web documents.

TIP

To perform a quick Yahoo search, type *GO* in the Address box, followed by one or more search words, and press Enter.

To use Lycos, follow these steps:

1. On the Internet Explorer toolbar, click Search. You see the Internet Searches page, shown in Figure 2-7 earlier in this chapter.

2. Type several words that describe the subject in which you're interested. Because the Lycos database is so huge, it pays to be very specific here. Suppose, for example, you're looking for the prospectus of the Gabelli fund. Type *Gabelli fund prospectus*.

3. Click OK. You'll see a Lycos Search Results page, such as the one shown in Figure 2-9.

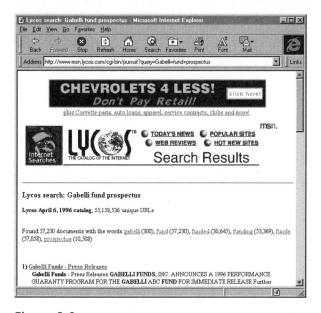

Figure 2-9

The result of a Lycos search.

At the top of the page, you'll see the documents that, according to Lycos' calculations, are most likely to match your interests. Read the descriptions to make sure. When you find a document that looks good, click its link to go to it directly. If you don't see anything good, go down to the bottom of the page and click the link for the next 10 "hits," or matches.

CHAPTER 2

From Here

🌐 In Chapter 3, take a tour of the best of the Web.

🌐 What do the rest of those tools on the toolbar do? Find out in Chapter 4.

🌐 Favorites list clogged with items you've added? Get it organized in Chapter 8.

🌐 Search didn't work out very well? Improve your search tactics in Chapter 10.

🌐 Couldn't access a Web page for some reason? Find out why in Chapter 11.

CHAPTER 3

Exploring the Web

Once you've learned the basics of using Internet Explorer, there's no reason to delay your exploration of the Web. In fact, you've probably already spent some time surfing around (maybe too much time), and you've likely found some cool stuff.

You've also probably found that quality varies. The Web runs the gamut from responsible, professional publishing to hotheaded ranting from the reality-challenged. It's wonderful that almost anyone can afford to publish on the Web, but the medium's inherent democracy means that the diamonds are well buried in dreck.

What's the solution? Get some help to find the best of the Web. To give you the flavor of the excellent material that's out there and to equip you with tools to find more, this chapter introduces you to the many services that guide you to the best sites, judged in a number ways (ranging from content reviews to pure, statistical popularity). And just in case you're wondering what the *worst* of the Web looks like, you'll find a couple of sites that list pages from the other end of the quality spectrum.

HELP

I've been up all night surfing—quick, I need an excuse!

Here are a few excuses I've tried. For some reason, they didn't work very well, but maybe you'll have better luck.

"I just lost track of time—I couldn't *believe* it when I saw the sun come up."

"The Information Superhighway will change society. I must be prepared."

"I realize that finding every Star Trek site on the Web could be seen as a waste of time, but I feel that I am learning highly marketable computer skills."

"A new form of consciousness is emerging, and I want to be part of it."

"It beats watching old movies, doesn't it?"

What Makes a Web Site Great?

You'll have your own ideas about what makes a Web site great after browsing for a while, but really great sites have several or all of these characteristics:

- **Rich content.** Not just a bunch of splashy graphics (which take forever to download).

- **Interactivity.** You can type something into an on-screen form and get a response.

- **Frequently updated, timely information.** The site's content changes frequently, and it's worth visiting again and again.

- **Free, useful goodies.** Downloadable images and software, useful information, and more.

TIP

Like to see Microsoft's cool site picks of the day? Just click Today's Links on the Links toolbar. (To bring this toolbar into view, click Links and drag so that you can see all the buttons.) If today's cool site doesn't interest you, you'll find links to other cool sites, including previous links of the day.

The Top 100

Ready to see the best of what's out there? You'll find several pages on the Web that list picks for the Top 100 pages on the Web. They vary, based on the interests and expertise of the people who put them together. Hyperlinks take you directly to pages that look interesting.

🌐 **MacUser 101 Must-See Sites.** Although this list includes some Mac-specific sites, it's really of general interest to any Web user. The touch here is decidedly artistic and zany (one of the Top 101 Must-See sites is "The Foolproof Guide to Making Any Woman Your Platonic Friend"), but there's some solidly useful stuff, too, including a great page of reference links ("When You've Misplaced Your Library Card").

```
http://www.zdnet.com/macuser/mu_0396/feature/feature1.html
```

🌐 **PC Magazine's Top 100 Sites.** Great links to computer companies and computer resources on the Web, with an emphasis on Windows systems and Windows-compatible computers. You'll also find useful sections on entertainment, news, sports, and reference.

```
http://www.pcmag.com/special/web100/1_atoz.htm
```

🌐 **The Web 100.** User ratings determine the rankings, so here's a great way to find out which pages Web users prefer. You can view them by rank, in groups of ten at a time, or by topic (including arts and entertainment, business and commerce, computers and the Net, education and reference, government and politics, health and medicine, news and information, sports and leisure, science and technology, and other). In the top 10 when the screen shown in Figure 3-1 was captured: Word, the Doonesbury Electronic Town Hall, the Internet Movie Database, *Wall Street Journal* Interactive Edition, and CNN.

```
http://www.web100.com
```

CHAPTER 3

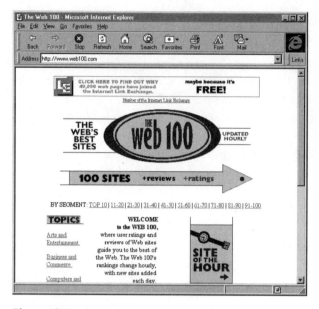

Figure 3-1

The Web 100.

More Ways to Find Great Sites

For lists of more great Web sites, try the following (but remember, sites come and go all the time, and the ones listed here are no exception). As you're typing these Web addresses, remember that they're case-sensitive. If you're having trouble accessing one of these sites, a possible reason is that you typed a lowercase letter where you should have typed a capital letter. Bear in mind, too, that these sites are often very busy, and sometimes the server can't respond. Try again later.

🌐 **c|net's Best of the Web.** Is this the best place to look for great Web sites? Take a look. What you'll find here is a preference for Web presentations with solid content, Web technical savvy, and great design. A recent example: "The Heart: A Virtual Exploration" at http://sln.fi.edu/biosci/.

`http://www.cnet.com/Content/Reviews/Website/`

🌐 **Magellan Stellar Sites.** This site features varying topics each week, and it's well worth visiting. The archives contain dozens of high-quality Web offerings in the arts, business and economics, career and employment, communications, computing, daily living, education, engineering, technology and mathematics, entertainment and pop culture, environment, food and beverages, government and politics, health and medicine, humanities and social sciences, the Internet, kidzone, law and criminal justice, music, news, religion and spirituality, science, sports and recreation, and travel and tourism.

`http://www.mckinley.com/feature.cgi?hot_bd`

🌐 **Point Communications Top Ten.** The top ten sites of the week, based on content, experience, and presentation. The rankings are based on Point's 50-point rating scheme. When you click one of the links, you'll see an in-depth critical review.

`http://point.lycos.com/topsites/`

🌐 **The Seven Wonders of the Web.** A new site is picked every day, seven days a week.

`http://www.penncen.com/7wonders/7wonders.html`

🌐 **WebCrawler Select.** The best sites of the Net, as selected by WebCrawler Select's critical reviewers. Categories include arts and entertainment, business, computers, daily news, education, government and politics, health and medicine, humanities, Internet, life and culture, personal finance, recreation and hobbies, science and technology, sports, and travel.

`http://webcrawler.com/select/`

What's Cool

Apart from the gold and the dreck, there's the *cool*. And what does cool mean? As my Generation X friends say, "If you have to ask, you're never gonna know," but here's a Web-specific definition: A cool Web site seems to capture the spirit of the Web as a new, multimedia communication medium.

Admittedly, "cool" is hard to define. At the Cool Site of the Day (http://cool.infi.net) you'll find a FAQ (short for "Frequently Asked Questions") that employs scientific research in an effort to pin down just what makes certain Web sites cool. According to the FAQ, a site's coolness is attributable to a trace element called "coolium." However, most of the sites that wind up on "what's cool" lists tend to have one or more of these characteristics:

🌐 **Awareness of the potential of the Internet as a new medium.** One of the most popular sites on the Web and frequently named in "what's cool" lists is Word, an online magazine, shown in Figure 3-2. A literary magazine stressing Generation X sensibilities, Word combines text, graphics, animations, and photographs in a full expression of the Web's multimedia possibilities.

`http://www.word.com/index.html`

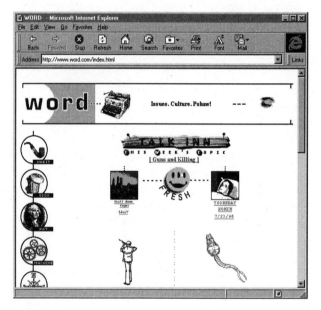

Figure 3-2
Word.

🌐 **Slightly over-the-top humor.** A parody of Word, sort of, and most of all a parody of itself, Suck, shown in Figure 3-3, affects a stridently anticommercial stance in defense of the Internet while at the same time nakedly soliciting advertising. Caustic but tongue-in-cheek ridicule is the order of the day.

`http://www.suck.com`

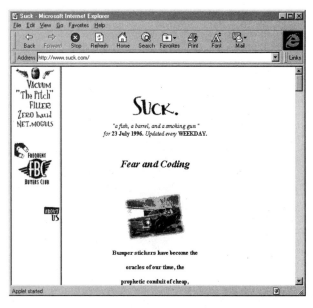

Figure 3-3
Suck.

🌐 **Savvy music stuff.** I wonder how many otherwise obscure bands have become major sellers because of the Internet? Word about music that's unusual, interesting, or hip gets around quickly on the Net. Don't miss the Ultimate Band List, which keeps tabs on the pages—both amateur and record-company sponsored— about bands of all kinds, ranging from the best-known acts to obscure (but up-and-coming) local ensembles.

http://american.recordings.com/wwwofmusic/ubl/ubl.shtml

🌐 **Techno-zaniness.** At last count, there were over one hundred devices connected to the Web, including a talking machine (what you type is spoken out loud), a lava lamp, a CD player, a hot tub, and dozens of live cameras. For a list, see this one:

http://www.yahoo.com/Computers_and_Internet/Internet
/Entertainment/Interesting_Devices_Connected_to_the_Net/

(Type this address all on one line, with no spaces.)

CHAPTER 3

Secret knowledge revealed. As you'll see in the Hidden Mickey page, Disney World's designers embedded Mickey shapes here and there throughout the park, as a joke; here's how to locate them:

```
http://iu.net/tshaw/trs/HiddenMickey.html
```

 Hip graphics. Some of the world's best graphic designers are working on the Web—it's an exciting new medium for them. Currently, there's a preference for 1950s nostalgia graphics (for an example, see the home page of the Internet Underground Music Archive, shown in Figure 3-4).

```
http://www.iuma.com/IUMA-2.0/home.html
```

Figure 3-4

Internet Underground Music Archive (IUMA).

You'll find several sites that offer lists of what's cool:

 Spider's Pick of the Day. This is an interesting list, with lots of diversity—and it's often over the edge.

```
http://gagme.wwa.com/~boba/pick.html
```

⊕ **Cool Site of the Year.** From the folks who bring you the Cool Site of the Day, here's the Cool Site of the Year, along with some runners-up.

```
http://cool.infi.net/csoty.html
```

⊕ **Netscape's What's Cool.** This page should be titled "What's cool in corporate America," but it's well worth a visit.

```
http://home.netscape.com/home/whats-cool.html
```

⊕ **Coolest on the Web.** If your preference is for sites with hip graphics and great design, check out this list of the very coolest of the Web.

```
http://www.projectcool.com/coolest/
```

What's Hot

This isn't exactly the opposite of what's cool: *hot* sites are the most popular, and some of them are cool, too. You can find out what's hot by checking out the following:

⊕ **100 Hot Games.** The hottest 100 sites for games of all kinds (including computer games, video games, chess, cards, role-playing, and more), based on Web traffic statistics.

```
http://www.100hot.com/games/
```

⊕ **100 Hot Web Sites.** This list is compiled objectively, using Web traffic statistics. The list doesn't include college sites or home pages. Categories include models and celebrities, the best of the Web, games, show business, online services, sports, live audio, places, travel, technology, chat lines, kids, business, jobs, service providers, and shopping.

```
http://www.100hot.com
```

⊕ **PC Magazine and Web 21 Hot 25.** Web 21 is a new Web service that analyzes Web traffic and generates lists of the most frequently visited sites. This site lists the top 25 from this week's Web 21 list.

```
http://www.pcmag.com/IU/web/hot25.htm
```

CHAPTER 3

- 🌐 **Point Communications Most Visited.** Point's reviewers rank sites according to a 50-point scale. Of the sites Point has reviewed, these are the most frequently visited.

  `http://point.lycos.com/topsites/`

- 🌐 **WebCrawler Top 25.** The 25 most popular documents retrieved by the WebCrawler search service.

  `http://webcrawler.com/WebCrawler/Top25.html`

What's New

Hundreds, sometimes thousands, of new Web sites appear daily. There's no way to keep up with all of them, but the following Web services keep track of some of the most interesting and useful new sites:

- 🌐 **What's Hot in the iZone.** A list of new sites from InfoSeek Guide, with an emphasis on glitzy commercial sites.

  `http://guide.infoseek.com/izone?pg=izone.html`

- 🌐 **New and Noteworthy.** Point Communication's picks of the most interesting new sites reviewed this week.

  `http://point.lycos.com/columns/new/`

- 🌐 **WebCrawler Select New Sites.** New sites that have been critically reviewed by the WebCrawler Select staff.

  `http://webcrawler.com/select/nunu.new.html`

- 🌐 **What's New?** The very newest sites on the Web, submitted by their creators—and not ranked or reviewed. Very much a mixed bag, but interesting to browse.

  `http://www.emap.com/whatsnew/`

- 🌐 **Netscape What's New.** A list of interesting new sites compiled by Mozilla, Netscape Communication's reptilian mascot.

  `http://home.mcom.com/escapes/whats_new.html`

- 🌐 **What's New On Yahoo.** Hundreds of new sites daily, and they'll appear in Yahoo, the Web's best subject tree. (See Chapter 10.)

  `http://www.yahoo.com/new/`

PART

Daily Inspiration

Here are some great Web sites that change every day, bringing you new information that will make you learn and laugh:

🌐 **Cool Jargon of the Day.** Those ever-enterprising techno-babblers are sure to come up with ever-more-confusing terms.

http://www.bitech.com/jargon/cool/

🌐 **Cool Site of the Day.** Every day there's a new, cool site. Check it out!

http://cool.infi.net/

🌐 **David Letterman's Daily Top Ten List.** Did you miss the *Late Show?* Check out this site for the latest Top Ten List. (Today's list: rejected names for the new show.)

http://www.cbs.com/lateshow/

🌐 **Deep Thought of the Day.** Can the Web be profound? You be the judge.

http://www.eecs.nwu.edu/cgi-bin/deepthought/

🌐 **Today in History.** You think today's news is bad?

http://www.unison.com/wantinfo/today/

🌐 **Urgent News of the Day.** Skip the newspaper, skip Dan Rather—it's all here.

http://www.yahoo.com/headlines/current/news/

The Worst of the Web

Now for the dreck. Actually, this site is one of my favorites on the Web: Mirsky's Worst of the Web (Figure 3-5 on the next page), located at:

http://mirsky.com/wow/Worst.html

CHAPTER 3

Mirsky, a mild-mannered white-collar worker by day, spends his evenings roaming the Web in search of the worst, and there's a new one every day. Some characteristics of "worst-while" sites:

- **Unintentional self-parody.** At a site containing train sounds, you can download "the high-pitched whistle of an Amtrak Superliner coach toilet flushing, from outside the car."

- **Bad taste.** It just isn't cool to create Web pages about your former significant other.

- **Complete waste of Internet resources.** For reasons inexplicable to most of us, people have posted lists of items in their personal possession, such as T-shirts and CDs.

Figure 3-5

Mirsky's Worst of the Web.

TIP

Mirsky has some competition. Check out Anthony's Most Annoying of the Web:

`http://www.cs.vassar.edu/~anschorr/annoying.html`

You're not going to believe the background he's using. In addition, don't miss The Useless WWW Pages Hall of Fame:

`http://www.chaco.com/useless/useless/hall-of-fame.html`

Also check out The Useless Pages:

`http://www.chaco.com/useless/`

From Here

🌐 Learn more about Internet Explorer in Part II, "Using Internet Explorer," beginning with Chapter 4, "What's on the Screen?"

🌐 Customize your start page so that it contains your favorite sites, as explained in Chapter 8.

🌐 Master the intricacies of surfing in Chapter 9, "Surfing Tips and Tricks."

🌐 Can't find the site you're looking for? Check out Chapter 10, "Tracking Down Information."

CHAPTER 3

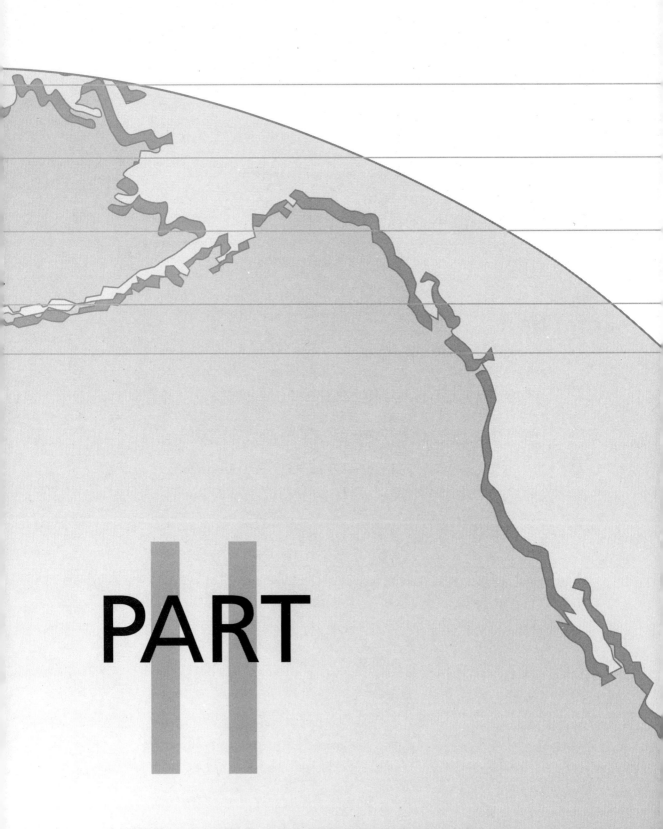

PART

II

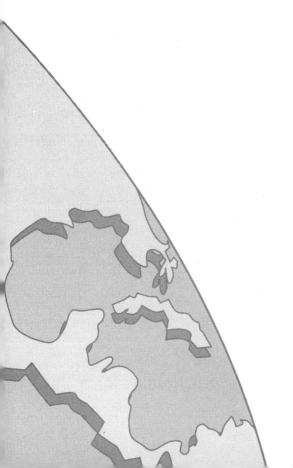

Using Internet Explorer

CHAPTER 4

What's on the Screen?

Microsoft Internet Explorer turns your computer into a window on the Internet, including the World Wide Web. As you learn more about Internet Explorer, you'll come to think of it as a wonderful tool for exploring the riches of the Internet—and what's more, keeping a record of your favorite World Wide Web sites. In time, Internet Explorer will become a personalized tool for you, chock-full of shortcuts that enable you to access your favorite Web sites with the click of a mouse button.

As with any tool, Internet Explorer will make more sense to you if you learn the basics before putting it to work. In this chapter, you'll learn how to use the tools and options that the Internet Explorer window makes available.

A Quick Guide to the
Internet Explorer Window

From top to bottom, here's what you'll see in Internet Explorer's window, shown in Figure 4-1.

Figure 4-1

Internet Explorer window.

🌐   **Title bar.** At the top of the window, this bar shows the name of the Web document you're currently accessing. It also contains tools for managing the window. For more information on these tools, see "Window Management Basics" on page 57.

🌐   **Menu bar.** Here, you'll find the names of Internet Explorer's menus. If you click one of the menu names, a menu drops down, giving you additional options. For more information on menus, see "Using the Menu Bar" on page 60.

PART

- **Toolbar.** The tools on the toolbar provide quick access to the most frequently used Internet Explorer commands and options. **New In Version 3:** The toolbar contains three moveable panels, including the Address and Links panels. For a quick introduction to these tools, see "Using the Toolbar" on page 63.

- **Program icon.** The Internet Explorer insignia becomes animated while Internet Explorer is retrieving a document for you. (Retrieving a document is sometimes called *downloading.*) The animation ceases when the whole document has been downloaded.

- **Workspace.** Here, you see the Web document you're currently accessing. If the document is bigger than the current window size, you'll see an active scroll bar, which you can use to bring additional portions of the document into view.

- **Status bar.** This bar is used to display short messages from Internet Explorer.

TIP To make Internet Explorer's screen less complex, you can hide the toolbar, Address panel, and status bar, as explained in Chapter 8. However, there are good reasons to keep these features in view, as you'll learn in the following chapters. For example, many times it's necessary to type a Web site's address to access it. With the Address panel in view, you can easily do so by selecting the current address and simply typing the new address in the box.

Window Management Basics

Internet Explorer is an application for Microsoft Windows 95, and its window features work just like the other applications you'll run on Windows 95. If you already know the basics of Windows 95, you can skip this section.

Moving the Internet Explorer Window

To move the Internet Explorer window (it must not be maximized), just drag the title bar until the window is where you want it. If you'd prefer to use the keyboard, press Alt+Spacebar to activate the application menu and then press M to select the Move command. ("Alt+Spacebar" means you hold down the Alt key while you press the Spacebar key.) The mouse pointer changes to an arrow pointing in four directions. You can then use the arrow keys to move the window. When you're done, press Enter.

Scrolling the Internet Explorer Window

If the current window size doesn't show the whole Web document, you'll see scroll bars on the right side of the window, the bottom of the window, or both. To bring additional portions of the document into view, click the scroll arrows, drag the scroll boxes, or click in the scroll bar above or below the scroll boxes.

New In Version 3: Are you viewing a document with frames? Some Web authors divide a page into two or more independent panels, as shown in Figure 4-2. If the panel is scrollable, you'll see scroll bars on the left border, bottom border, or both.

For information on navigating with frames, see Chapter 9.

TIP

Some Web authors let you adjust the size of a frame's panels. You can tell if you can change a frame's size by moving the mouse pointer to the frame's border. If the pointer changes shape to arrows, you can adjust the frame border's position.

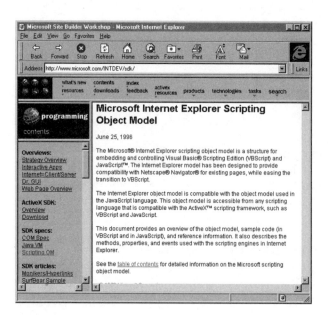

Figure 4-2

Frames with independent scrolling.

Sizing the Internet Explorer Window

The appearance of most Web documents changes when you adjust the width of the Internet Explorer window. Some documents may not look good unless you widen the window a little.

To size the Internet Explorer window, move the mouse pointer to one of the window's borders or corners. The mouse pointer will change shape, indicating the direction in which you can size the window. To size the window, drag the border in the desired direction.

If you'd prefer to use the keyboard to size the window, press Alt+Spacebar to activate the application menu and then press S to choose the Size command. Press one of the arrow keys to choose which border you will adjust, and then use the arrow keys to move that border in or out. When you're satisfied with the size of the window, press Enter.

Sometimes you'll run into a site that asks you to size your window to a certain width, such as the one shown in Figure 4-3. Nothing bad will happen if you don't; the request is made purely for aesthetic reasons. As new technologies give Web authors more control over document layout, you'll see this request less frequently.

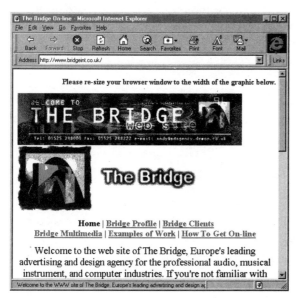

Figure 4-3
Site that requests you to size your window.

Maximizing, Restoring, and
Minimizing the Internet Explorer Window

Most Web sites look best with a relatively narrow window, just wide enough to accommodate the graphics and produce a pleasing layout. In addition, narrow text columns are easier to read. For these reasons, you probably won't want to maximize Internet Explorer's window unless you run across some exceptionally wide data or a large graphic.

To maximize Internet Explorer's window (zoom it to full size), click the Maximize button. After you've maximized the window, the button changes to the Restore button. To restore the Internet Explorer window to its previous size, click the Restore button. (The button changes back to the Maximize button.)

If you want to minimize the Internet Explorer window, click the Minimize button. The window disappears, and you see its icon on the taskbar. To see the Internet Explorer window again, click the Internet Explorer button on the taskbar.

Using the Menu Bar

The menu bar provides access to all of Internet Explorer's commands.

To open a menu, click the menu's name. You'll see the menu, such as the View menu, shown in Figure 4-4. To choose a command from the menu, click it. To exit the menus without choosing anything, click a blank area on the menu bar or press Alt or Esc.

In this book, I'll refer to a particular menu command by simply combining the menu name and the command name. For example, to tell you to select the View menu and then choose the Refresh command, I'll simply say, "Choose the View Refresh command."

HELP

I can't choose one of these commands!

If a command is unavailable for some reason, it is dimmed and you can't choose it. For example, suppose you're viewing the start page at the beginning of an Internet Explorer session. Since you've displayed only one Web document, you can't go back or forward. For this reason, the Go Forward and Go Back commands are both dimmed.

PART

TIP

To maximize the Internet Explorer window quickly, double-click the title bar. To restore the maximized window to its previous size, double-click the title bar again.

Figure 4-4

The View menu with dimmed and undimmed options.

What's on the Menus

Here's a quick overview of the menu names you see on the menu bar:

🌐 **File.** On this menu, you'll find commands for opening Web sites, saving documents, mailing documents to friends or coworkers, creating shortcuts, and printing.

🌐 **Edit.** You can select any text that's displayed in the workspace and then copy it to the Clipboard using the Edit Copy command (or the Ctrl+C shortcut). Whenever you're typing text (for example, a Web page's Internet address), you can also use the Edit Cut (Ctrl+X) and Edit Paste (Ctrl+V) commands. This menu also contains the Edit Find command, which you can use to search for text in the currently displayed Web document.

🌐 **View.** This menu contains commands to hide or display the toolbar and status bar. You can also choose the font size of the display, stop an unwanted download, reload a fresh copy of the document from the network, and view the underlying source (HTML) code. You can choose additional options using the View Options command.

🌐 **Go.** This menu contains menu equivalents of the Back, Forward, Home, and Search buttons, as well as the Best Of The Web button on the Links toolbar and the Mail button. It comes in handy if you've hidden the toolbar, but you'll probably prefer the buttons if the toolbar's visible. This menu also lists the last few sites you've accessed, enabling you to return directly to one of them without clicking Back. Also available on this menu is a command that opens the History window, enabling you to return directly to all the sites you've recently visited.

 Favorites. This menu enables you to record the location of particularly cool or useful Web documents that you discover. You can start by adding favorites directly to the menu, but soon you'll have so many of them that you'll need to organize your Favorites list. Chapter 8 shows you how to do this.

 Help. This menu provides Help for Internet Explorer. You can also run the Internet Tutorial again, if you want. In addition, you'll find lots of links to Microsoft's Web pages.

Accessing Menus with the Keyboard

The mouse provides the easiest way to access Internet Explorer's menus, but you can also use the keyboard. To open a menu, press the Alt key to activate the menu bar, and then use the left and right arrow keys to select the menu you want. Press Enter or the down arrow key to open the menu. Use the down and up arrow keys to highlight the command you want, and then press Enter. To exit the menu without choosing anything, press Alt or Esc.

TIP

Here's another way to open a menu: Hold down the Alt key and press the underlined letter in the menu name you want. For example, pressing Alt+V opens the View menu. To choose a command after the menu is open, press its underlined letter. (Don't press Alt again at this point.)

Using Keyboard Shortcuts

Some menu options have direct keyboard shortcuts. For example, you can start printing a document by pressing Ctrl+P. The following table lists the most common keyboard equivalents for Internet Explorer menus. If you prefer to use the keyboard rather than the mouse, you'll find these very handy.

New In Version 3: If you're used to the keyboard shortcuts in previous versions of Internet Explorer, note a few changes. Previously, the View Refresh command didn't have a shortcut, but now you can refresh the screen by pressing F5 (which is in line with the keyboard shortcut to refresh a window in Windows Explorer). Also, note the new keys for Go Back and Go Forward.

Menu	Command	Keyboard Shortcut
File	New Window	Ctrl+N
File	Open	Ctrl+O (the letter)
File	Save	Ctrl+S
File	Print	Ctrl+P
Edit	Cut	Ctrl+X
Edit	Copy	Ctrl+C
Edit	Paste	Ctrl+V
Edit	Select All	Ctrl+A
Edit	Find (on this page)	Ctrl+F
View	Stop	Esc
View	Refresh	F5
Go	Back	Alt + Left Arrow
Go	Forward	Alt + Right Arrow

Using the Toolbar

New In Version 3: Internet Explorer's toolbar now consists of three panels, as shown in Figure 4-5, which you can move and size independently:

🌐 The tool panel includes the commands you'll use most frequently, including Back, Forward, Stop, Home, and Print.

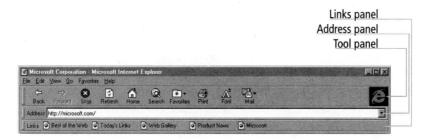

Figure 4-5
The Internet Explorer toolbar.

🌐 The Address panel shows the Web address of the site you're viewing.

4 CHAPTER

HELP

I can't see the toolbar!

That's because you or somebody else chose the command that hides it. To view the toolbar, choose the View Toolbar command.

 The Links panel gives you quick access to up to five cool and useful sites. You can use the links included with Internet Explorer, or you can add your own, as explained in Chapter 8.

By default, you see two rows of toolbar panels. On the top, you see the toolbar proper, with all the buttons you'll access frequently. On the bottom, you see the Address and Links toolbar panels. The Links panel is reduced to its smallest size; you can't see any of the buttons on this panel unless you move it or enlarge it.

You can also adjust the size of the toolbar by dragging the toolbar's thick bottom border up or down. When you drag up, the program reduces the number of rows, reducing the size of the panels as necessary. When you drag down, the program adds rows, enabling the panels to reach their full size, as shown in Figure 4-5 on the preceding page.

If you prefer, you can arrange the panels in one, two, or three rows, and you can size them to your heart's content. You can also change their order. You do this by moving and sizing the panels, as described in the following section.

TIP

If you'd like to reduce the amount of room the toolbar takes up, choose View Options and click the General tab. In the Toolbars area, deselect Text labels, and click OK. The toolbar will display the graphics for each button, but not the text.

Like to get rid of the toolbar's background graphic? In the same area of the Options dialog box, deselect Background bitmap.

Moving and Sizing the Toolbar Panels

Each of the toolbar's panels has a handle, as shown in Figure 4-6. To move or size a toolbar, move the mouse pointer to the handle, hold down the left mouse button, and drag up, down, left, or right.

PART

Toolbar panel handle   Address panel handle   Links panel handle

Figure 4-6
Toolbar panel handles.

To maximize a toolbar panel quickly, click its name. For example, to see the whole Address panel, just click the word *Address*. To reduce the panel to its smallest size, click the name again. Use this trick to take advantage of Internet Explorer's default panel layout, which displays the Address and Links panels on the second row. To work with the Links panel, click Links to enlarge it. The program automatically reduces the Address panel to its minimum size. To work with the Address panel and reduce the Links panel, click Address.

What Do All Those Toolbar Buttons Do?

The toolbar, shown in Figure 4-7, provides quick access to many of Internet Explorer's most frequently accessed commands—especially Web navigation commands. Here's a quick overview of the tools and a brief description of what they do.

Figure 4-7
The toolbar.

New In Version 3: If you've used previous versions of Internet Explorer, note that the new toolbar sports far fewer buttons—and that's all to the good. The buttons you see are the ones you'll use every day, and they're big enough to hit with a casual swipe of the mouse.

CHAPTER 4

Name	Action
Back	Goes back one document in the list of documents you have retrieved in this session and displays the document in the workspace. (This tool is unavailable if you've just started Internet Explorer and haven't accessed anything but the start page.)
Forward	Goes forward one document in the list of documents you have retrieved in this session and displays the document in the workspace. (This tool is unavailable if you haven't clicked the Back tool or chosen the View Back command.)
Stop	Stops downloading the current document. This tool is handy if the document you're downloading seems to take forever or doesn't look very interesting anyway.
Refresh	Downloads a new, fresh copy of the current document from the Internet. This tool is useful if you've clicked the Stop tool and then decide you'd still like to see the whole document.
Home	Redisplays the default start page.
Search	Displays a page that enables you to search for Web and Usenet information.
Favorites	Displays a drop-down menu that enables you to add favorites or open the Favorites window.
Print	Prints the Web document you're currently displaying.
Font	Cycles through larger and smaller font sizes.

Using the Address Panel

The Address panel, shown in Figure 4-8, shows the Web address of the document you are currently viewing.

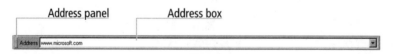

Address panel   Address box

Figure 4-8

The Address panel.

The Address panel isn't just for viewing:

If you would like to give a friend this document's address, you can select the address and copy it to the Clipboard (Ctrl+C).

🌐 To access a Web site by typing its address directly, click in the Address box. The current address is selected. Type the new address, and press Enter.

🌐 The down arrow at the right of the Address box gives you a way to redisplay documents you've previously viewed in this and earlier sessions, if you opened them by typing the address directly in the Address box. Click the down arrow, and select the document from the drop-down box.

Using the Links Panel

The Links panel, shown in Figure 4-9, contains up to five quick links to useful Web documents.

Figure 4-9
The Links panel.

Name	Action
Best Of The Web	Each week feature articles are chosen from some of the best sites on the Web. You'll find a directory of hot links to Today's Picks, Find It Fast!, News, Business & Finance, Computers & Technology, Sports & Health, Living, and Travel & Entertainment.
Today's Links	Displays Today's Pick of the Day, plus links to the hottest news-breaking events. The picks cover a wide range of subjects from Life On Mars to Authors On The Highway.
Web Gallery	Displays a collection of Microsoft's multimedia elements that you can use to publish your own Web pages. You'll find images, sounds, style sheets, ActiveX controls, Java applets, and True-Type fonts.
Product News	Click this button to download the most recent version of Internet Explorer and to learn more about developing pages for the Web.
Microsoft	Click this button to see the home page of Microsoft. Visit often: It's updated daily!

CHAPTER 4

Using Hyperlinks

In the documents you'll display with Internet Explorer, you might see *hyperlinks*, shown in Figure 4-10, as briefly discussed in Chapter 2. A hyperlink (also called *link* or *shortcut*) is an underlined word or phrase that you can click to access another Web document.

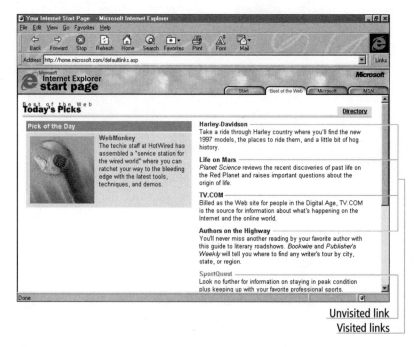

Unvisited link
Visited links

Figure 4-10

Visited and unvisited hyperlinks.

Hyperlinks are shown in color, underlined text. Hyperlinks you've already visited are shown in underlined text of a different color.

Sometimes pictures, called *clickable maps* or *imagemaps,* can serve as hyperlinks. These pictures contain embedded hyperlinks. You can tell whether an image contains a hyperlink by moving the mouse pointer over it. If the pointer changes to a hand shape, you've found a hyperlink.

Figure 4-11 shows an example of this kind of picture. You can click in any region of the world to see more information specific to that region.

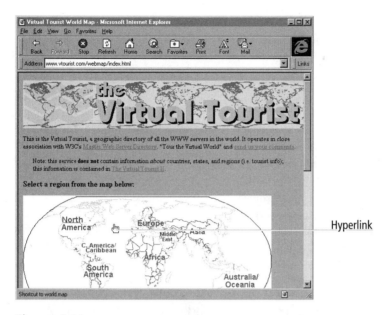

Figure 4-11

Clickable map (The Virtual Tourist).

Using Pop-Up Menus (Right-Clicking)

Take a minute or two now to explore a useful feature of Internet Explorer: the pop-up menus that appear when you point to something and click the right mouse button. These menus list the things you can do to whatever you clicked. For example, try right-clicking the background of a document. This menu lists all the things you can do when you click within a document's text or white space areas. As the following sections discuss, the pop-up menus differ depending on which part of the screen you right-click.

The Title Bar Pop-Up Menu

If you right-click Internet Explorer's title bar, you see the pop-up menu shown in Figure 4-12, with the options listed on the following page.

Figure 4-12

The title bar pop-up menu.

Name	Action
Restore	Restores the window to its previous size. (This command is available only if the window is maximized.)
Move	Enables you to move the window by using the keyboard's arrow keys.
Size	Enables you to size the window by using the keyboard's arrow keys.
Minimize	Minimizes this window.
Maximize	Maximizes this window. (If the window is already maximized, this command is dimmed.)
Toolbar	Displays or hides the toolbar.
Status Bar	Displays or hides the status bar.
Close	Closes this window.

The Document Background Pop-Up Menu

If you right-click the document background (or any text that isn't part of a hyperlink), you see the pop-up menu shown in Figure 4-13, with the following options:

Name	Action
Save Background As	Saves the background graphic to your computer's hard disk.
Set As Wallpaper	Saves the background graphic to your Windows directory and modifies Windows so that this graphic appears as your computer's default wallpaper graphic.
Copy Background	Copies the background graphic to the Clipboard.
Select All	Selects all the text in the document but not the graphics.
Create Shortcut	Creates a shortcut for the current document and places the shortcut on the Windows desktop.
Add To Favorites	Adds the current page to your Favorites folder.
View Source	Displays the source (HTML) code underlying this document.
Refresh	Retrieves a fresh copy of this document from the current Internet address.
Properties	Displays the Page Properties dialog box, which contains information about the document's type, address, size, and its creation date. You can also see information about the document's security.

Figure 4-13

The document background (white space) pop-up menu.

The Hyperlink Pop-Up Menu

The following lists the commands that appear in the pop-up menu shown in Figure 4-14 when you right-click a hyperlink.

Figure 4-14

The hyperlink pop-up menu.

Name	Action
Open	Follows the link and displays the linked document (the same as clicking the hyperlink with the left mouse button).
Open In New Window	Follows the link and displays the linked document but displays the new page in a new Internet Explorer window.
Save Target As	Saves the document that this link would display but without opening the page.
Copy Shortcut	Copies the Web address to the Clipboard.
Add To Favorites	Adds this Web address to your Favorites folder.
Properties	Displays general information about the document connected to this link.

The Graphic Pop-Up Menu

If you right-click a graphic, the pop-up menu shown in Figure 4-15 displays the following options:

Figure 4-15

The graphics pop-up menu.

Name	Action
Open	If the graphic contains a hyperlink, follows the link and displays the linked document (the same as clicking the hyperlink with the left mouse button). If this option is dimmed, the graphic doesn't contain a hyperlink.
Open In New Window	If the graphic contains a link, follows the link and displays the linked document but displays the new page in a new Internet Explorer window. If this option is dimmed, the graphic doesn't contain a hyperlink.
Save Target As	If the graphic contains a link, saves the document that this link would display but without opening the page. If this option is dimmed, the graphic doesn't contain a hyperlink.
Save Picture As	Saves this graphic to your hard disk.
Set As Wallpaper	Saves this graphic to your Windows directory and modifies Windows so that this graphic appears as your computer's default wallpaper graphic. (This command doesn't appear on the pop-up menu if the pointer is positioned over a hyperlink.)

Name	Action
Copy	Copies the graphic to the Clipboard.
Copy Shortcut	If the graphic contains a link, copies the Web address to the Clipboard. If this option is dimmed, the graphic doesn't contain a hyperlink.
Add To Favorites	If the graphic contains a link, adds the Web address to your Favorites folder.
Properties	Displays general information about the graphic connected to this link.

Using the Status Bar

Internet Explorer uses the status bar to send messages to you and to indicate the program's status—what it's doing and what kind of document it's displaying. Unless you're downloading a document, the status bar displays three panels, from left to right:

🌐 **The Message Panel.** Here, you'll see the messages that Internet Explorer gives you. For example, position the pointer over a hyperlink; you'll see this hyperlink's Web address on the status bar. At some sites, Web authors use Java to display a scrolling message in this space.

🌐 **The Progress Indicator.** When Internet Explorer is busy downloading a graphic or a lengthy document, this area shows a progress indicator that lets you know how the download's going.

🌐 **The Program Status Indicator.** In this panel, you see tiny graphics that indicate what Internet Explorer is doing. A yellow page with a globe indicates that the program is displaying a document. A gold lock indicates that you're viewing a secure document (see Chapter 16). A globe with a spyglass indicates that the program's roaming the Internet for you, trying to find something. If you see an hourglass, the program's too busy to enable you to click anything just now—wait a second or two.

CHAPTER 4

**About Internet Explorer's
Abbreviated Web Addresses (Shortcuts)**

By default, Internet Explorer displays abbreviated Web addresses on the toolbar. For example, if you move the pointer to a hyperlink that jumps to http://www.microsoft.com/ie/support/revguide, the program displays "Shortcut to revguide" on the status bar. If the document is located at a different server, you also see the server's name, as in this example: "Shortcut to index.html at members.aol.com."

This information isn't very helpful if you're trying to figure out the full Web address that's embedded within a hyperlink. For example, the abbreviated address "index.html at members.aol.com" isn't sufficient to enable you to locate the document by typing the address manually. Nevertheless, these abbreviated addresses are easy on the eyes, and you can go to the document simply by clicking the link. If you would like to see the full Web address on the status bar when you point to links and download documents, choose View Options, click the Advanced Panel, and deselect the option called Show Friendly URLs.

From Here

- Experience the richness of Web multimedia with Chapter 5 as your guide.

- Found something you like? It's a keeper. Chapter 6 shows you how to download it, save it, make it a favorite, or print it.

- Is the Net a little slow today? Find out how to improve Internet Explorer's performance in Chapter 7.

- Customize Internet Explorer so that the program works the way you want. Find out how in Chapter 8.

PART

CHAPTER 5

Hypermedia! (Sounds, Videos, and Plug-Ins)

What's the coolest thing about the World Wide Web? Many people would say it's the Web's multimedia capability—sound, graphics, video, and animation. On the Web, multimedia can become something even richer—*hypermedia,* which employs multimedia (sound, graphics, video, or animation, or a combination of these) as an integral part of a Web presentation. With the introduction of Java, a programming language that enables you to download miniprograms to run, and Microsoft's new ActiveX technology, hypermedia comes alive with eye-popping special effects, such as rotating graphics, scrolling banners, and much more. If you've thought of the Web as a static medium, hold on to your seat belt.

New In Version 3: Thanks to Internet Explorer's amazing new technology, hypermedia isn't the hassle it used to be. With previous versions of Internet Explorer and with other browsers, you needed the assistance of accessory programs (called *helper applications*) in order to deal with all the different types of multimedia *file formats* you encountered on the Internet. A multimedia file format refers to the method used to store multimedia material (sounds, animations, and graphics) on disk. Users were left to their own devices when it came to obtaining and installing these accessory programs, most of which had to be downloaded from the Internet and installed in a laborious, error-prone process. Internet Explorer completely eliminates the need to obtain and configure accessory programs.

In this chapter, you'll learn how to deal with all the types of multimedia that the Web can sling at you. In addition, you'll learn how Internet Explorer version 3 can work with Netscape *plug-in programs,* which greatly enhance the program's ability to deal with rich data on the Internet. You'll also learn how Internet Explorer deals with the Java programs you've heard so much about, and you'll visit some cool Java sites. Finally, you'll take a closer look at Microsoft's exciting new ActiveX technology, which can make the Web come alive with safe, secure programs that Internet Explorer automatically downloads from the Internet.

Multimedia File Formats

Multimedia resources, such as sounds or movies, are stored using a number of differing file formats. Each has it own identifying extension. For example, Windows movies are stored in files with the avi (*.avi) extension. There are over a dozen multimedia file formats in use on the Internet.

Before ActiveMovie, you needed to know quite a lot about these file formats. Happily, that's no longer necessary. Still, you might want to know what kinds of sounds and movies ActiveMovie can handle. It's an impressive list:

- Sun/NeXT sounds (*.au)
- Apple/Silicon Graphics sounds (*.aiff)
- Windows WAV sounds (*.wav)
- QuickTime movies (*.mov)
- Windows AVI movies (*.avi)
- MPEG movies (*.mpg)
- MPEG audio (*.mp2)

There's only one other thing about this chapter that you need to know and get ready for: You're about to see the future of computing. That's no exaggeration, since it's clear that tomorrow's computers will make use of software obtained from the Internet in addition to software that's already present on the user's hard disk. Internet Explorer's ActiveX technology, as you'll see, shows how this can be done—and what's more, how to do it without the threat of computer viruses.

What's the Difference Between Multimedia and Hypermedia?

You've surely heard about multimedia, one of the most hyped concepts in contemporary computing. In brief, multimedia involves the use of more than one medium—for example, text supplemented by animations—to get your point across. There's plenty of multimedia on the Web. In fact, your basic Web page is generally a multimedia effort, blending graphics with text.

So what's hypermedia? It's the use of multimedia as an integral part of a Web presentation, not as a mere sideshow. This distinction isn't understood by all Web authors. Too many of them think they're doing hypermedia by including a few graphics or a couple of sounds. In a well-conceived hypermedia presentation, the graphics, sounds, and videos stand equal to the text, both as a means of understanding the material and of navigating the site.

Puzzled by what all this means? Take a look at what the masters are doing. At Disney's home page (http://www.disney.com), you'll find links to Disney's online "theaters," one of which is shown in Figure 5-1 on page 81. In this presentation, the entire means of navigation is visual; in Figure 5-1, for instance, you stand at the entrance to the theater's stage door. You can learn more about the featured play by clicking any of the text links you see— this is a clickable map (also called an imagemap), as you can see by moving the pointer over the graphic. When the pointer changes to a hand shape, it's over a hyperlink.

Whether you're looking for education or entertainment, multimedia provides a much richer experience than mere text. When multimedia is blended with hypertext in a focused, high-quality presentation, the result is doubly interesting.

CHAPTER 5

What Equipment Do You Need?

To enjoy the sounds you can access on the Web, you need to equip your system with the following:

- **A stereo sound card.** You have a choice of three kinds of sound cards: non–MIDI capable, FM synthesis, and wave-table synthesis. A non–MIDI capable sound card will do a good job of reproducing the *wave* sounds you'll download from the Web. A wave sound is an exact digital reproduction of an actual sound, such as music or voice, that is made using recording techniques similar to those used in making audio CDs. However, if you want to download and listen to *MIDI* files, your sound card must have FM synthesis capability. I'd recommend that you spend the extra money it takes to get a wave-table synthesis sound card. MIDI files do not contain recorded sounds—they contain instructions that tell a sound card how to synthesize the sound. Wave-table cards do a much better job of playing MIDI files than do FM synthesis cards. It still doesn't sound like real music, but it's closer.

- **Self-powered stereo speakers.** If you plan to put your speakers next to your monitor, be sure they are shielded speakers so that their electromagnetic fields don't distort the image on your monitor.

You don't need any additional equipment to view video with Windows 95, but ActiveMovie will automatically take advantage of any hardware MPEG support that your computer has. With hardware MPEG support, you will be able to view MPEG movies with better resolution and larger display sizes.

PART

II

Figure 5-1

Disney's virtual theater.

Introducing ActiveMovie

New In Version 3: Internet Explorer's facility with sounds and movies is due to ActiveMovie, an add-on program that you can download for free from Microsoft. In brief, ActiveMovie replaces all the previous Windows utilities for playing back sounds and movies. If you've used previous versions of Internet Explorer or some other browser, you had to link multimedia file types (such as Windows or MPEG movies) with specific players. But that's no longer necessary. After you install ActiveMovie, it's all automatic.

Playing Sounds and Movies with ActiveMovie

There's nothing simpler than playing sounds and movies with ActiveMovie: You simply click the link that leads to the sound or movie. Embedded within the page you're viewing, or sometimes a new page, you'll see a set of VCR-like controls that enable you to begin playing (click the Play button), stop

CHAPTER 5

playing (click the Stop button), or rewind the sound or movie (drag the slider control back). Figure 5-2 shows these controls as they appear when you're playing an MPEG video.

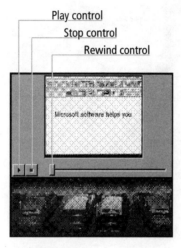

Figure 5-2

ActiveMovie controls.

Using the ActiveMovie Pop-Up Menu

You can control movies by moving the pointer within the movie or sound control panel and clicking the right mouse button. The pop-up menu contains the Run, Pause, and Stop controls. From this menu, you can also access the Properties dialog box, discussed in the following section.

Controlling Sound and Movie Properties

If you would like to gain more control over the playback of sounds and movies, display the ActiveMovie pop-up menu by right-clicking the ActiveMovie control and choose Properties. You'll see the Properties dialog box, shown in Figure 5-3 on page 84. The Playback page, shown in the figure, enables you to adjust the sound volume and balance, view the timing, choose a play count, turn on auto repeat, and enable auto rewind. The following table sums up the options you can choose on this and the other tabbed pages of the Properties dialog box:

PART

To Do This	Click This Tab	And Do the Following
Adjust the volume.	Playback	Adjust the volume slider control.
Adjust the balance.	Playback	Adjust the balance slider control.
Change the start and stop timing.	Playback	Type new start and stop times in the Start and Stop text boxes. By default, playing automatically starts with the beginning of the sound and ends with the end of the sound.
Specify the number of times to play the sound.	Playback	Type a number in the Play Count box (the default is 1).
Repeat the sound automatically.	Playback	Select the Auto Repeat option.
Rewind the sound automatically when it finishes playing.	Playback	Select the Auto Rewind option (the default is 1).
Select the movie size.	Movie Size	In the list box, choose Original Size, Double Original Size, 1/16 of screen size, 1/4 of screen size, or 1/2 of screen size.
Zoom the movie to the full size of the screen.	Movie Size	Click Run Full Screen.
View a digital display panel showing timing and tracks.	Controls	Select Display Panel.
View the control panel.	Controls	Select Control Panel (the default is on).
Add position controls to the control panel.	Controls	Select Position Controls.
Change the control panel's foreground color.	Controls	Click Foreground Color, and choose a color.
Change the control panel's background color.	Controls	Click Background Color, and choose a color.

CHAPTER 5

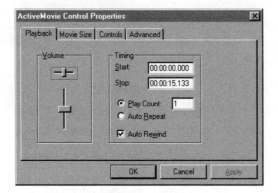

Figure 5-3

ActiveMovie Properties (Playback page).

NOTE

ActiveMovie supports *progressive playback* of sounds and movies. This means that you can start playing the sound or movie before it finishes downloading. Although you can't hear the complete sound or see the whole movie until downloading is complete, progressive playback enables you to determine whether it's worth downloading the entire file.

Using Netscape Plug-Ins

New In Version 3: If you switched to Internet Explorer from Netscape, you might want to continue using the *plug-ins* you downloaded and installed. In brief, plug-ins are accessory programs that extend Netscape's capabilities. A popular Netscape plug-in program is Macromedia Shockwave, which enables Netscape users to view Macromedia Director animations within a Web page displayed by Netscape.

To use your Netscape plug-ins with Internet Explorer, you needn't do anything special. Just use Internet Explorer to access the sites you formerly viewed with Netscape. Internet Explorer will detect the need for a plug-in, locate the plug-in on your disk, run the plug-in program, and display the data. That's all there is to it.

TIP

If you've never used Netscape or Netscape plug-ins, don't bother downloading Netscape plug-ins, even though Internet Explorer can use them. It's much better to look for ActiveX controls, many of which perform exactly the same functions that Netscape plug-ins do. ActiveX controls use superior technology and function more efficiently with Internet Explorer. For more information on ActiveX controls, see "Using ActiveX Controls," later in this chapter.

Running Java Programs

New In Version 3: A creation of Internet pioneer Sun Microsystems, the Java programming language enables professional programmers to prepare miniprograms (called *applets*) that can be downloaded from a Web page. A browser capable of interpreting Java, such as Netscape or Internet Explorer version 3, runs the program while the page is being displayed. There are thousands of Java applets on the Web. Examples include scrolling stock tickers, tic-tac-toe and Solitaire games, spreadsheet-like calculators, and much more. In Figure 5-4, you see Java in action: in this case, a Java clock.

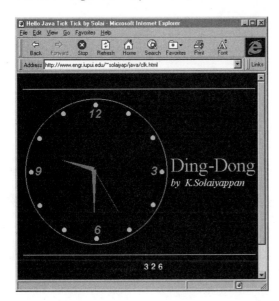

Figure 5-4
Java in action.

Is Java Secure?

Internet Explorer's Java capabilities enable you to enjoy sites with Java applets, but be cautious: Experts disagree on just how safe Java really is. Although Sun's design team made every effort to make Java safe to use, some critics believe that computer criminals could write rogue Java programs. These programs, like computer viruses, could damage your data. It's certainly possible to write prank applets, which can be rather annoying even if they don't actually harm your data. (An example is a prank applet that purports to perform a useful function, but the only way you can stop it is to turn off your computer.) If you want to experience Java on the Web, you'll be wise to visit Java sites maintained by reputable companies such as Sun or Microsoft.

Trusted Java Sites

The following sites offer excellent examples of Java applets, and you can be reasonably certain that you won't run into a prank program if you visit them:

- **Gamelan.** You'll find over 3,000 applets at this well-organized site.

  http://www.gamelan.com

- **Java Center.** Lots of applets to try, plus information and links.

  http://www.java.co.uk/javacentre.html

- **Java Applets Rating Service.** Here you'll find ratings of hundreds of popular applets.

  http://www.jars.com

TIP If you're nervous about Java and don't want to take any risks with your data, you can disable Internet Explorer's Java support. Choose View Options, and click the Security tab. In the Security panel, deselect Enable Java programs and click OK.

PART

Using the Just-In-Time (JIT) Compiler

Internet Explorer includes a *just-in-time (JIT)* Java compiler that can speed up the display and execution of Java applets, but it doesn't work with some of the Java applets you'll find on the Web. For this reason, the JIT compiler is turned off by default. If you'd like to speed up the execution of most Java applets, at the risk of not being able to run a few of them, choose View Options and select the Advanced tab. Click Enable Java JIT Compiler, and choose OK. You'll need to quit Internet Explorer and restart the program in order to use the JIT compiler.

Using ActiveX Controls

New In Version 3: Microsoft's new ActiveX technology enables Web authors to prepare programs, called ActiveX Controls, which can be downloaded to run on your computer. These programs help bring Web pages alive, with effects such as live audio, scrolling banners, and much more. In this sense, ActiveX Controls resemble Java applets, but there are a couple of major differences. ActiveX offers the security protection that Java lacks, and ActiveX controls can be written in any popular programming language, including Java and Microsoft Visual Basic.

As an Internet Explorer user, you don't need to worry about the sophisticated technology that underlies ActiveX. You just need to devote some thought to whether you should download the control or not, as the following section explains.

Deciding Whether to Download an ActiveX Control

If you encounter a site that has an ActiveX control, Internet Explorer checks to see whether the control has been digitally signed. A digitally signed control has been independently certified to be free from computer viruses or destructive effects. You'll see the certificate, as shown in Figure 5-5 on the next page. It's safe to install this software, and you'll probably want to choose the options (below the certificate) that hide this message for additional controls made by the same company.

CHAPTER 5

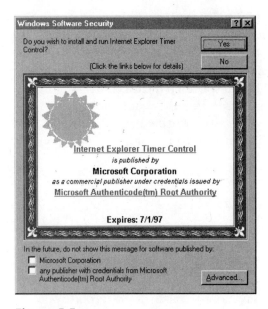

Figure 5-5

ActiveX Control certificate.

When the control doesn't have certification, you see the alert box shown in Figure 5-6.

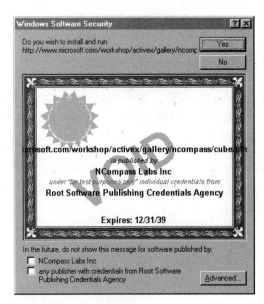

Figure 5-6

Noncertified alert box.

This doesn't mean you're about to download a destructive program—it just means that the author hasn't obtained certification. If you're downloading the program from a trusted site, and you're sure you've backed up all your important work, click Yes. However, if you have any reason to suspect that the site you're accessing isn't all that it says it is (for example, you're rummaging around in college students' home pages), click No.

ActiveX Controls in Action

Dozens of software companies are busily preparing ActiveX controls for use on the Web. To see what they've come up with, visit the ActiveX Component Gallery (http://www.microsoft.com/activex/controls/), shown in Figure 5-7. You'll find examples and links to many interesting and useful ActiveX controls. Here's a brief summary of some of the goodies currently available or slated for availability in the near future:

Figure 5-7
ActiveX Component Gallery.

🌐 **Adobe Acrobat.** This control will enable you to read and browse richly formatted Adobe Acrobat documents on the Web.

- 🌐 **Real Audio Player.** With this control, you can listen to Real Audio voice recordings, which are widely available on the Web. What's neat about Real Audio is that the recording starts playing immediately; you don't have to wait for a lengthy download.

- 🌐 **Macromedia Shockwave.** With this control, you'll be able to view Web pages that contain Macromedia Director animations.

From Here

- 🌐 Find a keeper? Chapter 6 tells you how to download it, add it to your Favorites list, save it to disk, or print it.

- 🌐 Is the Net bogged down? Find out how to speed up Internet Explorer in Chapter 7.

- 🌐 Like to customize Internet Explorer, including creating your own custom start page? See Chapter 8.

CHAPTER 6

Keepers (Downloading, Saving, and Printing)

Found something you like? Like to keep it? Just what you do depends on what you've found.

- If it's software, you can *download* (copy) the program to your computer. Internet Explorer will handle the whole process for you, and you can browse the Web while the download's taking place.

- Found a graphic you like? You can copy it to the Clipboard or save it to your hard drive. You can even make a Web graphic your default Windows Desktop wallpaper.

- Like to have a printout of the site you're viewing? Fire up your printer, because you can print anything you can display (and that includes graphics). **New In Version 3:** Tables print correctly, just as you see them on screen.

🌐 Found some text you like? You can copy it to the Clipboard, from which you can paste the text into other applications. Or you can save just the text from a document, in a plain-text file.

This chapter details all these procedures.

Downloading Software

At last count, some 250,000 freeware or shareware programs were available on the Internet—that's right, a quarter of a million! (The term *freeware* refers to programs that are copyrighted but freely redistributable, as long as this is not done for commercial gain, while *shareware* refers to programs that require payment of a registration fee if you want to keep using them.) These programs range from the not-very-impressive efforts of beginning programmers to highly professional, full-featured programs.

About Computer Viruses

It isn't much fun to think about, but hundreds—perhaps thousands—of programmers worldwide are busily trying to create rogue programs, called *viruses,* that are capable of harming computer systems and data. A computer virus replicates itself willy-nilly, infecting your computer and traveling outward by means of disk and Internet file exchanges. Why do virus authors create these vexing programs? Their motivations vary, but they stem from an inability or unwillingness to put technology in context—to realize that there are *people* involved in computing.

(continued)

About Computer Viruses *continued*

Virus authors focus narrowly on trying to outwit the software industry, which is doing all it can to prevent your computer from getting infected.

One to watch out for: There's a fake version of PKZIP (PKZIP300.EXE or PKZ300B.EXE), the popular file-compression program, that reformats your hard drive. Also, consider purchasing an antivirus program, which scans your drive and your computer's memory for viruses.

Formerly, you could avoid computer viruses by practicing safe computing, but the rise of the Internet creates a new distribution medium for virus authors. In safe computing, you never run programs unless you've obtained them from a reputable source. With so many shareware and freeware programs on the Internet, however, can you be sure your sources are reputable?

The safest course of action is to avoid downloading software altogether, but this takes away a lot of the Internet's fun and usefulness. A reasonable compromise is to download with caution. Begin by establishing a regular backup program so that your valuable data is protected if you should encounter a virus despite all your precautions. If you're searching for a program, use a reputable search service to locate and download software from the Internet, such as c|net's shareware.com (discussed in this book's next section). If you know which program you're looking for, search for the software company's home page and download it directly from there. You'll be sure that you're getting the most recent version. Just try to make sure that the page you're accessing really is the company's home page and not some imposter loaded with rogue programs. Think long and hard before downloading executable files from Usenet!

Above all, don't succumb to virus paranoia. I've seen too many computer users panic when something seems odd about their computer system. Often, the problem is just a minor software glitch that can be cured by a good, healthy restart. Also, remember that there are plenty of virus hoaxes on the Internet; they're all designed to make fools of novices. To avoid getting hoodwinked, bear in mind that viruses can propagate only by means of executable programs. They aren't present in graphics files or e-mail.

If you really do suspect that you've contracted a virus, check out the Anti-Virus Resource Center (http://www.symantec.com/avcenter/index.html). You'll learn about the latest virus and rogue program threats (the real ones, that is).

CHAPTER 6

Searching for Software on the Internet

Looking for freeware or shareware? Here are two great places to start:

- **Microsoft Free Product Downloads.** For Windows users, this site, shown in Figure 6-1, is a computer playground from heaven. You'll find free TrueType fonts, games, accessories for Internet Explorer and Microsoft Office products, monthly content updates for Cinemania and Music Central, Windows 95 updates and up-grades, and tons more. Hope you have lots of free disk space!

  (http://www.microsoft.com/msdownload/

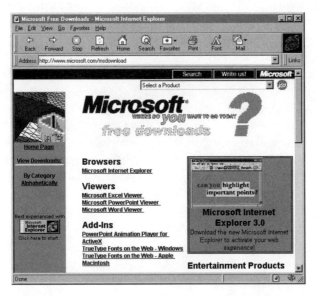

Figure 6-1
Microsoft Free Downloads.

- **shareware.com.** This outstanding Web site, shown in Figure 6-2, is a production of c|net and enables you to search a database of more than 190,000 freeware and shareware programs by typing one or more key words. The search engine looks for the key words in the product description database as well as in the file name, so the chance is good that you'll find what you're looking for, if it exists at all.

  http://www.shareware.com/

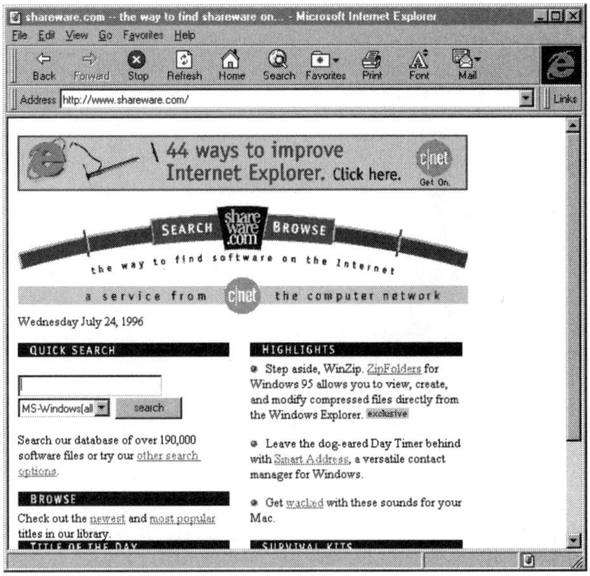

Figure 6-2

shareware.com (c|net).

TIP

Keep your version of Internet Explorer up-to-date by downloading the latest version; you'll find it at the Download Area (http://www.microsoft.com/ie/down-load/). Don't forget to check out the latest features and accessories, including NetMeeting and Comic Chat, which you can obtain from the Additional Features & Components page at http://www.microsoft.com/ie/download/ieadd.htm/.

Deciding Whether to Download Software

If you click a link to a downloadable program, you might see the dialog box shown in Figure 6-3 on the next page.

TIP

Here's a necessity for Windows computing, especially once you've got your Internet connection: a program that can decompress *.zip files. The standard is WinZip for Windows 95, available for downloading from Niko-Mak Computing's home page (http://www.winzip.com/). The program is shareware and requires the payment of a $29 registration fee.

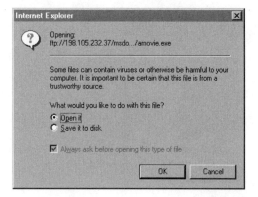

Figure 6-3

The download security dialog box.

Are you sure the file is from a trustworthy source, such as Microsoft's Free Product Download page? If so, choose one of the following options:

- **Open It.** If you choose this option, Internet Explorer will download the file and look for an application that can open the file. If the file is an executable (*.exe) file, Internet Explorer will tell Windows to run it. If the file is a compressed (*.zip) file, Internet Explorer will look for a decompression program, such as WinZip for Windows 95. If the program is a document (*.doc), Internet Explorer will open the document with Word for Windows. As long as you have installed software that can deal with files with the same extension as the one you're downloading, this is the best option to choose.

- **Save It To Disk.** If you choose this option, Internet Explorer will download the file to your hard disk. You'll see a Save As dialog box, enabling you to specify where the file should be stored. This is the best option to choose if you don't have a program capable of opening the file. After you obtain the necessary program, you can open it at a later time.

Downloading the File

New In Version 3: While the file is downloading, you'll see a message box that keeps you informed of the download's progress, such as the one shown in Figure 6-4.

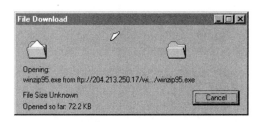

Figure 6-4
The File Download message box.

If Internet Explorer was able to determine the size of the file, you'll see a progress indicator that visually shows how much of the file has been downloaded. In addition, you'll see an estimate of how much time is required to complete the download. While downloading is in progress, you can return to the Internet Explorer window and browse other sites.

If you're using Internet Explorer on a 14.4- or 28.8-Kbps modem line, avoid downloading more than one file at a time. Internet Explorer doesn't prevent you from doing this—you can just click file after file, and Internet Explorer will start downloading—but your Internet connection will bog down to the point that each of the downloads slows to a crawl. One at a time, please!

About Windows Software Security

If you chose the Open option when you began downloading an executable (*.exe) file, you might see the alert box shown in Figure 6-5 when the download is complete.

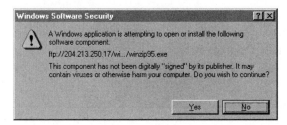

Figure 6-5
The Windows Software Security alert box.

This alert box appears if you've downloaded an automatic software installation program, which is very common. It informs you that the software has not been digitally "signed" by the publisher. Don't be alarmed; very few of the programs you'll download have been signed in this way. Digital signatures are used for ActiveX Controls, described in the previous chapter. As long as you're still sure that you downloaded the software from a reputable source, choose Yes to open the program and let it make changes to your system.

Mailing a Web Address

As you're browsing the Web, you'll run across pages that may interest friends or coworkers. If so, you can let them know by e-mailing the Web address to them so that they can see the page for themselves.

Here's how to e-mail the address. Choose the File Send To command, and choose Mail Recipient from the pop-up menu. Windows will start the e-mail program that's currently listed in the Programs page of the Options dialog box. (For more information on choosing your e-mail program, see Chapter 12.) Enter the recipient's e-mail address, a subject line, and some explanatory text, and click the command that sends the mail.

Copying and Saving Graphics

You can copy or save any graphic that you see in a Web document. If you copy a graphic, you can paste it into a document that you're creating with another application. If you save the graphic, you can open it later with a graphics program, through which you can display, modify, copy, or print the image. The following sections explain how to copy or save a graphic.

Copying a Graphic

If you see a graphic that you would like to use in one of your documents, you can copy it to the Clipboard. From there, you can paste it into a document in another application.

To copy a graphic to the Clipboard, right-click the graphic and choose Copy from the pop-up menu.

To paste the graphic into a document that you're creating with another application, position the insertion point where you want the graphic to appear and choose the Edit Paste command, press Ctrl+V, or click Paste on the toolbar.

TIP

When you copy a graphic to the Clipboard, Microsoft Windows 95 automatically converts the graphic to the Windows bitmap format. If you want to preserve the original graphics file format of the graphic, save the graphic to your hard disk, as described in the following section, "Saving a Graphic."

Saving a Graphic

Internet Explorer enables you to save a graphic to a disk file so that you can reuse it anytime you want. Windows will preserve the graphic's original file format.

To save a graphic, follow these steps:

1. Right-click the graphic.

2. From the pop-up menu, choose Save Picture As. You'll see the Save As dialog box, shown in Figure 6-6. In the File Name box, Internet Explorer displays the document's name. In the Save As Type box, Internet Explorer displays the document's file format. There's no need to change either of these settings.

3. If you want, choose a different location for the saved graphic.

4. Click the Save button.

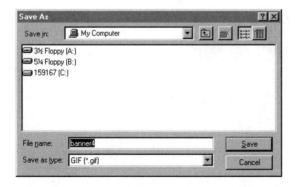

Figure 6-6

The Save As dialog box.

Making a Graphic the Default Wallpaper

With Windows 95 and Windows NT, you can choose a graphic to serve as *wallpaper,* the image that's displayed on the desktop. If you run across a graphic on the Web that you think you can live with every day (think about it), you can quickly make the graphic the default wallpaper.

To make a graphic the default wallpaper, do this:

1. Right-click the graphic.
2. From the pop-up menu, choose Set As Wallpaper.

Copying and Saving a Background Graphic

Some of the documents you'll encounter on the Web have fancy graphical backgrounds, which range from tasteful to annoying. (For an example, see Figure 6-7.) If you'd like to copy or save the background graphic, or save it as your default Windows wallpaper, you can do so by following the instructions in this section.

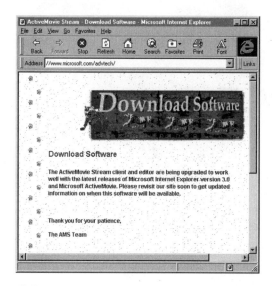

Figure 6-7

A Web document with a background graphic.

Copying a Background Graphic

To copy a background graphic to the Clipboard, right-click the background and choose Copy Background from the pop-up menu.

To paste the graphic into a document that you're creating with another application, position the insertion point where you want the graphic to appear and choose the Edit Paste command, press Ctrl+V, or click Paste on the toolbar.

Saving a Background Graphic

To save a background graphic, use these steps:

1. Right-click the background.

2. From the pop-up menu, choose Save Background As. You'll see the Save As dialog box. In the File Name box, Internet Explorer displays the document's name. In the Save As Type box, Internet Explorer displays the document's file format. There's no need to change either of these settings.

3. If you want, choose a different location for the saved image.

4. Click the Save button.

Copying and Saving Text

If you find some text on the Web that you'd like to reuse in a document you're creating, you can copy it to the Clipboard or save it to your hard disk, as explained in the following sections.

Copying Text to the Clipboard

To copy text from a Web document to the Clipboard, follow these steps:

1. Position the pointer at the beginning of the text you want to copy. The pointer changes from an arrow to an I-beam shape.

2. Drag to select the text.

3. Choose the Edit Copy command. Alternatively, you can either right-click your selection and choose Copy from the pop-up menu, press Ctrl+C, or click Copy on the toolbar.

TIP

To select all of the text in the document, choose the Edit Select All command or press Ctrl+A. You can also point to any of the document's text and right-click; from the pop-up menu, choose Select All.

Viewing the Source HTML

If you're an aspiring Web author and would like to see the HTML code producing the document you're viewing, you can display it using the Notepad utility. From there, you can save or print the HTML code, if you want.

To view the HTML code, follow these steps:

1. Right-click the document's background.

2. From the pop-up menu, choose View Source. You'll see the HTML code in a Notepad window, as shown Figure 6-8.

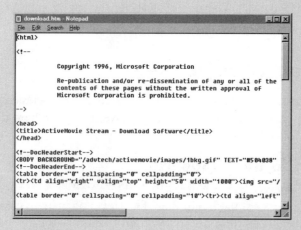

Figure 6-8
HTML source code.

3. To print the HTML code, choose the File Print command in Notepad.

4. To exit Notepad, choose the File Exit command.

You can also save the HTML code to disk by choosing the File Save As command in Notepad. This has the same effect as saving a document in HTML from within Internet Explorer, as explained in the section titled "Saving a Document as HTML."

PART

Saving Text

You can save any document that Internet Explorer can display, and you can do so in two ways:

 As plain text. Internet Explorer strips all the HTML code from the document, producing a plain-text document that you can later modify easily with a word processing program such as Notepad or WordPad.

 As HTML. Internet Explorer saves the HTML source code, just as you see it when you use the View Source command. (See the sidebar titled "Viewing the Source HTML.") However, Internet Explorer does not save any graphics in the document. If you want to save the graphics, you must use the right-clicking technique (described earlier in this chapter) and you must save each graphic individually. However, it might not be worthwhile to go to all of this trouble. If you merely want to make sure you can visit some site again later, save it as a favorite, as described in Chapter 2. Be aware, however, that the site may change and a particular document may no longer be available.

Saving a Document as Plain Text

This is a good option if you want to have a plain-text version of the document you are viewing on screen, shorn of graphics and HTML codes. (Plain text is also known as ASCII text, which stands for American Standard Code for Information Interchange, a standardized coding method for letters, numbers, and other characters.)

To save a document as plain text, follow these steps:

1. Choose the File Save As File command. You'll see the Save As dialog box. In the File Name box, type a name for the document. In the Save As Type box, choose Plain Text (*.txt).

2. Click the Save button. Internet Explorer saves the document in plain-text format.

Saving a Document as HTML

This procedure isn't recommended unless you are an aspiring Web author and want to save the HTML code for later experimentation or inclusion in your own HTML documents. Save a site as a favorite or make it a desktop shortcut (see Chapter 2) if you just want to make sure you can get back to it.

CHAPTER 6

To save a document as HTML, follow these steps:

1. Choose the File Save As File command. You'll see the Save As dialog box. In the File Name box, type a name for the document. In the Save As Type box, choose HTML (*.htm, *.html).

2. Click the Save button. Internet Explorer saves the document in HTML format.

HTML—The Web's Language for Document Design

HTML is the basis for those cool Web documents you're seeing on screen. But what is it?

HTML (HyperText Markup Language), as its name indicates, is a *markup language*—in other words, it lets a document designer mark the parts of a document, such as the title, headings, and body text. Marking a document isn't the same as formatting it, as you would format a document with a word processing program. In formatting, you control the document's final appearance (the fonts, font sizes, alignments, emphasis, and spacing). Markup identifies some text as belonging to a certain part of the document; a part is called an *element*. The *appearance* of the element is left up to the browser. The browser "reads" the HTML and formats the document on screen.

What are the advantages of a markup language? The two biggest advantages are cross-platform compatibility and speed. Cross-platform compatibility means the ability of people using lots of different kinds of computers—Sun workstations, Macintoshes, IBM compatibles, and more—to exchange HTML documents. That is possible because HTML documents contain nothing but plain ASCII text, which almost any computer can handle. HTML documents lend themselves to speed because they tend to be compact, and that's because, once again, HTML consists of nothing but text. (Document retrieval slows down significantly when people load up their Web pages with graphics, as you may have noticed.)

HTML is easy to learn. To mark up a document, you can use any word processing program to insert the HTML codes, which are called *tags*. Most tags are paired: There's a beginning tag and an ending tag.

(continued)

PART
II

106

HTML—The Web's Language for Document Design *continued*

All the tags are enclosed in angle brackets. Here are the tags used to mark a Level 1 heading:

```
<H1>This is a Level 1 Heading</H1>
```

If you want some help creating HTML code, you can obtain a *converter* designed to work with your word processing program. A converter transforms your formatted documents into HTML code (which, you'll find, will almost certainly need some hand coding before it looks just right). You can also use an HTML editor, a program that lets you choose the tags from menus. There still isn't a true "what-you-see-is-what-you-get" HTML program, which would let you forget about HTML code and concentrate on your document's look.

HTML is changing rapidly, and what's more, it's not entirely clear where it's headed. That's because the language is being pulled in two directions. On the one side are HTML purists who want the language to remain a "pure" markup language, in which the formatting is left up to browsers. On the other side are Web document designers who want more control over the appearance of their Web pages. They want tags that let them specify font sizes, text alignment, and other aspects of document formatting. Stepping into the fray recently was Netscape Communications Corporation, whose Netscape Navigator—the most widely used browser before Internet Explorer—incorporated the Netscape Extensions, a set of nonstandard tags that give greater formatting control. In an effort to restore standards to the HTML community, the World Wide Web Organization—the closest thing to a standards body that the Web currently has—plans to incorporate some (but not all) of the Netscape Extensions into the next standard version of HTML, version 3.

Printing Documents

Printing documents with Internet Explorer is easy, and the results look great—especially if you have a color printer. If you want, you can print all or part of a document, and you can also make changes to the default page format. The following sections explain how.

CHAPTER 6

Printing a Document

To print the document you're currently viewing, follow these steps:

1. Choose the File Print command, press Ctrl+P, or click Print on the toolbar. You'll see the Print dialog box, shown in Figure 6-9.

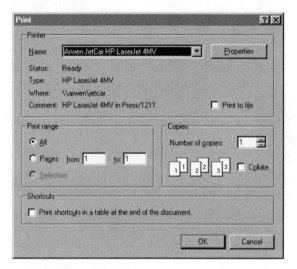

Figure 6-9
The Print dialog box.

2. If you want to print a specific page range, click to select the Pages option in the Print Range area. Then type the beginning page in the From box, and type the ending page in the To box.

3. If you want to print more than one copy, type a number in the Number Of Copies box or click the up and down buttons to specify the number of copies you want printed. Then click the Collate check box if you want Internet Explorer to collate your copies.

4. **New In Version 3:** If you would like Internet Explorer to print a table containing all the Web addresses (shortcuts) found in the document, click the Print Shortcuts option in the Shortcuts area.

5. Click the OK button to initiate printing.

PART

Setting Up the Page Format

By default, Internet Explorer formats your printout with 0.75 inch margins on all four sides of the page. In addition, the program prints a header with the document's title positioned flush left and the page number positioned flush right. It also prints a footer with the current date positioned flush left and the current time positioned flush right.

As the following sections explain, you can change the paper size, paper tray, print orientation, margins, and headers. To change these settings, choose the File Page Setup command. You'll see the Page Setup dialog box, shown in Figure 6-10.

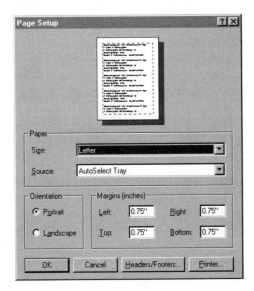

Figure 6-10
The Page Setup dialog box.

Choosing Paper Size

If your printer can print with more than one size of paper, you can choose the paper size that you want Internet Explorer to use.

To choose the paper size, follow these steps:

1. Choose the File Page Setup command. You'll see the Page Setup dialog box, shown in Figure 6-10.

2. From the Size list box, choose the paper size you want to use. The options you see depend on your printer's capabilities.

3. Click OK.

Choosing the Paper Tray

Some printers have more than one paper tray. If your printer has two or more trays, you can select the tray that you want your printer to use when it prints your Internet Explorer document.

To choose the paper tray, follow these steps:

1. Choose the File Page Setup command. You'll see the Page Setup dialog box, shown in Figure 6-10.

2. From the Source list box, choose the paper tray you want to use. The options you see depend on your printer's capabilities.

3. Click OK.

Changing the Printing Orientation

Some Web pages look best when printed with a portrait orientation, while others look best when printed with a landscape orientation. Internet Explorer can print Web pages either way.

To choose the print orientation, follow these steps:

1. Display the document you want to print.

2. Choose the File Page Setup command. You'll see the Page Setup dialog box, shown in Figure 6-10.

3. In the orientation area, click the orientation you prefer (Portrait or Landscape).

4. Click OK.

5. Print the document, as described in the previous section. Internet Explorer will print the document using the current settings in the Page Setup dialog box.

Setting Margins

By default, Internet Explorer formats your printout with 0.75 inch margins on all four sides of the page. You can change the margins, if you want.

TIP

Internet Explorer uses the current Windows 95 settings for measurements. For example, copies of Windows 95 that are sold in the U.S. display measurements in inches. If you would like to change the measurement format, click the Start menu, choose Settings, and click Control Panel. In the Control Panel window, double-click Regional Settings. In the Regional Settings Properties dialog box, choose the Number tab, if necessary. From the Measurement System list box, choose the number system you want to use, and click OK.

To change the margins, do the following:

1. Choose the File Page Setup command. You'll see the Page Setup dialog box, shown in Figure 6-10 on page 109.

2. In the Margins area, type the margin values you want to use.

3. Click OK to confirm the new margins.

Defining Headers and Footers

By default, Internet Explorer prints a header with the document's title positioned flush left and the page number positioned flush right. It also prints a footer with the current date positioned flush left and the current time positioned flush right.

Internet Explorer can print four header and footer areas:

- **Left Header.** The text is flush left at the top of the page.
- **Right Header.** The text is flush right at the top of the page.
- **Left Footer.** The text is flush left at the bottom of the page.
- **Right Footer.** The text is flush right at the bottom of the page.

Internet Explorer uses codes, preceded by an ampersand (&), to define the contents of headers and footers. You can see the current codes by clicking the Headers button in the Page Setup dialog box. After clicking this button, you'll see a second Page Setup dialog box showing the current headers codes. The table on the next page explains the codes you can use.

Enter	To Print
&w	Window title
&u	Page address (URL)
&d	Date in this format: mmm dd yyyy
&D	Date in this format: dd mmm yyyy
&t	Time in 12-hour format
&T	Time in 24-hour format
&p	Current page number
&P	Total number of pages
&&	A single ampersand (&)

You can also enter text in the header and footer fields. If you type *Web document* in the Left box of the Page Header area, that's what you'll get on the printouts. The codes extract current information from the document (such as the page address) or from your computer system (such as the current date and time).

You can combine text and codes. For example, the text (Page &p of &P) prints the current page number and the total number of pages, as in the following example: "Page 7 of 10."

From Here

🌐 If Internet Explorer seems to be performing too sluggishly for your tastes, check out the next chapter.

🌐 Customize Internet Explorer so that the program works the way you want. Get the lowdown in Chapter 8.

C
H
A
P
T
E
R

7

Improving Internet Explorer's Performance

Internet Explorer version 3 incorporates numerous advanced features that greatly speed the program's performance:

🌐 **Small and efficient code.** Internet Explorer's program code is small and efficient, ensuring that the program runs at a good clip. It also takes full advantage of Windows 95's multithreading capabilities, enabling the program to perform several actions at once.

🌐 **Fast text mode.** Internet Explorer downloads text first and uses placeholders while graphics are downloading. You can read the text and scroll through the page while graphics downloading is taking place. If the page turns out to be irrelevant to your interests, you can move on without having to wait for all the graphics to download.

🌐 **Progressive rendering of graphics.** Complex graphics are downloaded sequentially, beginning with a low-resolution version of the graphic and gradually adding more detail. If the low-resolution version of the graphic reveals that the picture is as un-interesting as the text, you can move on without having to wait for the whole graphic to download.

These important technical innovations help make Internet Explorer the fastest browser around. If you're using Internet Explorer on a slow modem line, however, you might want to take steps to improve the program's performance, such as turning off the automatic display of graphics. In addition, you can further improve the program's performance by disabling active content and increasing the storage space for the program's temporary files. All these performance-improvement tricks are discussed in this chapter.

Switch Off
Graphics, Sound, and Video

Sure, multimedia's great. But multimedia files are *huge,* and they take time to download. Are you more interested in the text than the pictures and design glitz? If so, consider turning off the automatic downloading of multimedia files. The Web won't look as pretty, but you won't believe how much faster you can browse. You can still view individual pictures, if you want.

Turning Off Multimedia

Here's how to do it. Choose View Options, and click the General tab. In the General panel, shown in Figure 7-1, deselect Show Pictures, Play Sounds, and Play Videos, and click OK.

NOTE

If the page you were viewing contained pictures, you'll still see them after turn-ing off multimedia—but don't worry, Internet Explorer is still working just fine. Your choices in the Options menu affect only the new pages you download af-ter turning multimedia off. To hide the pictures in the current page, click Refresh (which forces Internet Explorer to download a new copy of the page from the network).

After you turn off graphics, sounds, and video, the Web won't look or sound as nice but it will download a lot faster. In place of graphics, you'll see *placeholders*, as shown in Figure 7-2. In well-designed sites, you'll see text that describes what the pictures show.

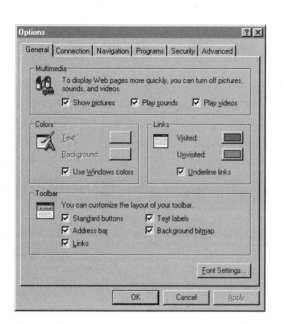

Figure 7-1

General Options.

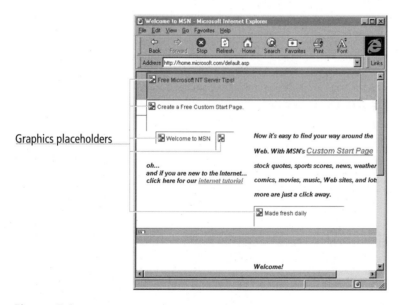

Graphics placeholders

Figure 7-2

Placeholders appear after switching off multimedia.

CHAPTER 7

Selectively Viewing Graphics

If you want to see one of the pictures on a page, move the pointer to the placeholder, click the right mouse button, and choose Show Picture from the pop-up menu. You see just this one picture; the rest of the placeholders aren't affected, as shown in Figure 7-3.

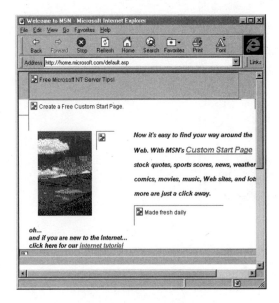

Figure 7-3

Graphic displayed with Show Picture command.

Restoring Multimedia

To view pictures and movies and hear sounds again, choose View Options, click General, select Show Pictures, Play Sounds, and Play Videos, and choose OK. This action won't affect the page you're viewing until you click Refresh on the toolbar. You won't have to choose Refresh for any new pages that you access.

Disable Active Content

Although Java applets and ActiveX Controls add diverting and sometimes useful effects to Web pages, they—like sounds and graphics—take time to download. If you're interested in high-speed browsing, you can turn off the downloading of these programs. To do so, choose View Options, and click Security. In the Active content area, deselect all four options (Allow Downloading Of Active Content, Enable ActiveX Controls And Plug-ins, Run ActiveX Scripts, Enable Java Programs) and click OK.

To restore active content, select all these options and click OK. Click Refresh to download the active components.

NOTE

Why are the Active content area options available on the Security page of the Options menu? Because they pose a security issue. So Internet Explorer gives you the option of preventing Java applets and ActiveX controls from downloading. There is always the danger of encountering a rogue or malicious Java applet or ActiveX control. Note, however, that ActiveX is much safer than Java, as Chapter 5 explained. When Internet Explorer encounters an ActiveX control, the program checks for a security certificate. The certificate attests that the program is safe and that you're downloading it from a reputable site.

Increase the Cache Size

Like all good browsers, Internet Explorer keeps copies of previously accessed documents—including graphics, sounds, videos, and animations—in a *cache* (pronounced "cash"). A cache is a special section of your hard disk that's set aside as an extension of a program's memory.

Why Does Increasing the Cache Size Speed Up Browsing?

When Internet Explorer encounters a Web site, the program first checks to see whether there's a copy of the site and its various components, including graphics, in the cache. Next, it checks to see whether anything on the page has changed since you last accessed it. If not, the program loads the page from your hard disk instead of the network.

Now you know why it's so much faster to go back to the previous Web page (by clicking the Back button) than it is to access sites you've never visited. When you click Back, Internet Explorer restores the page by loading it from your computer's hard disk. When you access a site you've never visited before, the program must retrieve the page and its components from the network, which is much slower.

The cache greatly speeds up Internet Explorer's performance, but the cache fills up quickly. When it does, the program erases previously visited pages to make room for copies of new ones. If you subsequently return to one of those previously visited pages, the program will not be able to find a copy on your disk, so it must retrieve a fresh copy from the network.

By increasing the size of the cache, you allow more room for storing copies of Web pages. You also increase the chance that the cache will contain a copy of a page that you previously visited. As a result, Internet Explorer will often seem to perform more speedily—and that's a decidedly good thing.

Increasing the Cache Size

By default, Internet Explorer stores copies of the Web pages you access in a folder called Temporary Internet Files, within the Windows folder. This folder fills up very quickly with all the pages, graphics, sounds, videos, applets, and controls you're downloading.

TIP How much disk space should you set aside for Internet Explorer's use? It depends on how much you have free. If you're using a 1.2 GB (gigabyte) drive and you've only used 220 MB, you have lots of free space. You can set aside 15 percent of your drive (150 MB) and still have plenty of room for new programs and data. If you're really low on disk space, you'll be wise to free up some space before proceeding. You can do this by erasing unwanted programs and moving infrequently accessed data to backup files. Also, consider running Drivespace 3, the excellent compression program included in Microsoft Plus!. On my system, Drivespace 3 effectively doubled the size of my hard drive without causing noticeable performance loss.

To increase the size of Internet Explorer's cache, choose View Options and click the Advanced tab. In the Temporary Internet files area, click Settings. You'll see the Settings dialog box, shown in Figure 7-4.

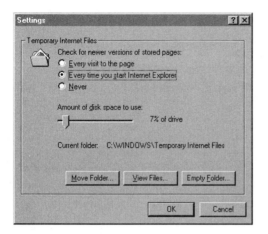

Figure 7-4

The Settings dialog box.

Adjust the disk space slider to increase the percentage of your drive that's set aside for storing temporary Internet files, and click OK.

NOTE If you run low on disk space in the future, remember that you can free up lots of disk space—dozens of megabytes, potentially—by reducing the size of the cache. You can free up a great deal of disk space by returning to the Settings dialog box, erasing all the cache files by clicking Empty Folder, and reducing the amount of disk space to set aside for temporary files.

Decrease the Cache Update Frequency

This section describes a super speed-improvement trick—but it's risky.

The trick has to do with cache updates, which Internet Explorer performs automatically to see whether a page has changed. (If the page hasn't changed, the program retrieves the page from the cache rather than the network, as you learned in the previous section.)

By default, the program updates pages just once during a session. Suppose it's Monday morning, and you turn on your computer. You access the MSNBC news page, which you last viewed on Friday. Sure enough, Internet Explorer finds that the page has changed, so the program downloads the fresh copy instead of retrieving the Friday page from the cache. Obviously, this is a good thing, because you don't want to read Friday's news.

If you choose View Options and click the Advanced tab, and then select Settings (see Figure 7-4 on the preceding page), you'll see that you can choose several update options. If you select Every Visit To The Page, Internet Explorer will always check to see whether a page has changed before retrieving a page from the cache. This really slows things down. The default setting, Every Time You Start Internet Explorer, performs a check just once in an Internet Explorer session. The third setting, Never, prevents Internet Explorer from *ever* performing a check.

You can greatly speed up Internet Explorer's performance by choosing Never, but here's the risk: You might be looking at old or outdated copies of a page without realizing it. The page may have changed, but you won't know. The change will be pretty obvious, however, if you check out a news page on Tuesday and the news is from days earlier—the day you chose Never. While we're on the risk topic, note that there's a small risk with the default setting, too, especially if you leave Internet Explorer running for more than one day at a time: Because the default setting performs updates only once in an Internet Explorer session, you might not realize that a page has changed if you access it more than once during a session.

New In Version 3: In version 3 of Internet Explorer, pages generated by scripts—for example, pages created by search engines such as Alta Vista or Lycos—are automatically updated, even if you've chosen Never.

What about pages that aren't automatically updated? To make sure you're viewing the latest copy of a page, click Refresh on the toolbar. The Refresh command forces Internet Explorer to retrieve a fresh copy.

TIP
Should you choose Never? For most users, I'd say no. You might forget to click Refresh, and you'll see outdated data without realizing it. A worst-case scenario: You're checking out your mutual fund prices, and you make a sell or buy decision based on incorrect figures! If you're working with time-sensitive data like this, I'd recommend choosing Every Visit To The Page. This setting slows down the program somewhat, but it assures you that you'll never see outdated data.

From Here

🌐 It's time to personalize your copy of Internet Explorer, as described in Chapter 8. You'll love the results. And as you'll see, they can save you even more time.

🌐 Still looking for ways to browse faster? Check out Chapter 9, which describes a number of speed-enhancing browsing tricks.

CHAPTER
7

CHAPTER 8

Personalizing Internet Explorer

Imagine starting Internet Explorer and seeing a start page that's loaded with information of direct, personal use to you: your favorite links, quotes for your stocks and mutual funds, weather reports for your area, scores for your favorite sports leagues, your favorite comics, and more. A click away is MSNBC, where you'll find an equally customized look at fast-breaking news, featuring just the stories of interest to you. And, as this chapter explains, it's easy.

In addition to creating a personalized start page, you can choose from a slew of program customization options. For example, wouldn't you like to have your favorite sites on the Links toolbar? How about getting your Favorites folder organized so that you can easily retrieve all those cool favorite sites you've saved? You'll find out how to perform this and many other useful modifications in this chapter. For information on privacy and security options, flip to Chapter 17.

Personalizing the Start Page

Personalizing your start page takes only a few minutes. As I'm sure you'll agree, it's time well spent. This is one of the coolest things you can do with Internet Explorer. To get started, click the MSN.com link on the Internet Explorer Start Page (http://home.microsoft.com/). Find and click the Custom Start Page link on the Custom Start Page (http://www.msn.com/). At the bottom of the first Custom Start Page, click the link that gets the ball rolling on personalizing your start page.

As with everything on the Web, all that follows is subject to change. Microsoft is sure to make additions and improvements to this procedure, so don't be surprised if there's even more to choose from when you give this a try.

TIP
Before you get started, write down the ticker symbols for up to seven of your favorite stocks or mutual funds. You'll need this information if you'd like to see a streaming ticker showing current price quotes. Also, make a list of the URLs (Web addresses) of up to six of your favorite Web sites.

Your Personal Preferences

The first page you'll see asks you to fill out your personal preferences, including your name and address, as shown in Figure 8-1. Don't forget to supply your zip code; it's essential for television listings and weather reports. You can also select the type of music you'd like to hear when you're at the start page (click None if you'd rather not hear music). If you don't want your name to be added to Microsoft's mailing list, don't check the mailing list box. If you'd like to include a link for kids, select this option. When you're finished with this page, click the link that sets up the page and you'll see the Services page.

Choosing Services

On the Services page, you'll be asked to choose the services you'd like to see on your start page, as shown in Figure 8-2. Here's where you'll need to type the ticker symbols for the stocks or mutual funds you want to track. You can also choose sports scores, movies, music (including concert listings, record reviews, articles, and interviews), and family information. When you're finished with this page, click the link that sets up this page and you'll see the News & Entertainment page.

PART

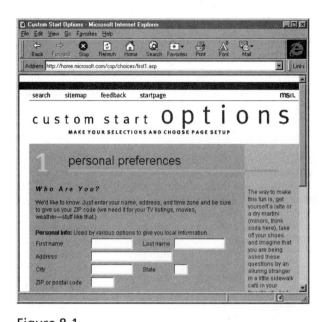

Figure 8-1

The Personal Preferences page.

Figure 8-2

The Services page.

News & Entertainment

On the News & Entertainment page, shown in Figure 8-3, you can choose additional elements to appear on your custom start page, including links to news articles, TV listings for your area, comic strips, technology news, and more. Choose what you like, and click the link that sets up this page. You'll see the Internet Searches page.

Figure 8-3
The News & Entertainment page.

Internet Searches

On the Internet Searches page, shown in Figure 8-4, you can choose which search services you'd like to use. (My favorite is Alta Vista.) In addition, you can specify up to six Web sites (you'll need to type the full Web addresses), and you can ask to see MSN's picks in a variety of subject areas. When you're done, click the link that sets up this page. You'll see your custom start page, similar to the one shown in Figure 8-5.

Figure 8-4

The Internet Searches page.

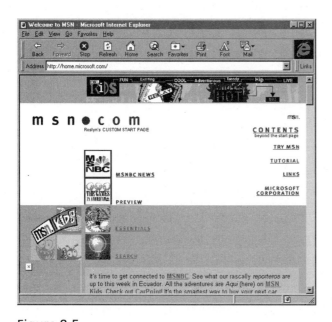

Figure 8-5

A custom start page.

Making Changes to Your Custom Home Page

It's easy to make changes or additions to your custom home page. Just look for the links that enable you to change your options for each category. You'll see one of the pages where you made your initial choices. Change your options, and click the link that sets up the page.

HELP

Hey! Who can access all this personal information about me?

Nobody but you. Actually, it's stored on your hard disk, not on Microsoft's computers. This is done by means of *cookies,* discussed in Chapter 17.

Personalizing MSNBC

Microsoft and NBC's joint news venture, MSNBC, enables you to create a customized news page. To access the customization form, open the MSNBC home page (http://www.msnbc.com/) and follow the links to the Personal Front Page. Choose the information that you'd like to appear on your Personal Front Page, and click the option that displays your page. You'll see a Personal Front Page with the choices you've selected.

Adding Your Own Sites to the Links Toolbar

The Links toolbar contains up to five Web sites, enabling you to choose them very quickly. By default, the Links toolbar contains sites that point you back to Microsoft, which makes sense when you're learning Internet Explorer and need support and additional tools. After you've learned the program, you might want to change the Links toolbar sites to something more to your personal taste.

TIP

You can add the Web addresses to the Links toolbar in two ways: by navigating to the site and clicking an option that configures one of the buttons for the current site, or by typing the Web address (URL) manually. The most convenient way to change one of the buttons is to display the Web page first and then make the change. If you want to change all five buttons, write down the Web addresses before proceeding because you'll need to type the addresses.

To change the Links toolbar sites, choose View Options and click the Navigation tab. In the Navigation panel, as shown in Figure 8-6, find the Page list box and select the Quick Link button you want to alter (they're numbered 1 through 5). In the Name box, type a name for the button. In the Address box, type the Web address or click Use Current to add the page that Internet Explorer is currently displaying. You can change other buttons by choosing them in the Page list box, if you want, and repeating these steps. Click OK when you're done.

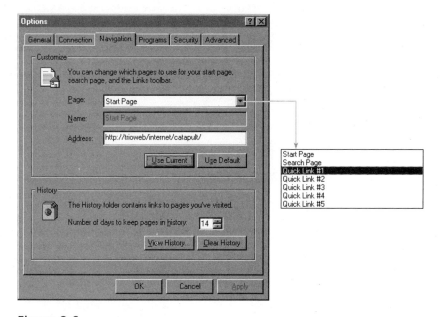

Figure 8-6

The Navigation panel (Options).

Organizing Your Favorites Folder

By now, you've surely saved many sites to the Favorites folder, as described in Chapter 2—and as a result, your Favorites menu now might have too many sites. The more sites you add, the longer the list grows. Before long, the Favorites list becomes less useful. Time to organize your Favorites list.

In this section, you will learn how to organize your Favorites list into folders. As you'll see, the folders you create appear as commands on the Favorites menu—commands that, when you click them, display submenus listing Web sites according to whatever categories you've created.

It's a little bit of work to get your Favorites list organized, but after you do, you'll be glad you did. With an organized Favorites list, you can add hundreds of sites without overburdening the Favorites menu. In time, your copy of Internet Explorer will become a treasure trove of the Web sites you've found most useful.

Planning Your Folders

To get the most out of Internet Explorer's Favorites list, you should organize it so that few or no Web documents appear in the menu's top level. As you'll see in the section titled "Creating a Folder," this is easy to do: Every folder you create within the Favorites list automatically establishes a new command on the Favorites menu. When you click one of these commands, you see a submenu containing all the Web sites you placed within that folder.

Keeping individual Web sites off the top level of the Favorites menu helps to keep its size within bounds. Remember, adding sites to the top level of the menu causes problems with the Favorites menu (which gets too long too fast). By placing new favorites within folders, you can keep the top level of the menu under control and still have room for hundreds, even thousands, of stored sites. Figure 8-7 shows a nicely organized Favorites menu.

Take a moment to plan your Favorites categories. What types of Web documents are you most likely to save in your Favorites list? Jot them down, and don't forget that you can also create folders within folders. Here's a sample folder organization:

Investing
    Bonds
    Mutual Funds
        Balanced Funds
        Bond Funds
        Growth Funds
        Income Funds
        Small-Cap Funds
    Quick Quotes
    Stocks
Sailing
    Boatyards
    Chesapeake Bay
    Marinas
    Rappahannock Weather

Figure 8-7

A Favorites menu with folder names directly on the menu and document names on submenus.

New In Version 3: The Organize Favorites window, shown in Figure 8-8, gives you easy-to-use tools to create new folders. To display this window, choose Favorites Organize Favorites. The changes you make here will be automatically reflected in the Favorite menu's submenus and in pop-ups.

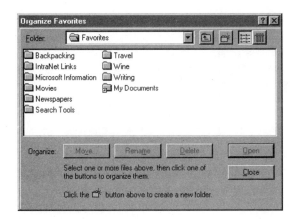

Figure 8-8

The Organize Favorites window.

133

Creating a Folder

After you decide how to organize your Favorites list, it's time to create some folders by following these instructions:

1. Open the Organize Favorites window, if necessary, by choosing the Favorites Open Favorites command.

2. Click the New Folder button on the toolbar. You'll see a new folder in the window.

3. Type a name for your new folder.

Adding Favorites to a Folder

Now that you've created a new folder, you can move existing favorites into it. To add a newly discovered favorite site to one of the folders within the Favorites window, use these steps:

1. In the Organize Favorites window, select the favorite that you want to move.

2. Click Move. You'll see a Browse For Folder dialog box, as shown in Figure 8-9.

Figure 8-9

The Browse For Folder dialog box.

3. Click the folder in which you'd like to add the favorite, and click OK. Internet Explorer moves the favorite into the folder.

Renaming a Favorite

To rename a favorite or folder in the Organize Favorites window, select the favorite and click Rename. Windows will highlight the current name. Just start typing to replace this name with the new one.

Deleting Favorites from a Folder

Sometimes favorite sites fall out of favor—you don't visit them anymore, and you can't remember exactly why you thought they were so hot in the first place. Others summarily disappear or move to new locations so that the connection on your Favorites list no longer works. To keep your Favorites list well organized, you should periodically delete unwanted sites.

To remove unwanted sites from the Favorites list, do this:

1. Display the Organize Favorites dialog box by choosing it from the Favorites menu.

2. If necessary, open the folder that contains the site you want to delete.

3. Select the site you want to delete. To delete more than one site, hold down the Ctrl key and click all the sites you want to delete.

4. Click Delete.

5. You'll see an alert box asking whether you're sure you want to move the deleted item to the Recycle Bin. If you're sure you're deleting the correct site, click the Yes button. (If you're not sure, click the No button and check what you've selected.)

HELP

I deleted the wrong site!

Never fear. On the desktop, double-click the Recycle Bin. Select the site that you deleted accidentally. Choose the File Restore command. Windows 95 will return the deleted item to the place from which you deleted it.

Reorganizing Folders

The Organize Favorites window is actually a standard Windows 95 Explorer window, meaning that you can use familiar drag-and-drop techniques to reorganize files and folders. To do so, use Windows Explorer to open the

Favorites folder, which you'll find within the Windows directory (see Figure 8-10). Your reorganization efforts will be reflected in the organization of the Favorites menu's submenus and pop-ups.

Figure 8-10

Favorites folder viewed by Windows Explorer.

Additional Personalization Options

This chapter has already covered the most important customization options. In this section, you'll learn about some additional ways you can customize Internet Explorer. This is strictly fine-tuning, however, so you can skip this section if you like.

Choosing Toolbar and Status Bar Options

Are you strapped for screen space? Here are some tricks you can use to reduce the amount of space the toolbar and status bar take up:

- To hide the text labels (thus reducing the size of the buttons), choose View Options, deselect Text Labels in the General tab, and click OK.

- To selectively hide one or two of the toolbar panels, choose View Options, and in the General tab, deselect the panels you don't want to see. (If you don't use Quick Links, for example, deselect Links.) Click OK.

To hide the toolbar entirely, choose View Toolbar so that the check mark on this menu disappears. I don't recommend this, however, because those navigation tools are very handy.

 To hide the status bar, choose View Status Bar so that the check mark on this menu disappears. If you're really strapped for screen room, this is a better choice than deleting the toolbar—and what's more, you won't have to read those annoying scrolling messages that some Web authors place on the status bar using a Java trick.

Choosing Font Options

Thanks to Internet Explorer's HTML innovations, fonts are finally coming to the Web. Competitor Netscape quietly introduced the <FONT FACE> tag in its most recent version of the popular Navigator browser, so there's every reason for Web authors to start adding font specifications to their site. Still, there are lots of sites out there that don't specify a font, so you might want to change Internet Explorer's default font specification (particularly if you find the default fonts hard to read for some reason).

By default, Internet Explorer displays proportionally spaced type in Times Roman and displays monospace (typewriter) type in Courier. If you'd like to change these settings, choose View Options and click the General tab. In the General panel, find the Fonts area and choose new fonts from the list boxes. Click OK to confirm your choices.

TIP

Are you having trouble reading the type that you see on the screen? The solution might be just a click away. Try clicking Font on the toolbar to cycle through a series of increased and decreased font sizes. Maybe you'll be able to stop squinting at the screen.

Changing the Start And Search Pages

When you start Internet Explorer, it automatically displays the default start page. However, you can use any existing Web page as your start page—and if you don't like the change, you can restore the default start page easily. You can also change the page that's displayed when you click Search The Internet.

Rather than changing the start page, I'd recommend that you create a custom start page, as described earlier in this chapter. The default search page is pretty neat, too. There's really no need to change these settings unless you have something special in mind.

To change the start or search page, follow these steps:

1. Display the Web page that you want to use as your new start or search page.

2. Choose the View Options command, and click the Navigation tab.

3. In the list box, choose Start Page or Search Page.

4. Click the Use Current button, or type the Web address in the Address box.

5. Click OK.

If you get tired of your change, you can restore the default start and search pages by choosing Start Page or Search Page in the Page list box and clicking Use Default.

Increasing the History List's Time Depth

The history list keeps track of all the sites you've visited within a specified period of time—by default, the past two weeks. The history list comes in handy when you're trying to get back to a site you previously visited, as discussed in Chapter 9. By increasing the retention time of the history list, you increase the chance that you'll be able to find your way back to a previously visited site.

Don't worry about eating up too much disk space. Unlike the cache, the history list is just a collection of Web addresses.

To change the retention time of the history list:

1. Choose the View Options command. You'll see the Options dialog box.

2. Select the Navigation tab. This tab is shown in Figure 8-11.

3. In the History area, enter the maximum number of days you want to retain each Internet address on the history list.

4. Click the OK button.

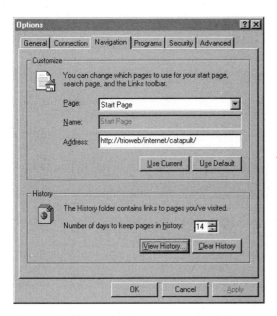

Figure 8-11

The Navigation tab on the Options dialog box.

HELP

I caught my coworker looking at my history list!

That wasn't very nice, but let's face it—people do it. Maybe they're looking for something that could embarrass you, or maybe they're just curious. Either way, you should be aware that even a relatively unsophisticated intruder can tell where you've been browsing by looking at your history list, just by clicking the View History button in the Navigation panel, by clicking the Open History in the Go panel, or by opening the History folder in the Windows directory. If you'd like to cover your tracks, click the Clear History button. (Please note that, even if you erase your history list, your employer can use other methods to tell where you've been browsing. If you're using a computer at work, make sure you're using it for professional purposes, and do your surfing at home.)

Sundry Additional Tweaks

You'll find a few more customization options in the Advanced page of the Options menu (to view this page, choose View Options and click Advanced).

- **Show Friendly URLs.** This option, enabled by default, displays "friendly" (abbreviated) versions of Web addresses (also known as shortcuts) on the status bar. Personally, I prefer the "unfriendly" (full) versions.

- **Highlight A Link When Clicked.** This option, enabled by default, highlights a link when you click it. The highlight makes it easier to tell that you've successfully clicked the link, I suppose, but the hourglass symbol (which tells you it's time to wait) does the job, too. Your call, but I'm leaving it on.

- **Enable Java JIT Compiler.** This option, mentioned in Chapter 5, turns on the Java Just-in-Time Compiler, which greatly speeds up the execution of Java applets. However, it's not compatible with all the applets out there. Try leaving it on; if you run into problems downloading Java applets, turn it off.

- **Use Smooth Scrolling.** What's not to like about the cool, liquid feel of scrolling with this option on?

- **Use Style Sheets.** Enabled by default, this option allows Internet Explorer to use the font and layout specifications in *style sheets,* a new addition to the tools Web authors can use to design Web pages. Internet Explorer's style-sheet smarts conform to international specifications, so this one's a no-brainer: Keep it on.

- **Enable Java Logging.** This option is of interest only to Java developers. It directs the output of Java programs to a text file, called MSJAVA.LOG, found in the Java subdirectory of the Windows directory.

From Here

- You're an expert on Internet Explorer now—so let's surf! In Chapter 9, you'll learn a number of tricks you can use to make your surfing speedier, easier, and more satisfying.

- Trying to find specific information on the Web? Check out Chapter 10. You'll learn how to use subject trees and search engines to locate just the information you're looking for.

- Can't access a Web site, or got a weird message? Find out what to do in Chapter 11.

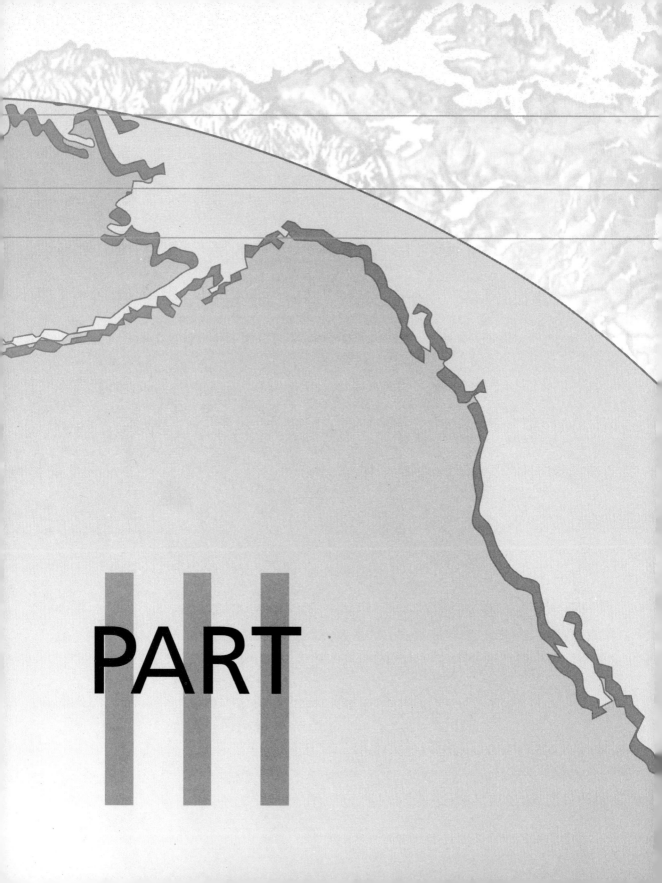

PART

III

Surfing the World Wide Web

CHAPTER 9

Surfing Tips and Tricks

You've learned the basics, and now it's time for some fine-tuning. In this chapter, you learn how to deal with some subtle but vexing surfing mysteries, such as how to return to that cool site you saw a few days ago, how to make the best of Internet Explorer's ability to open more than one window, how to navigate in framed documents, and how to make full use of Internet Explorer's keyboard navigation tools.

Returning to Previously Visited Sites

You want to go back to a site you previously visited, so you start clicking Back. Trouble is, the site you're looking for is *way* back there. It's going to take a good bit of time to reload all those pages as you click Back, Back, Back. Why not use the Go menu, or the History window? They enable you to "leapfrog" back to a previously viewed site.

Retrieving a Site from the Go Menu

If you click the Go menu, you'll see a list of the last several sites you've visited, such as the one in Figure 9-1.

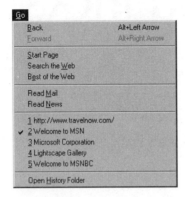

Figure 9-1

The Go Menu.

From this menu, you can choose one of the sites you visited most recently. However, this menu holds a maximum of five sites. If you're trying to get back to a site you visited 10 or more sites ago, you'll need to use the Address panel list box or the History window, as explained in the following sections.

HELP

Where'd that site go?

Sometimes the Go menu doesn't list a site you've recently visited, even though you viewed it just two or three sites ago. To understand why, see the section titled "Why Did That Site Disappear from the Go Menu," later in this chapter.

Note that the Go menu is erased when you quit Internet Explorer. If you're looking for a site that you visited in a previous session, use the History folder, as described in the following section.

Retrieving a Site from the History Folder

If you're trying to return to a site you visited in a previous session or one that isn't in the Go menu for some reason, try the History folder. The History folder contains the Web addresses of all the sites you've visited in the past two weeks. (For information on changing the retention time, see Chapter 8.) This is the place to look for that cool site you visited a few days ago.

PART
III

To view the History folder, choose Go Open History Folder. You'll see your History folder, as shown in Figure 9-2. This is a standard Windows Explorer window, which you can navigate using the familiar Microsoft Windows 95 tools and techniques.

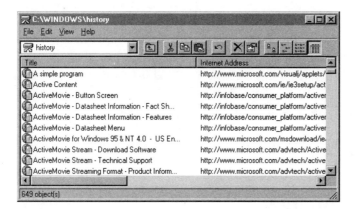

Figure 9-2
The History folder.

Why Did That Site Disappear from the Go Menu?

Let's start with a problem that beginning surfers soon notice. You're visiting a site, and you go down deeply into a series of links and then click Back. You do a little more surfing. Then, remembering something you saw that was cool, you try to go back again, looking for a document you *know* you displayed a few minutes ago—but clicking Back doesn't display it. Worse, you don't see the document in the Go menu.

What's going on? You can see for yourself. Go to a site (let's call it Page 1) that has lots of links, and click one. You'll see a new page (let's call it Page 2). Look at the Go menu; you'll see Page 1 and Page 2. Now click one of the links on Page 2. You'll see a page we'll call Page 3. If you look at the Go menu now, you'll see Page 1, Page 2, and Page 3. Now click Back to go back to Page 2, and click a *different* link. You'll see Page 4. If you look at the Go menu now, you'll see Page 1, Page 2—and Page 4! But no Page 3!

What's going on here? It's simple. The Go menu tracks only one *lineage* at a time. A lineage is a series of hyperlinks that continue in one unbroken stream. If you go back in the stream and branch off in a new direction, the Go menu lops off sites you went back from.

So *that's* what happened to the mysterious missing page.

New Lineage, New Window

Now that you know what a lineage is, you're about to learn what I consider to be the best surfing trick in this book. To reduce confusion while browsing and maximize your ability to go back to a previously viewed site, remember the motto "New lineage, new window." This motto reminds you to open a new window whenever you've gone back to a previously viewed site and want to head off in a new direction. If you do this consistently, each Internet Explorer window will preserve all the sites you've visited in a given session, and you won't have any trouble returning to any of the sites you've visited.

Using More Than One Window

You can open more than one window on the Internet with Internet Explorer. As you've just learned, you can use this capability to reduce confusion while browsing.

Multiple-Window Tricks

Here are some other good reasons to open more than one window:

- 🌐 **Keep working while downloading a lengthy document.** Suppose you're waiting for a lengthy document to download. To keep working with Internet Explorer, you can open another Web document in a new window. The lengthy document will continue downloading in the original window.

- 🌐 **Keep reference information in one window while you're reading another document.** For example, you could display a glossary of terms in one window while reading text in another window.

- 🌐 **Keep a search engine or a subject tree visible in one window.** You can return to your search or your subject tree quickly and easily as you browse through the results.

How to Open a New Window

You can open a new Internet Explorer window by right-clicking or by using the File menu.

Right-Clicking to Open a New Window

If you see a hyperlink that you'd like to display in a new window, you can do so by following these steps:

1. Right-click the hyperlink.

2. From the pop-up menu, choose Open In New Window. Internet Explorer opens the document in a new window.

Using the File New Window Command

To open a new Internet Explorer window, choose the File New Window command or use the Ctrl+N shortcut.

Stopping an Unwanted Download

After you click a hyperlink, Internet Explorer starts downloading a new document. If you decide you're not interested in seeing the document, you can stop the download before it's complete.

To stop downloading a document, Click the Stop tool, choose the View Stop command, or simply press Esc.

Dealing with Frames

Framed documents (for an example, see Figure 9-3) pose special problems for navigation, as you'll doubtless discover the first time you click Back in a framed document. Once you understand what's going on, though, you won't have any trouble.

Figure 9-3

A site with frames.

CHAPTER 9

Keep the following in mind when you're navigating a framed document:

🌐 Some frames are scrollable, and others aren't. You can tell the difference by looking to see whether there's a scroll bar.

🌐 Sometimes Web authors enable you to adjust the frame borders. You can tell whether a border is adjustable by moving the mouse pointer to the border. If the pointer changes shape to arrows, you can adjust the border.

🌐 Only one frame is active (selected) at a time. When you click Back or Forward, your action affects only that frame (but not the others).

🌐 If you've viewed many pages within the frame site and want to go back to the previous site you viewed, it's faster to choose the previous site from the Go menu rather than clicking Back. You might have to click Back many times to exit the framed site.

🌐 If you're at the beginning of the framed site (the welcome page), clicking Back takes you out of the current site to the previously viewed site.

NOTE

Thanks to innovative new HTML technology from Microsoft, you might soon see framed documents that don't have those big, intrusive, ugly borders.

Saving Passwords

More and more Web sites are requiring authentication to access their goodies, even if they're freebies. Why? They need to prove to their advertisers that people are actually visiting their sites.

You know the drill. You access one of these sites, and you're asked to specify a user name and password. Cheerfully, you supply these and enjoy the site. A few days later, you visit the site again—but you've forgotten your password. You'll have to send e-mail to the site's Webmaster to find out which password you've used, or you'll need to register all over again (with a different user name). Increasingly, that means filling out a long, detailed questionnaire.

Internet Explorer saves the day by remembering your password for you. The first time you access the site after registering, you'll see a dialog box such as the one in Figure 9-4.

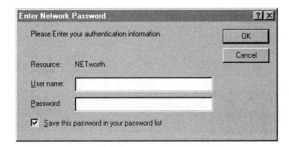

Figure 9-4
A password dialog box.

To direct Internet Explorer to memorize your login name and password so that you don't have to type them again, click Save This Password In Your Password List.

NOTE

Not every Web site demands passwords in the same way. Password memorization works only for those sites that direct the browser to display a dialog box. If the authentication is handled by means of a special Web page, Internet Explorer can't memorize your password.

Browsing with the Keyboard

New In Version 3: In general, browsers are click-intensive. Since excessive mouse usage may be associated with repetitive strain injuries (RSI), you might want to explore a very nice feature of Internet Explorer version 3: You can use the Tab and Shift+Tab keys to select hyperlinks (including hyperlinks embedded in imagemaps), and you can select a hyperlink by pressing Enter. Try it!

Choosing Ratings

If you want to let children browse the Web on their own with Internet Explorer, you can choose options that control the level of sexual content, nudity, violence, and adult language that they'll encounter. This is done by means of the Ratings dialog box. To display this dialog box, choose View Options, click the Advanced tab, and click Enable Ratings. You'll be asked to set a supervisor password. (If a password has already been set up, you'll be asked to supply it.) You'll see the dialog box shown in Figure 9-5.

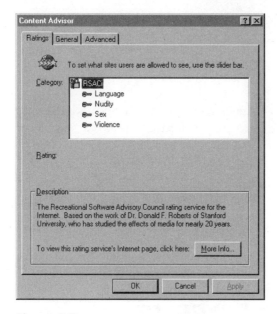

Figure 9-5
The Ratings dialog box.

To set ratings, click a category and adjust the slider to choose the restrictions you want. To make sure viewers can't see sites that aren't rated, click the General tab and deselect Users Can See Unrated Sites. When you're finished choosing restrictions, click OK.

NOTE
Internet Explorer depends on site ratings, but relatively few sites are rated at this time. (More are expected to adopt ratings in the future.) Until rating becomes common, you might prefer to turn off ratings restrictions and supply some good old parental supervision when the kids use the Internet.

From Here

🌐   With more than 55 million resources on the Web (at last count), it's a challenge to find the information you're looking for. In Chapter 10, you learn how to put the Web's powerful search tools to work on your behalf. If it's out there, you'll find it.

🌐   Run into error messages or problems while surfing? Find out what to do in Chapter 11.

CHAPTER 9

Tracking Down Information on the Web

Writing in the *Wall Street Journal,* Walter S. Mossberg points out something that millions of dismayed Web users are discovering for themselves:

"Everybody who's anybody wants to set up shop on the World Wide Web. The trouble is, it's not easy to locate a brand new Web site" ("Everybody's Jumping Onto the Internet, but Just Try to Find Them," July 6, 1995, p. B1).

With more than an estimated 55 million Web documents in existence and thousands more being added each day, the Web is becoming one of the richest treasure troves of information in the world—but it's difficult to *find* the information you're looking for.

What's the result? After logging on to the Web and surfing around for a while, too many people conclude that they've entered an impenetrable maze. They get lost. They get frustrated. They can't find what they're looking for. Too many search tools exist, and people don't know how to coordinate them. Some even conclude there's nothing out there for them.

If that's how you feel, take heart. Chances are there *is* something out there for you—and maybe lots of good stuff. You just don't know how to find it.

In this chapter, you'll learn a strategy for searching the Web that's virtually certain to locate documents in a specific area of interest—if such documents exist.

A Quick Guide to the Web's Search Services

- **Alta Vista.** This search service currently has the largest database of Web documents. Also, this service indexes the entire text of each document. For these two reasons, Alta Vista is great if you're looking for something fairly obscure, or if you want to find every possible Web document on a given subject. It's not such a good choice if you're just looking for a few good documents on a subject. Most Alta Vista searches retrieve a lot of documents that aren't relevant to your interests. Alta Vista enables you to search Usenet newsgroups, but there are no reviews of Web sites.

- **Excite.** Currently in transition to a database containing 50 million Web documents, Excite promises to become one of the Web's best services. A plus: you can search reviewed sites as well as Usenet news and classified ads.

- **InfoSeek Guide.** Although this search service has a small database, you'll find that InfoSeek searches generally produce a more useful retrieval list than most other search services. However, the small database means that there are surely more documents of interest out there. A very nice feature of InfoSeek Guide: the search service tries to match your search terms with site categories from the Guide, a collection of high-quality sites. You can search the database of Web documents, a much smaller collection of InfoSeek Select Sites, site categories, Usenet newsgroups, or Usenet FAQs (Frequently Asked Questions).

(continued)

A Quick Guide to the Web's Search Services *continued*

🌐 **Lycos.** Like Alta Vista, Lycos offers a huge database of Web documents. However, this service does not index the full text of Web documents. Instead, it concentrates on important words in the first 20 lines or so of text and gives preference to titles. As a result, Lycos searches seem somewhat more accurate than Alta Vista searches (that is, a higher percentage of retrieved documents actually pertain to your search interests), but you might miss documents in which your subject is mentioned only peripherally.

🌐 **Magellan.** Like Excite, Magellan enables you to search reviewed sites. A major plus: you can search for *green light* sites, which are OK for kids. You can search the rated and reviewed sites only, or you can search the entire database.

🌐 **Yahoo.** When you search Yahoo, you search among thousands of reviewed sites and site categories. In comparison to Alta Vista and Lycos, the database is small, but the quality of retrieved documents is high. Yahoo is a good place to look if you're trying to find a few good sites on a subject.

Step 1: Develop a List of Key Words

Take out a sheet of paper—or if this is too low-tech, open WordPad—and make a list of all the words that somebody would include in a document of interest to you. Be sure to include all possible forms of each word (such as "kayak," "kayaks," and "kayaking").

For example, suppose you're interested in making a visit to North Carolina's Outer Banks, and you're hoping to do some kayaking. Your first list might look like the following:

Outer
Banks
North
Carolina
kayak
kayaks
kayaking

Step 2: Check the
Subject Catalog (Yahoo)

Remember your first grammar school library assignment? You start researching by checking the subject catalog—you know, the one that organized all
those library cards using headings like Transylvania—Fiction—Vampires.
With any luck, you'll find something in the subject catalog that will get you
started, and its bibliography will help you find additional items of interest.

Unfortunately, there's no subject catalog for the Internet that comes even
close to indexing the many millions of Web documents. That's because
computers aren't smart enough (yet) to do subject indexing, which must be
done by hand. The folks at Yahoo are hard at work, indexing up to several
thousand documents per day, but currently Yahoo was just breaking the
100,000 mark. Still, Yahoo provides a great place to start.

To get started, click the Search button on the toolbar. You'll see the
Internet Searches page shown in Figure 10-1. Think of this page as a Grand
Central Station for Internet searching.

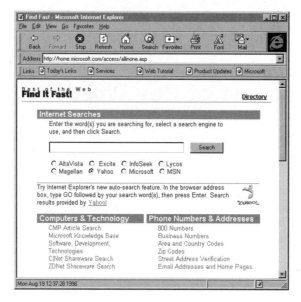

Figure 10-1

The Internet Searches page.

Searching Yahoo

You can search Yahoo from the Internet Searches page. To get started, try to think of some combination of your search words that expresses what you're looking for in the most general terms (for example, "Outer Banks" rather than "Outer Banks kayaking rentals"). Type just one or two of your words in the text box, and click Search. If Yahoo found anything that matches your search terms, you'll see a page such as the one shown in Figure 10-2.

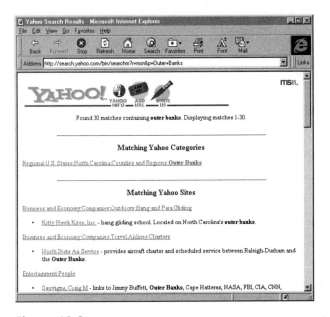

Figure 10-2
The results of a Yahoo search.

If you're really lucky, Yahoo will have found a Yahoo Category that matches your search terms. In Figure 10-2, you see a category for Outer Banks ("Regional:U.S. States:North Carolina:Counties and Regions:Outer Banks"). If you click this link, you'll find a good sampling of high-quality documents about this subject, as shown in Figure 10-3. Below the Categories links, you see a lengthier list of Yahoo sites whose names or descriptions contain the words "Outer Banks." You can scroll through these to see if there's anything of interest.

CHAPTER 10

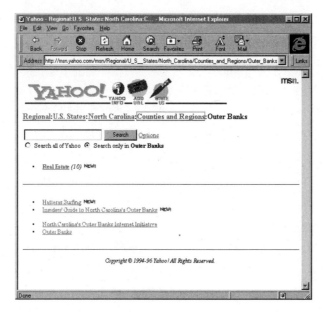

Figure 10-3

Yahoo subject page for Outer Banks.

Sometimes your Yahoo search will generate too lengthy a list. If so, go back to the search page and add one or more additional terms to your search.

Looking at Yahoo Search Results

Once you've displayed a subject page, such as the one shown in Figure 10-2, you can perform an additional search that's restricted to the sites listed in this subject. (In Figure 10-3, for example, you would do this by clicking Search only in Outer Banks.) This feature comes in handy when a Yahoo subject page contains hundreds of links.

Step 3: Look for Reviewed Documents

Another way to find high-quality Web documents is to search the Web site reviews offered by Excite, InfoSeek, and Magellan. Only a very small proportion of Web sites have been reviewed by these services. Still, you might get lucky and find a site that's gotten rave reviews. This search doesn't take very much time, so it's worth a try.

Looking for Reviewed Sites in Excite

To search for reviewed sites in Excite, click the Excite hyperlink (instead of typing your search terms and clicking Search). You'll see the Search Excite page, shown in Figure 10-4. This page enables you to choose advanced search options. Type your search terms in the text box, and then click Reviews. For an example of a positively reviewed page retrieved in a search for the Outer Banks, see Figure 10-5. It's the home page for The Insider's Guide to the Outer Banks (http://www.insiders.com/outerbanks/index.htm).

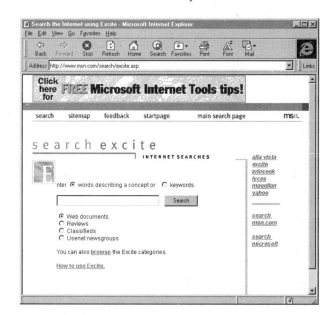

Figure 10-4

The Search Excite page with advanced options.

10
CHAPTER

Figure 10-5

Insider's Guide to the Outer Banks (site reviewed by Excite).

Looking for Reviewed Sites in InfoSeek

To search for reviewed sites in InfoSeek, click the InfoSeek link on the Internet Searches page. You'll see the Search InfoSeek page, shown in Figure 10-6. In the text box, type your search terms. Then choose Infoseek Select Sites from the list box, and click Search. The reviews aren't as extensive or critical as Excite's, but you'll find a few good links.

Looking for Reviewed Sites in Magellan

Magellan has embarked on the daunting task of rating Web sites using a four-star system. An additional and praiseworthy feature is Magellan's Green Light rating system, which indicates whether a site is appropriate for kids. Great work, Magellan!

To search for reviewed sites in Magellan, click the Magellan link on the Internet Searches page. You'll see the Search Magellan page, shown in Figure 10-7. In the text box, type your search terms. From the list box, choose Green Light sites if you're interested in seeing only those sites appropriate for kids. Click Search, and you'll see a page that combines items retrieved from Magellan's reviews and the larger Web database. There's a link at the top of the page that restricts the list to reviewed sites—give it a try. (Figure 10-8 shows the results.)

Figure 10-6
The Search InfoSeek page.

Figure 10-7
The Search Magellan page.

163

Figure 10-8

Magellan-reviewed sites.

I get different results from these services!

That's right—and that's why it's a good idea to try all of them. Indexing and reviewing the Web is a job akin to counting the grains of sand in all of California's beaches, so it's not surprising that there's so little overlap among the sites reviewed by Excite, InfoSeek, and Magellan. It all depends on where they started digging.

Step 4: Try a Quick Search of the Web

Still looking for something? Try a quick search using one of the services that maintains a database of Web documents. These databases are much, much larger than Yahoo's categorized links or the collections of reviewed sites (in Excite, InfoSeek, and Magellan).

Where do these databases come from? These services rely on automated programs called *spiders*. These programs roam the Web looking for new Web documents. When they find one, they download the document's text, index some or all of the words found in the document, and add the Web address to the database.

A good place to start is InfoSeek. This search service is easy to use and produces good results. Other search services offer larger databases, but they also hit you with lots of irrelevant documents in their retrieval lists.

A big advantage of InfoSeek is that this service enables you to perform *phrase searches*. In brief, a phrase search tries to match the exact phrase you typed and doesn't return documents that mention the individual words in the phrase unless they're next to each other (and in the same order you typed them). Phrase searches help to cut down on the retrieval of irrelevant documents. To perform a phrase search with InfoSeek, you enclose your search terms in quotation marks (for example, "Outer Banks").

Now you can start your search:

1. On the toolbar, click Search.

2. In the InfoSeek box, type one or more search terms. If you would like to perform a phrase search, enclose the phrase in quotation marks.

3. Click Search. You'll see a page of links matching the terms you typed, if any were found (see Figure 10-9).

4. To jump to one of these links, just click it.

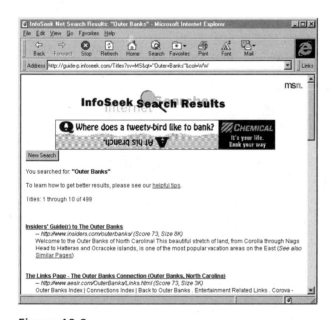

Figure 10-9
InfoSeek search results.

CHAPTER 10

Troubleshooting Your Search

If your search didn't work out well, consider the following:

- 🌐 **Did you spell the search terms correctly?** A typo or mis-spelling can ruin your search.

- 🌐 **Try a synonym.** If you're searching for a wine called Shiraz, you should also search for Syrah, a different name for the same wine.

- 🌐 **Did you use the wrong capitalization pattern?** Use capital letters only when they're appropriate. Don't type your search terms in all capital letters.

Step 5: Perform a Deeper Search

Still haven't found what you're looking for? Hard to find, isn't it? It's time for Alta Vista.

Currently, Alta Vista has the largest of all Web databases—some 30 million documents, every word of which has been indexed by Alta Vista's powerful computers—but it has plenty of competition. Both Excite and InfoSeek plan to offer much bigger databases as well. Still, Alta Vista will continue to be a very good place for your needle-in-the-haystack search.

Performing Your Alta Vista Search

To perform your Alta Vista search, display the Internet Searches page, and type *all* your search terms (from step 1) in the Alta Vista text box. That's right—all of them. Why? Alta Vista's database is so huge that, in all likelihood, a search for a general subject will produce far too many retrieved items. You don't want to spend hours going through page after page of irrelevant junk, do you? Consider that Alta Vista currently has roughly 2000 documents containing the exact phrase "Outer Banks"—and that excludes all the documents that have nothing to do with North Carolina's Outer Banks, but do include phrases such as, "Spaceman Spif, hoping to avoid the alien's attack, *banks* his spacecraft sharply and heads for *outer* space."

Refining Your Alta Vista Search

Chances are your Alta Vista search will net some good documents, but I'll bet it's full of material that strikes you as erroneous. Sure, there's some good stuff in there, but maybe it's not near the top. Maybe it's buried on the 20th page of the retrieval list, and you'll get bored with the whole thing after reading two or three pages of junk.

PART
III

If that's how you reacted to your first Alta Vista search, there's good news. You can use a couple of super-easy tricks to increase the accuracy of your search. Here's a quick overview:

🌐 If you're looking for a phrase, surround the phrase in quotation marks. For example, type *"Outer Banks"* rather than *Outer Banks*, so you won't get the page describing the new banking ventures in Outer Mongolia.

🌐 Use a *wild card* to make sure you're getting all the documents relevant to your interests. Most Web search services don't enable you to do this, but Alta Vista lets you type an asterisk to match one or more characters at the end of a word. For example, you can type *kayak** to match *kayak*, *kayaks*, and *kayaking*.

🌐 Put a plus sign in front of your most important word (no space). If you see lots of stuff on the Outer Banks but nothing on kayaks, for example, type *"Outer Banks" +kayak**. The plus sign brings documents containing this word to the top of the list.

🌐 If the retrieval list is stuffed with documents pertaining to something you *don't* want, type a term describing these documents and place a minus sign in front of it (no space). For example, the Outer Banks kayak search nets a lot of documents, for some reason, that mention Asheville, N.C. To demote these documents to the bottom of the list, type *-Asheville*.

These nifty tricks enable you to perform a pinpoint search. Of the more than 3000 documents containing some or all of the search words, this strategy puts a hot one right at the top of the list: Kayak Touring of the Outer Banks (http://www.khsports.com/khs/kayaking.html).

HELP

I tried these tricks with another search service, but they didn't work!

That's right. Unfortunately, each of the Web's search services uses its own search *syntax,* the rules for typing search terms and search commands properly. But there's some overlap. For example, you can use the plus and minus signs in Lycos and InfoSeek, and you can perform a phrase search in InfoSeek by surrounding the search term in quotation marks.

CHAPTER 10

From Here

  You're browsing along happily, but all of a sudden you see a horrifying error message. Find out what it means in Chapter 11.

  If you've mastered searching and surfing, you've mastered the Web! Now tackle the rest of the Internet, including e-mail, Usenet news, Internet Relay Chat, and Internet telephony. It's all possible with Internet Explorer. Find out more in Part IV.

CHAPTER 11

Hey!
What's Wrong?

You're browsing the Web
innocently enough, and everything's going fine—but then
you see an alert box or encounter an error message. No, this
doesn't mean you're a failure with the Internet. It's a big network out there,
and all kinds of things can go wrong. Sometimes, try as you might, you just
can't get through to a Web site that worked fine just a few days ago. Still, there
are some tricks you can try, as you'll learn in this chapter.

It Says Other People
Can See What I'm Sending!

You've probably already seen this dialog box (shown in Figure 11-1) lots
of times.

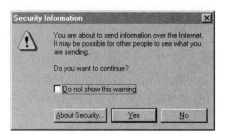

Figure 11-1

The Security Information dialog box.

This doesn't necessarily mean that the FBI or computer hackers are
tracking your every move on line, but it does call for caution. As you'll learn
in Chapter 17, it's quite true that the text you're typing can be intercepted
and read en route. It's nothing much to worry about if you're searching Alta
Vista for ways to make your kitty feel secure or for family bookstores in
Atlanta, but you'll definitely want to bear this mind if you're uploading sen-
sitive personal information (such as your credit card number) or something
naughty (such as a search query for fantasy leather sites). Flip to Chapter
17 for more information. For now, click Do Not Show This Warning; this dialog box cries "Wolf!" too often.

I Clicked the Hyperlink
and Nothing Happens!

This is probably the most frustrating problem you'll encounter when browsing
the Web. The program icon revolves and revolves, but you don't see a darned
thing on screen. After what seems like an eternity, you see a message like
the one in Figure 11-2 that says the site was not found.

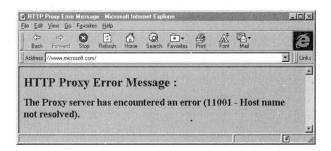

Figure 11-2

The "site not found" alert box.

Here are possible solutions:

🌐 **Did you type the address correctly?** It's pretty easy to make a typing mistake when you're typing those pesky Web addresses. Remember that you don't need to type the *http://* part; Internet Explorer will handle that for you. Carefully check what you've typed. In particular, look for spaces (not allowed within a Web address). If your eyesight isn't the greatest (like mine), look carefully to see whether you've typed a comma instead of a period (*www,microsoft.com*).

🌐 **Are you still connected to the Internet?** Sometimes line noise can cause modems to become confused—a very painful situation for modems, apparently, because they'll shut down the connection without so much as a by-your-leave. Check the Windows 95 status bar to see if the little modem icon is still there. If not, your modem has hung up on you. You'll need to dial the connection again.

🌐 **Are you browsing between 11:30 AM and 1:30 PM?** Sometimes Web servers get so overloaded that they can't even respond to a request by saying, "Try later, I'm too busy." This is a likely culprit if you're searching at lunchtime, since people are increasingly spending their lunch breaks surfing the Web instead of doing something healthy like going to the gym.

It Says, "404 Not Found"!

And you weren't even searching for 404, right? Well, there's good news and bad news here (see Figure 11-3). The good news is that part of the Web address you're using is correct. Internet Explorer was able to find the server you're trying to contact. The only problem is that the server couldn't locate a document with the name you supplied.

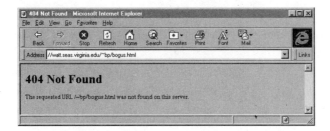

Figure 11-3

You found the server, but the document's missing.

Possible solutions:

- **Did you type the address correctly?** I hate to sound like a broken record, but this is a good possibility. In particular, check to see whether you typed the document's extension correctly. Lots of Web documents use the extension .html, but many—dating back to the glory days of Windows 3.1, when three-letter extensions were the order of the day—use *.htm. If you type *.html* when the server expects *.htm, it might not retrieve the document.

- **The document might have been moved, and the author didn't have the courtesy of leaving a forwarding address.** To see whether it's available on some other server or in a different directory location on the same server, try an Alta Vista search, as described in the previous chapter.

🌐 **The document might have been yanked from the Web.** This happens—all too frequently. It even happens when you link to a document from a search service, such as Excite or Alta Vista. Sometimes these services take a few days or even a few weeks to discover that a page has disappeared from the Web.

🌐 **The author might be in the middle of updating the page.** Try again later.

It Says, "Forbidden"! (Error 403)

This one's a shock (see Figure 11-4). And it's *rude*, too—but it's intended to be. Basically, you've accessed a document that isn't designed for access outside the organization or regional area that it calls home. It's designed for local consumption only. Too bad. Go away!

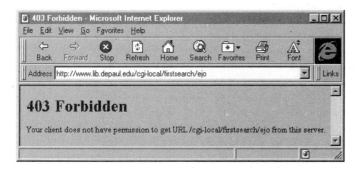

Figure 11-4

You can't access this document from outside the originating organization.

It Says, "This Site Has Moved!"

Now here's a thoughtful Web author, with the courtesy to give you a forwarding address (see Figure 11-5 on the next page). If there's a link to the new location, click it.

Figure 11-5

Follow the link from the old site (top) to the new site (bottom).

It Says, "Cannot Open Internet File"!

You're trying to download a file from an FTP site, as discussed in Chapter 15, but you can't get through to the overloaded server. (This is common if you're accessing a popular site.) The message, shown in Figure 11-6, adds, as if in triumph, that the "operation was completed successfully."

Figure 11-6
The "Cannot Open" dialog box.

It wasn't so successful from your point of view, was it? Here's what's going on. You were trying to download a file, and you clicked a link that accesses an FTP file server. (For more information on FTP, see Chapter 15.) Unfortunately, the server is busy. Most FTP servers can't handle more than 250 downloads at once.

The solution's simple: Try later. Maybe like about 2 o'clock in the morning.

From Here

- 🌐 You've mastered Internet Explorer, and you've mastered the Web. What's left? There's lots more to the Internet, as you'll discover in Part IV: e-mail, Usenet, Internet Relay Chat, and Internet telephony and conferencing.

- 🌐 To get started with Internet Mail, see Chapter 12.

- 🌐 Get going with Usenet, but don't get burned. Find out how in Chapter 13.

- 🌐 Get into the swing of things on Internet Relay Chat with Comic Chat, covered in Chapter 14.

- 🌐 Explore the "old" Internet—FTP, Telnet, Gopher, and WAIS— which still has plenty of useful information left in it. Find out how in Chapter 15.

CHAPTER 11

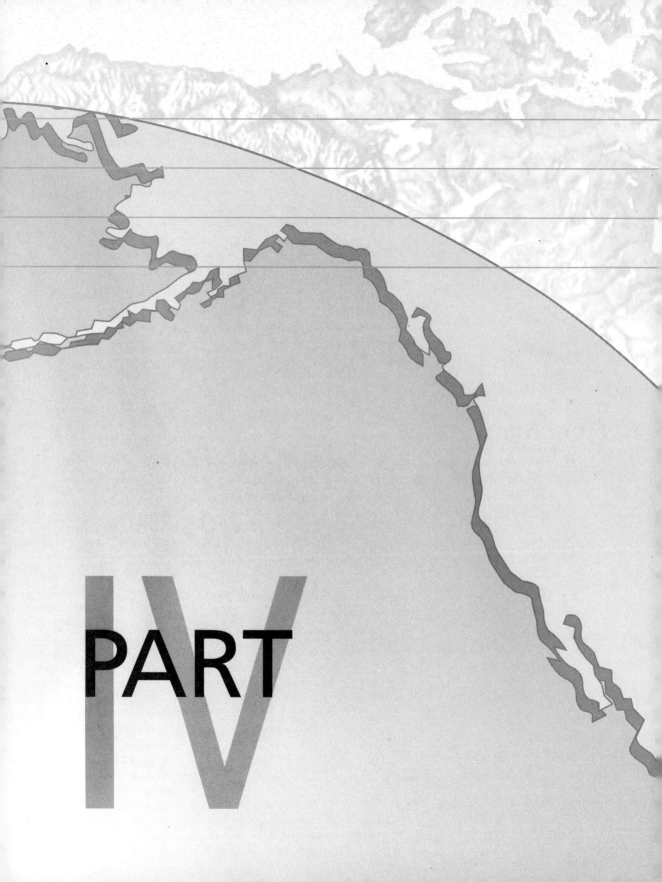

PART IV

Exploring the Internet

1 2

CHAPTER

Using Internet Mail

The Web is cool and extremely useful, provided you don't waste too much time browsing all those fun sites. However, when asked what they like best about the Internet, most people reply unhesitatingly, "Internet e-mail." In profession after profession, people soon conclude that they would be at a serious disadvantage if they couldn't communicate via e-mail.

What's so great about e-mail? It's faster than the U.S. Postal Service, for one thing, and that's a major attraction. What's also great about e-mail is the possibility of getting in touch with people who share your interests, whatever those might be, in a medium that obliterates geography. You might soon have e-mail pen pals all over North America and beyond. There are

CHAPTER 12

potentially millions of people—as many as 50 million by one recent estimate—you can reach in this way. Global in scope, the reach of Internet e-mail is actually much broader than the Internet itself, thanks to *e-mail gateways,* which permit Internet users to exchange e-mail messages with users of other computer networks.

New In Version 3: Gone are the days when Internet Explorer users had no other option besides Microsoft Exchange, a mail client designed for big corporate networks rather than the Internet. Nicely integrated with Internet Explorer version 3 is Internet Mail, a mail client that puts many commercial programs to shame. An Internet-savvy program, Mail includes exactly the features that Internet users want and includes some cool innovations. For example, you can choose to format your outgoing messages in HTML so that your recipient can view your message with rich formatting (including fonts, colors, sizes, bullets, and justification).

Even if you've never sent or received an e-mail message before, you'll be up and running with Internet Mail by using this chapter as your guide. You'll learn how to make good use of all the Internet Mail features, including:

- Downloading and reading your mail messages.
- Writing and sending replies and new messages.
- Including attachments (files) with your messages.
- Formatting your outgoing messages with HTML.
- Adding a personal signature to your messages.
- Organizing the message list.
- Searching for text within the message list.
- Creating an address book of frequently used e-mail addresses.
- Creating your own folders to organize and store incoming messages.
- Defining rules that automatically store incoming messages in the correct folder.

NOTE

Internet Mail isn't designed to work with online services, such as the Microsoft Network (MSN), CompuServe, or America Online. To send and receive internal as well as Internet electronic mail with these services, use the software provided by your online service. To use Internet Mail, you need a subscription with an Internet service provider.

Understanding Internet E-Mail

If you've never used e-mail before, you need to know that it's not like tra-ditional communication systems. Unlike ordinary mail, transmission is fast—you can send a letter halfway around the world in a matter of minutes. But it's by no means guaranteed that your recipient will actually read your message. It all depends on whether your correspondent logs on and checks his or her mail. Not everyone does so daily, or even weekly. It's even con-sidered good manners to tell people when you're going to be on vacation or otherwise not checking your e-mail for long periods.

When somebody sends you an e-mail message, it's stored temporarily in your electronic *mailbox*. Generally, this mailbox is part of the file stor-age system of an Internet service provider or an online service such as the Microsoft Network, or MSN. You don't get your messages until you log on to the service provider and start your e-mail program. The program then checks your electronic mailbox and downloads any new messages to your computer. You can then read them, reply to them, delete them, or forward them, just as you please. When you finish dealing with your messages, the e-mail program sends any new messages you've created to the service pro-vider, where they're zinged on their way to their destinations.

About Internet E-Mail Addresses

To get your e-mail message across, you need to know how to use Internet e-mail addresses, which look like this:

`frodo@bagend.shire.org`

Every Internet e-mail address has three parts:

- 🌐 **User name (for example, "frodo").** This isn't a person's name; it's the name given to a person's electronic mailbox, which is often made up of components of the person's name.

- 🌐 **At sign (@).** This is needed to separate the user name from the next part, the domain name.

- 🌐 **Domain name (for example, "bagend.shire.org").** This is the Internet address of the computer that contains the person's electronic mailbox. Note that the various parts of the domain name are separated by dots; if you're telling someone your e-mail address, you pronounce the dots by saying "dot," as in "frodo at bagend-dot-shire-dot-org."

CHAPTER 12

What It's Like to Use E-Mail

To use Internet e-mail, you use your computer to connect to your *mail server*, the computer that stores your incoming mail. When you log on, you supply your account name and password. The mail server then checks to see whether there's any e-mail for you. If so, Internet mail begins downloading the messages to your computer.

Once you've downloaded the messages, you can read them, store them in folders, reply to them, forward them to another e-mail address, or delete them. You can also write and send messages of your own. When you've completed downloading and sending your messages, you log off the server.

E-Mail and Privacy

Before using e-mail, you need to understand clearly that U.S. and state governments provide little or no privacy protection for your messages. The Electronic Communications Privacy Act of 1986, the only federal legislation that governs electronic mail, requires U.S. government agencies to obtain search warrants to intercept and read electronic mail messages while they are en route. What the computer-illiterate authors of this bill did not realize, however, is that all mail servers maintain backup tapes, sometimes for *years,* of all the e-mail messages that pass through their systems. Any investigator can obtain access to these tapes and use them for any purpose whatsoever.

As for e-mail that you send and receive on your employer's computer, the courts have consistently found that employees deserve no privacy protection at all when they're using their company's computers. Your boss is quite free to read your e-mail and use it in a termination proceeding, and there's nothing you can do about it.

You'll be very, very wise to follow the following rule:

Never, never, never write anything in e-mail that you wouldn't want to see the next morning on your boss's desk, on your mother's coffee table, or on the front page of your hometown newspaper.

An Internet domain name can give you hints about where a person's mail is coming from. At the end of the name is the *top-level domain,* which is a general category. If the message originates outside the United States, the top-level domain usually indicates the country of origin ("uk," for example, is United Kingdom, and "fr" is France). Within the United States, messages from universities and colleges use the top-level domain "edu," government agencies use "gov," corporations use "com," and nonprofit organizations use "org."

Introducing Internet Mail

Internet Mail is part of the Internet Mail and News software, which you'll find on the CD-ROM disc packaged with this book.

Should you use Internet Mail instead of other e-mail packages? You be the judge, but I think you'll conclude that Internet Mail is an impressive program. It includes the features that regular Internet mail users value the most, such as *signatures* (text added automatically at the end of every message you send), *filters* (rules that automatically file incoming messages into folders so that you aren't hit with hundreds of low-priority messages in the midst of your personal messages), and an address book to store frequently used e-mail addresses. Internet Mail compares favorably to the best mail programs on the market.

Installing Internet Mail

When you install Mail and News, you'll be asked to supply some important information about your e-mail account, so be sure to obtain this information before proceeding:

 Internet address for your incoming mail (POP-3 mail server). This is the name of the computer that stores your mail until you log on. It will have a name such as bagend.shire.org. (A POP-3 mail server employs an Internet standard, called the Post Office Protocol, to store your mail until you log on to retrieve it.)

 Internet address for your outgoing mail (SMTP mail server). Probably, this is the same as the computer that handles your incoming mail, but sometimes it's different. (An SMTP mail server employs another Internet standard, called the Simple Mail Transport Protocol, to send your e-mail over the Internet.)

CHAPTER 12

- **Your e-mail address.** Your Internet service provider will give this to you.

- **Your account name and password.** Often (but not always) your account name is the same as the first part of your e-mail address. The e-mail password might differ from the password you use to log on to the service provider. Be sure to write your password down somewhere in case you forget it.

NOTE

If you change Internet service providers, you will need to change the server information. With Mail, this is easy to do. Start Mail, and choose Mail Options. Click the Servers tab. In the Servers area, type the new information and click OK.

Running Mail for the First Time

To start Internet Mail, click Internet Explorer's Mail icon and choose Read Mail from the pop-up menu or choose Go Read Mail. When you run Mail for the first time, you'll see the Internet Mail Configuration Wizard. This wizard helps you supply the needed server information.

NOTE

Please be sure to type the server information correctly. One little typo is all that's needed to make connecting impossible. (If you later have problems connecting, you can check this information by opening Mail and choosing Mail Options and clicking the Servers tab. You can make any needed corrections here.) Also, be sure you have all the information you need. If not, call your Internet service provider.

To start the wizard, click Next. You'll be asked to supply your e-mail address, the Internet address of the computer that handles your incoming and outgoing mail, your e-mail account, and your password.

You'll also describe how you connect to the Internet (via a LAN at work, by means of a manual connection, or by modem). Here's what these options mean:

- **LAN At Work.** Choose this option if you're connected to a computer that's hooked up to the Internet via a local area network (LAN). If you're not sure, contact your network's administrator, who will be glad to help you.

- **Manual Connection.** This is the recommended option for most users who connect to an Internet service provider by means of a

PART
IV

modem. In order to use Mail, you will first have to establish your Internet connection (for example, by starting Internet Explorer or by clicking your service provider's icon in Dial-Up Networking).

🌐 **Modem Connection.** This option is *not* recommended unless you are paying a lot of money for a time-billed Internet connection and you want to keep your connect time to the absolute minimum. With this option, Internet Mail will start your Internet connection automatically when you open the program, download your mail, and log you off. If you were hoping to do something else on line, you might find this frustrating. For this reason, I recommend Manual Connection.

When you're finished with the wizard, you're ready to start Mail.

Connecting to Your Service Provider

If you chose Manual Connection as your preferred connection mode (this is the recommended option), you must connect to the Internet before starting Mail. To connect to the Internet, open My Computer, select Dial-Up Networking, and double-click your service provider's icon. (For more information on establishing your Internet connection, see Appendix A.)

To start Internet Mail, do one of the following:

🌐 From the Windows 95 Start menu, choose Programs Internet Mail.

🌐 From Internet Explorer, choose Go Read Mail, or click the Mail icon and choose Read Mail from the pop-up menu.

When you're successfully connected to the service provider, Mail will automatically check to see whether you've received any messages. If you're logging on for the first time, you might get a "Hello!" message from your service provider. If there aren't any messages for you, you'll see the message "No new messages" on the status bar.

HELP

I couldn't connect!

A lot can go wrong with a first-time mail connection, including problems with modems and log-on procedures. A very likely cause: You typed some of the setup information incorrectly. In Internet Mail, choose View Options and click the Server tab. In the Servers area, check this information carefully to make sure it's correct. If not, make the correction and click OK. For more information on troubleshooting your Internet connection, see Appendix A.

CHAPTER 12

Looking at Internet Mail

Internet Mail (see Figure 12-1) is designed to look and work like Internet Explorer. There's much that's familiar: the program icon and the toolbars that you can drag and position. You'll notice, however, that the toolbar buttons differ, and there are two panels within the workspace. These screen areas are dynamically linked: When you select a folder in the folder panel, you see that folder's message list, and the message window shows the message that's currently selected in the message list.

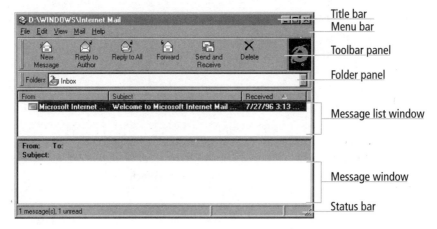

Figure 12-1

Internet Mail.

You'll see the following in Internet Mail's window (see Figure 12-1):

🌐 **Title bar.** To reposition the Mail window, drag the title bar. To maximize the window quickly, double-click the title bar. Double-click again to restore the previous size.

🌐 **Menu bar.** Here you'll find all the Mail commands, but the most frequently used commands are found on the toolbar.

🌐 **Toolbar.** The toolbar contains some useful tools. You'll find the following buttons: New Message, Reply To Author, Reply To All, Forward, Send And Receive, and Delete. (If you don't see the toolbar, choose View Toolbar.)

- **Folder list.** Internet Mail enables you to organize your mail into folders. You can create your own, as you'll learn later in this chapter. The default folders are described in the next section. By default, Inbox is selected.

- **Message list.** Here you see the contents of the folder you've selected in the Folder panel. You'll see your first messages, if you've received any.

- **Preview pane.** This window shows the text of the message that's currently selected in the message list. By choosing View Preview Pane, you can choose the display options for the preview pane. The options are Split Horizontally (the default option), Split Vertically, or None. You can also choose whether to display header information (the message's author, recipient, and subject). The defaults are fine for most people.

- **Status bar.** In this area, Mail displays messages and information about its status and what it's doing. You can hide the status bar by choosing View Status Bar, but it's worth keeping it visible because some of the messages are useful or important.

NOTE

You can drag and position the icon bar and folder list as you please: Just click the handles and drag up, down, left, or right.

The Default Folders

Mail is set up with the following folders:

- **Inbox.** Here's where your new messages show up—and here they stay unless you move them elsewhere.

- **Deleted Items.** If you delete an unwanted message from the Inbox, the Viewer puts it here. Think of the Deleted Items folder as if it were the Recycle Bin. To completely erase a message, you must open the Deleted Items folder and delete the message there.

- **Outbox.** Here's where your messages are temporarily stored until they're electronically transported to your service provider. You do this by clicking Send And Receive.

- **Sent Items.** Here you'll find copies of messages you've sent.

CHAPTER 12

TIP

You can set up Mail so that the program automatically empties the Deleted Items folder when you quit the program. Choose Mail Options, and click the Read tab. Select Empty Messages From The 'Deleted Items' Folder On Exit, and click OK.

Configuring Mail
for Offline or Online Usage

You can use Internet Mail in two different ways:

- **As an offline program.** This is a good option for people who have to pay by the minute for their Internet connection. You log on, get your messages, and log off. After logging off, you can read and reply to your messages. Your new messages go to the Outbox, where they stay until you log on the next time.

- **As an online program.** This is the right option for people who have unlimited Internet connectivity. Chances are you'll run Internet Mail for hours at a time—all the time you're connected. You read and reply to mail while you're logged on. You don't do any work off line.

By default, Internet Mail is set up as an offline program. (Isn't that nice? Microsoft doesn't want you to go broke paying for your Internet connectivity.) If you're using the program on line, however, you'll quickly become frustrated by the offline settings. But there's a cure for this. Change them.

To configure Internet Mail for online usage:

1. Choose Mail Options, and click the Send tab.

2. Select Send Messages Immediately.

3. Click the Read tab.

4. Select Check For New Messages. If you would like to change the frequency of checking for new messages, use the controls to increase or decrease the number of minutes between checks.

TIP

If you don't need to keep a message, click Delete immediately after reading it. The more unwanted messages you leave in your Inbox, the more time you'll have to spend housecleaning later on.

PART

IV

Reading Your Mail

To read your mail, choose Inbox in the folder list, if necessary, and select a message in the message list. Your unread messages are shown in bold. Next to unread messages, you see an unopened letter icon.

When you select a message, you'll see the text of the message in the preview pane, as shown in Figure 12-2 on the next page. At the top of the preview pane, you see basic information about the message (who it's from, who it's to, and the subject). This information stays put even if you scroll the message.

After five seconds, the bold formatting disappears and the icon next to the message shows an opened letter. (If you would like to increase the time it takes to mark a letter as read, choose Mail Options, click Read, and increase the time in Mark Messages As Read After Previewed For 5 Seconds. Click OK to confirm.)

Take a look at the sample message from Microsoft (which might be the only message you'll see, at this point, unless there's an automatic message from your service provider). This message, shown in Figure 12-2, gives you a good hint of what you're in for with Mail: Look at the formatting! With Mail, you can send and receive messages formatted with HTML, the same markup language that underlies the appearance of Web documents. You don't even need to know any HTML to do this, as you'll see; formatting your messages is as simple as using a few simple formatting commands that work just like the ones in a simple word processing program.

TIP After you've placed the highlight on a message for a few seconds, Mail removes the bold formatting from the message's name, indicating that you've read the message. If you haven't finished reading the message, you can restore the bold formatting by choosing View Mark As Unread or by just pressing Ctrl + Shift + Enter. (Should you want to do so, you can remove the bold formatting from unread messages by choosing View Mark As Read or by pressing Ctrl + Enter.)

CHAPTER 12

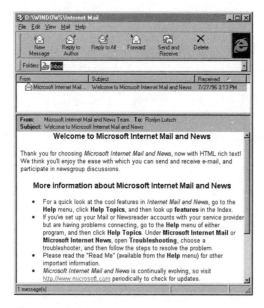

Figure 12-2

A message displayed with rich formatting (HTML).

Using the Message Window

A convenient way to read messages is to use the main Mail window, with its message list and preview pane. You can also read messages in the message window. To view a message in the message window, just double-click the message. You'll see the message there, as shown in Figure 12-3.

The message window's toolbar includes convenient tools for your reading purposes. Left to right, they include Save This Message, Print, Copy, Delete, Reply To Author, Reply All, Forward, Previous, Next, and Address Book. The Previous and Next buttons give you a convenient way of going through the messages in your list; try it.

NOTE

A good reason for reading your messages in the message window (rather than the preview pane) is that you can easily add your correspondents' addresses to your Address Book by double-clicking their names. For more information, see "Creating an Address Book," later in this chapter.

Figure 12-3
The message window.

Navigating in the Message List

To view the next message down in the list, just click it, press Alt + left arrow, press Ctrl + >, or choose View Next Message.

To view the previous message in the list, just click it, press Alt + right arrow, press Ctrl + <, or choose View Previous Message.

Sorting the Message List

By default, the message list is sorted by date, with the most recent message at the top. You can change the sort method by clicking the sort bars at the top of the message list. To sort by the sender, for example, click From.

For each of the three sort methods (From, Subject, and Received), you can sort in ascending or descending order. To sort in ascending order, choose View Sort Ascending so that a check mark appears next to Ascending. To sort in descending order, choose View Sort Ascending again (so that the check mark disappears).

TIP

For most purposes, the best way to display your messages is to sort them by the date you received them and in descending order. You'll see your new messages at the top of the window.

CHAPTER 12

Displaying Additional
Information in the Message List

Mail is configured to display three columns (From, Subject, and Received). If you want, you can display additional information and configure the columns as you please. This information includes a column indicating the date the message was sent, the name of the person to whom the message was sent, and the size of the message. This information really isn't necessary for most purposes, so you will probably want to stick with the three default columns.

To configure the message list columns, choose View Columns. You'll see the Columns dialog box, shown in Figure 12-4.

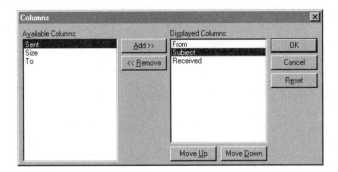

Figure 12-4
The Columns dialog box.

In the left panel, you see the additional information you can add (Sent, Size, and To). To add this information to the message list, highlight one item and click Add. To change the position of an item in the Displayed Columns list, click Move Up or Move Down. If you'd like to remove a column, highlight it and click Remove. To confirm your options, click OK.

TIP If you've done some experimenting with columns and regret doing so, you can quickly restore the defaults. Choose View Columns, click Reset, and click OK.

Receiving an Attachment

If you receive a message that has an *attachment* (a file sent along with the message), you'll see a paper-clip icon next to the envelope icon. To view the attachment, just double-click the message. You'll see a compose window,

PART IV

just like the one you use when you write a new message, as discussed later in this chapter, except that there's a special panel at the bottom that contains the attachment.

Mail displays the attachment as an icon. To view the attachment, just double-click it. Windows will attempt to find an application to view the file.

If no application exists that's capable of displaying the file, you'll see a dialog box asking you to associate this type of file with an application.

TIP

If somebody wants to send you an attachment, ask the sender to be sure the file is in a format that one of your applications can read. For example, if you have Microsoft Word for Windows 95 (version 7), you can read just about any Word file, but you won't be able to read a WordPerfect for Macintosh version 1.0 file.

Finding a Message

Once you've received and sent many messages, you might find that manual search techniques don't cut it. To search for a message, click Edit Find Message. You'll see the Find Message dialog box, shown in Figure 12-5.

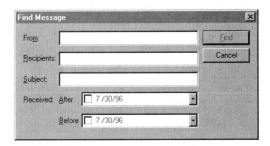

Figure 12-5
The Find Message dialog box.

You can search by the sender, the recipient, any text in the subject line, or the date. When you've made your choice, click Find. Mail will try to locate the message you're searching for; if the program finds a match, the program selects the message and displays the text in the preview pane. To repeat the search, choose Edit Find Next or just press F3.

Using the Pop-Up Menu

If you click the right mouse button with the pointer positioned within the message list, you'll see the pop-up menu shown in Figure 12-6.

Figure 12-6

The pop-up menu that appears within a message list.

This chapter hasn't covered all these options yet, so don't worry if you don't understand what all of them do. For now, just remember that this is a very convenient way to choose some of the most frequently used options in Mail.

Writing and Sending Messages

You can send messages in three ways:

- By composing a new message.
- By replying to a message you've received.
- By forwarding a message you've received.

The following sections introduce the fundamentals of sending messages, beginning with a look at the compose window. Later in this chapter, you'll learn how to get fancy by creating a signature, using an Address Book, attaching files to your messages, and adding rich formatting.

Understanding the Compose Window

No matter whether you're replying, forwarding, or composing a new message, you'll use the compose window to address, write, and edit your message. The compose window is shown in Figure 12-7.

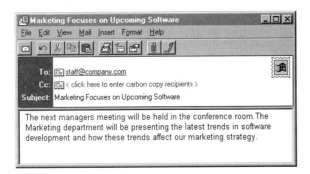

Figure 12-7

The compose window.

The following is a quick guide to the compose window's parts:

🌐 **Title bar.** To reposition the Mail window, drag the title bar. To maximize the window quickly, double-click the title bar. Double-click again to restore the previous size.

🌐 **Menu bar.** Here, you'll find all the Mail commands, but the most frequently used commands are found on the toolbar.

🌐 **Toolbar.** The toolbar contains some useful tools. You'll find the following buttons, from left to right: Send, Undo, Cut, Copy, Paste, Address Book, Check Names, Pick Recipients, Insert File, and Insert Signature. You'll learn more about what these tools do in later sections.

🌐 **Header information.** Here you type the recipient's e-mail address, the e-mail address for carbon copies (optional), and a brief subject line.

🌐 **Message body.** Here's where you type your information.

Sending a Message

It's easy to use the compose window to compose a message. On the Mail toolbar, click New Message (you can also choose Mail New Message or press Ctrl + N). When the compose window appears, you just type a recipient in the To box, add a brief subject line, type the message's text, and click Send.

If you've installed Word for Windows 95 or Microsoft Office 95, you can check your spelling in the compose window by choosing Mail Check Spelling or by pressing F7. If Mail finds a spelling error, the program highlights the error and displays the Spelling dialog box. You can ignore the error, change it by typing it manually or by selecting a suggestion, or add the word to the Office dictionary (if it's correctly spelled). When the spelling check is finished, you see a dialog box that confirms this.

TIP

If you're anxious to send a message to somebody, but you don't know anyone's e-mail address yet, take a tip from Elvis: You can sit right down and write yourself a letter. Just type your own e-mail address in the To box, write a brief subject line, and pour your heart out. After you click Send, click Send And Receive to send your letter, and then click Send And Receive a few moments later to download it and read it.

To change the message's priority, click the postage stamp icon. You can choose from High, Normal, and Low Priority. (The default is Normal.)

If you would like to send the message with rich HTML formatting, choose Format HTML in the compose window. You'll see a toolbar containing font, font size, emphases such as bold or italic, font color, alignment, and bulleted list options. You simply choose these options and format your letter as you would in a word processing program; Mail takes care of the HTML. Note, however, that your message won't come across with intact formatting unless your recipient's e-mail program can decode HTML. If your correspondent is also using Internet Mail, you can be sure that the message will be automatically displayed with the rich formatting. Otherwise, your correspondent will be able to read your message's text but it will be full of HTML tags.

Replying to a Message

To reply to a message, you have two options on the Mail toolbar:

- **Reply To Author.** If you choose this option, your reply goes only to the e-mail addresses included in the From line in the header information. (Note that this might include more than one address.) No copies are sent to anyone on the cc: (carbon copy) list of the original message.

- **Reply To All.** If you choose this option, your message goes not only to the author but also to everyone on the cc: list.

To reply to a message, select the message and click Reply To Author. (You can also choose Mail Reply To Author, press Ctrl + R, or choose Reply

To Author from the pop-up menu.) If you're *certain* that you really want to reply to everyone, select the message and click Reply To All. (You can also choose Mail Reply to All, press Ctrl + Shift + R, or choose Reply To All from the pop-up menu.)

HELP

I just sent a private letter to everyone in my company!

You wouldn't believe how often this happens, and here's how. Many e-mail addresses are actually distribution lists, which look like individual e-mail addresses but actually refer to a lengthy list of e-mail addresses that could potentially include everyone in an organization. If you don't notice such an address in the cc: line and unthinkingly click Reply To All, you could be sending your message to hundreds or even thousands of people! Don't make yourself look stupid in front of dozens or even hundreds of people. *Please* exercise caution when you click Reply To All. Examine the addresses carefully to make sure you understand who's getting it. If you aren't sure or don't feel quite comfortable for some reason, don't choose Reply To All.

You'll see a compose window. In Figure 12-8, you see that Mail has *quoted* the original text. This is a long-standing Internet convention; recipients (if they're familiar with the Internet) know that the quote symbols are used to demarcate the original text.

Figure 12-8
Replying to a message.

Note that Mail has automatically added the recipient and positioned the insertion point at the beginning of the letter, above the quoted text. In addition, the program has added *Re:* before the subject.

Forwarding a Message

Forwarding works exactly like replying, except that Mail doesn't automatically supply the recipient's address in the To box. To forward a message, select the message and click Forward. (You can also choose Mail Forward, press Ctrl + F, or click Forward on the pop-up menu.) Type an address. You can add some explanatory text above the message you're forwarding, if you like. Click Send to send your message.

If you want, you can forward the message as an attachment. As long as your recipient's e-mail program can handle attachments, this file can be opened, read, saved, printed, or stored. This is the best option to choose if you're forwarding something lengthy. (Just make sure your recipient's e-mail program can handle it.)

To forward a message as an attachment, select the message and click Forward. (You can also choose Mail Forward As Attachment, or click Forward As Attachment on the pop-up menu.) Type an address. You can add some explanatory text above the message you are sending as an attachment, if you like. Click Send to send your message.

Creating a Signature

A *signature* (*sig*, for short) adds a nice touch to your e-mail, as long as it isn't too lengthy. By convention, it's thought best to keep your sig to no more than four lines. That's enough for whatever identifying information you feel comfortable sending.

There's no need to include your e-mail address in your sig; people get that automatically. But you might want to include your full name, your work number, and your work address. Think long and hard before including personal information such as your home telephone number and address. If you really want to send this information to someone, you can do so in the body of the message.

To create your sig, choose Mail Options and click the Signature tab. You'll see the Signature panel, shown in Figure 12-9.

In the Text box, type a brief signature, or click File and use the Browse button to locate a text file containing your sig, if you want. At the bottom of this panel, you'll find two options:

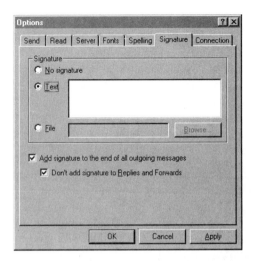

Figure 12-9
The Signature panel.

⊕ **Add Signature To The End Of All Outgoing Messages.**
When you open the compose window to start a new message,
Mail adds your sig automatically.

⊕ **Don't Add Signature To Replies And Forwards.** This is a
nice touch, since replies and forwards can get excessively lengthy
with all those repeated sigs.

Both of these options are selected by default, and that's probably the
best choice for most Mail users. If you decide against including the sig in
all your outgoing messages automatically, you can still include it selectively
by clicking Signature in the compose window's toolbar.

A cute trick, in which too many Internet users (including myself) indulge themselves, is to include a little ASCII art picture in their signatures. (Mine used to have
a sailboat.) As cunning as these works of art might appear to the eyes of those
who create them, they come across as gibberish to anyone who's chosen a pro-
portional font to read mail messages. Since that's increasingly common, it's time
to bid a fond farewell to these artistic efforts.

CHAPTER 12

Creating an Address Book

Typing e-mail addresses is a bother, and what's more, it's prone to error—if you make a typing mistake, your message won't get to its destination. To cure the problem (not to mention organize your e-mail addresses in a very convenient way), create an Address Book.

To begin creating your address book, click File Address Book. You'll see the Address Book dialog box, shown in Figure 12-10.

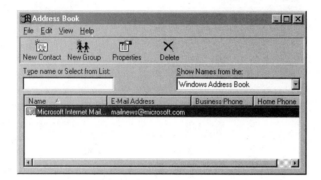

Figure 12-10

The Address Book dialog box.

Adding Entries to the Address Book

By far the easiest way to add a person's name and address to your Address Book is to display a message from this person in the message window and right-click the person's name or e-mail address in the From box and choose Add To Address Book. You'll see the Properties dialog box, as shown in Figure 12-11. Note that Mail has automatically added the recipient's e-mail address and taken a stab at the name.

Although Mail tries to parse the person's first and last names from the From box's information, it might not succeed, so you might need to edit this information. If you have additional information about this person, you can enter it by clicking Home (for home address and phone), Business (for business address and phone), or Notes (for your notes about this person). In both the Home and Business pages, there's even a space to put the Web address of the person's personal or business Web page—and after you enter it, you can view the page by clicking the Internet Explorer icon next to the Web Page box.

PART

To add an entry to the Address Book manually, click New Contact in the Address Book window. You'll see the first page of the Properties dialog box. Enter the person's name and e-mail address, and click Add.

If you need to edit a person's information later, highlight the person's name in the Address Book and click Properties.

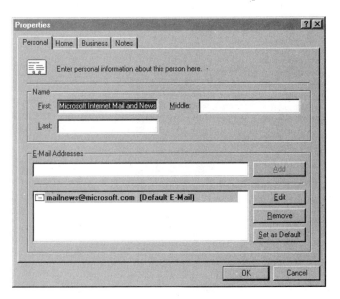

Figure 12-11

The Address Book Properties dialog box.

Creating a Group

Once you've entered two or more names in your Address Book, you can create a group. After you've created the group, you can send a message to the whole group by using the group address instead of individual e-mail addresses. To create a group, click New Group. In the Group dialog box, shown in Figure 12-12 on the next page, create a name for your group. Add members by clicking Add, selecting names from your Address Book, and clicking Add to add them to the list. Click OK to confirm, and then click OK to close the Properties dialog box. If you later want to add or remove people from this list, find the group name in the Address Book list—it has a distinctive icon showing two people hand-in-hand—and click Properties. To remove a name, highlight the name and click Delete.

TIP

If you created an address book with Microsoft Exchange, you can import your address book into Mail. To do so, choose File Import Address Book, click the Import button, and select the mail profile you want to import.

Figure 12-12
The Group dialog box.

Adding Addresses to Your Messages

Once you've created your Address Book, you can easily add addresses to your messages. In the compose window, just click the Address Book icon (which looks like a little Rolodex page) next to To or CC. Alternatively, click Pick Recipients on the Toolbar. You'll see the Select Recipients dialog box, shown in Figure 12-13.

To select the main recipient, select the name and click To. (You can add more than one main recipient, if you want, but this might complicate things for people if they would like to reply only to you.) To select a recipient for a carbon copy of the message, highlight the name and click CC. You can select as many CC names as you want without irritating your recipients.

PART
IV

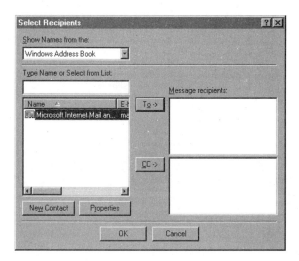

Figure 12-13

The Select Recipients dialog box.

Adding Attachments (Files) to Your Messages

One of the nicest things about e-mail is that you can send formatted documents over the Internet, including Word, Microsoft Excel, and Microsoft PowerPoint files. I don't doubt for a minute that this is going to eat into the profits of express services; almost all of my publishers can handle manuscript submissions this way. (That's how this chapter got to Microsoft Press, incidentally.)

It's easy to include an attachment. Just compose your letter or reply as you would normally, and click Attachment (or choose Insert File Attachment). You'll see an Open dialog box. Locate the file. (If you would like to include a shortcut to the file, rather than the whole file, click Make Shortcut To This File—but note that this probably isn't a very good idea, unless the person to whom you're writing is also running Windows 95 and Internet Mail and has permission to access your files.) Click Attach.

Organizing Your Mail into Folders

Once you've started getting e-mail messages, you'll find that it's convenient to sort your messages into named folders (rather than just keeping everything in your Inbox).

Creating a New Folder

To create a new mail folder, choose File Folder Create. You'll see the Create New Folder dialog box. Type a name for your folder, and click OK. After you create your new folder, you can see its name in the Folder list.

Adding Messages to Your New Folder

After you've created a new folder, you can easily add a message to it by selecting the message in the message list and doing one of the following:

- Choose Mail Move To or Mail Copy To, and select the folder to which you'd like to move the message.

- Right-click the message, choose Move To or Copy To, and select the folder to which you'd like to move the message.

Viewing Your Folders

To view the contents of one of the folders you've created, choose the folder name from the Folders list. To return to the Inbox, choose Inbox from the Folders list.

Compacting Folders

Mail messages can take up a lot of room. To reduce the space that a folder consumes, choose File Folder Compact and select the name of the folder you want to compact (choose All to compact all folders). After you compact the folder, you won't notice any difference in Mail's performance—the program needs a little more time to open messages in these folders—but they take up less disk storage space.

Deleting Folders

To delete an unwanted folder and all the messages within it, choose File Folder Delete and choose the name of the folder you want to delete. You'll see a confirmation message. Are you really sure that you want to delete all the messages in this folder? If so, click OK.

Diverting Incoming Mail to Folders

One of Mail's nicest features is Inbox Assistant, which can automatically route incoming messages to folders of your choice—which includes Deleted Items. Here's a great way to get rid of junk e-mail!

PART

IV

Inbox Assistant also comes in handy after you subscribe to mailing lists, as described later in this chapter. As you'll quickly discover after subscribing to a mailing list, you might get as many as dozens or even hundreds of messages per day, and they get in the way of your personal mail. By automatically routing these messages to a folder rather than sticking them in your face in the Inbox, Inbox Assistant frees you to read them at your convenience.

NOTE

Inbox Assistant shouldn't be used to store any incoming mail that you really need to read right away. The mail might go to a folder that you seldom look at. Rather, it's best used to deal with messages that aren't of pressing importance.

Creating Rules

To route your incoming messages to folders, you first need to create folders to store your messages. If you've subscribed to the Yachting-L mailing list, for example, create a folder called Yachting-L. (For information on creating your own folders, see "Organizing Your Mail into Folders," on page 205.)

Internet Mail relies on *rules* to divert your incoming messages into folders. A rule says, in effect, "If an incoming message contains such and such in such and such an area, move the message to the specified folder." An example, which should be sufficient to illustrate the usefulness of this feature: "If an incoming message is from Dave Rhodes and contains the text 'Make Money Fast' in the subject line, move it to Deleted Items." (The Rhodes 'Make Money Fast' text is an old Internet hoax that keeps cropping up.)

TIP

Plan your rules before trying to create them. Inbox Assistant can match any text in the To, CC, From, or Subject lines, so think about how you will instruct the program to recognize the correct incoming messages. Browse through your Inbox and display messages that you wish had been automatically diverted. For example, suppose you have subscribed to the Holt stock report, which sends a free daily e-mail newsletter containing stock market results. You want to divert the incoming messages to the Holt Report folder. As you examine the Holt messages, you see that every one contains *GEOHOLT <Geoholt@cris.com>* in the From line. This is good text to use for writing your rule.

It's simple to create rules. Just click Mail Inbox Assistant. You'll see the Inbox Assistant dialog box. Click Add, and you'll see the Properties dialog box, shown in Figure 12-14.

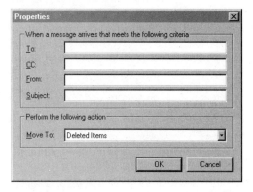

Figure 12-14

The Inbox Assistant Properties dialog box.

Type the criteria you want to match in one of the boxes, and choose the folder to which you'd like to move the mail. When you're finished, click OK.

Prioritizing Rules

If you write several rules, it's possible that more than one will apply to a given incoming message. For this reason, you can prioritize your rules. To change a rule's priority, highlight the rule in the Inbox Assistant dialog box and click the up or down arrow to move the rule in the list.

To illustrate how prioritization solves problems for you, suppose your friend Marvin likes to kid around a lot with silly subject lines (such as "Get a life," or "Make money fast"). You like Marvin's messages, but you can do without the other "Make money fast" messages, which persistently advertise some kind of Ponzi scheme. So you write a rule that sends Marvin's letters to the Marvin folder, and another rule that sends any message with "Make money fast" to the Deleted Items folder. To make sure Marvin's messages don't get trashed, even if they contain "Make money fast," place the Marvin rule higher in the priority list.

Printing and Saving Messages

You can print or save a message at any time.

To print a message, select the message in the message list and choose File Print. If you'd like to print multiple copies or choose other print options, choose File Print or press Ctrl + P. You'll see the Print dialog box, shown in Figure 12-15.

You can choose multiple copies, collation options, and print range options in this dialog box. When you've finished choosing your options, click OK.

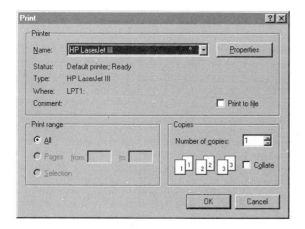

Figure 12-15
The Print dialog box.

Internet Mail enables you to save messages to a disk, but there's really no need to do so unless it's something ultra-important. Your incoming messages are saved in your Inbox or your folders unless you deliberately delete them. (And even then, they're routed to the Deleted Items folder, where you can recover them later.)

Mailing Lists

Mailing lists are one of the most rewarding aspects of the Internet. Imagine being able to join a few dozen or a few hundred people who all share your interest, whether it's collecting Barbie dolls or analyzing the human genome, entering into daily debate, discussion, and resource-sharing with mailing list members. There are thousands of mailing lists on every conceivable subject, and many of them are publicly accessible—which means *you* can join, even if you aren't an expert in a field.

Sounds great, doesn't it? Mailing lists *are* great. I'm always on three or four. But they come at a price. You get a *lot* more e-mail messages than you can easily cope with. If you're really interested in a given topic, however, it's worth the effort to plow through dozens of e-mail messages each day.

Before joining a mailing list, you should know what to expect. It isn't all sweetness and light:

🌐 Every once in a while, somebody posts a message that really pushes people's buttons, and you get a regrettable phenomenon called a *flame war*—lots of public name-calling and unpleasantness. Until cooler heads prevail, the mailing list will generate more heat than light.

🌐 People forget how to unsubscribe—there's a procedure you're supposed to follow, described later in this chapter—so they post pathetic messages with subjects such as, "Will somebody PLEASE tell me how to get off this list?" Your mailbox is cluttered enough as it is without this.

🌐 Personal and important messages to you alone can get lost amid the dozens or hundreds of messages from lists. Join one mailing list, or maybe two, but take care not to join too many.

Finding a Mailing List in Your Area of Interest

Thanks to the volunteer efforts of Stephanie da Silva, you can access a fantastic index of Internet mailing lists on the World Wide Web. Here's the address:

```
http://www.neosoft.com/internet/paml/
```

Note that the letter in "paml" is a lowercase "L."

You'll see the Publicly Accessible Mailing Lists page, shown in Figure 12-16. If you click the Index button, you'll find that you can search by Name or by Subject.

Subscribing to a Mailing List

After you locate information about a mailing list that looks good, try subscribing to it. Please be sure to follow the directions carefully. The following instructions will work for many (but not all) list servers:

1. Create a new e-mail message addressed to the list server.
2. Leave the Subject box blank.
3. Type *subscribe* in the body of the message, followed by a space and the name of the mailing list (for example, *subscribe ford-probe*).
4. Delete your signature, if it was automatically inserted.
5. Click Send.

You'll receive a confirmation, plus information about the mailing list, shortly. This information includes directions for unsubscribing to the list.

PART
IV

Figure 12-16

The Publicly Accessible Mailing Lists page.

Please print this information and file it away so that you can retrieve it if you decide to unsubscribe.

Replying to Mailing List Messages

Messages from the mailing list appear like any other e-mail messages—they show up in your Inbox. When you reply to a specific message, it goes to the person who created it—not to the list. That's as it should be, because you don't want to post something to the entire list unless you really have something worth saying.

Please don't post "me too" messages or anything else that you'd find irritating if it showed up in *your* mailbox.

So that mailing list messages don't get in the way of your personal mail, create a folder for the mailing list and write rules to divert messages from the list to this folder. (For more information on writing rules, see "Diverting Incoming Mail to Folders," earlier in this chapter.) By all means, write a rule that sends messages containing "unsubscribe" to the Deleted Items folder; as you'll learn in the following section, it's very common for people to forget how to unsubscribe to the list, and you'll get lots of these messages (which are very annoying).

12
CHAPTER

Unsubscribing to a Mailing List

There's a procedure for unsubscribing to a mailing list, similar to the one you used to subscribe in the first place. After you subscribe to a mailing list, you'll receive an automatic message from the server detailing how to unsubscribe. *Please create a folder called Unsubscribe Info, and save this message so that you'll know how to get off the mailing list later.*

For example, here's the procedure for unsubscribing to the Wine mailing list:

1. Create a new e-mail message addressed to the following:

    `Majordomo@ee.pdx.edu`

2. Leave the Subject box blank.

3. Type *unsubscribe wine* in the body of the message.

4. Send the message.

Unfortunately, it seems that very few people save unsubscribe information, so they try to post the unsubscribe message to the mailing list itself. *Please* don't do this. This is really irritating to people. You need to send your unsubscribe message to the server, not to the mailing list. The server has a different address!

From Here

- 🌐 Check out Chapter 13 for the lowdown on accessing Usenet newsgroups.

- 🌐 Once you've learned Mail and News, you've learned a great deal about Internet communication. But there's more! Chapter 14 introduces Internet Relay Chat and Comic Chat.

- 🌐 While we're on the subject of communications, don't miss Chapter 18, which covers NetMeeting, Microsoft's exciting new tool of Internet-based real-time collaboration.

CHAPTER 13

Using
Internet News

Wide-open, freewheeling, invaluable, shocking—these adjectives, and more, spring to mind when Usenet pops up on your screen, and for good reason: For those with access to a computer, Usenet is just about the most open and democratic communication medium that's ever been devised. All kinds of people contribute all kinds of material to Usenet, and it runs the gamut from garbage to gold.

This chapter fully introduces Usenet and shows you how to mine the gold (and avoid the garbage). You'll learn how to access Usenet by using Internet News, which is Internet Mail's companion program. As you'll see, Internet News is a feature-packed newsreader (a program that enables you to read and contribute to Usenet newsgroups), yet it's easy to use and nicely integrated with Internet Explorer.

TIP To access Usenet newsgroups with Internet News, you need an Internet subscription that includes access to a *news server.* (A news server is a computer that stores and organizes Usenet messages and enables you to download just the ones you want to read. In this sense, it resembles the mail servers discussed in the previous chapter.) Internet News requires the computer address of your mail server. If you don't know this or if you aren't sure whether you have access to Usenet news, call your service provider.

Introducing Usenet

Imagine a "letters to the editor" column, like the one in your local newspaper. Some of the letters are wise and worth reading; some are amusing; and some are loaded with false or misleading information. Got it? Now imagine that every letter to the editor written to every newspaper in North America was automatically reproduced so that every letter appeared in all the newspapers. The daily edition of the newspaper would be roughly 80,000 pages, requiring a fairly serious truck to deliver it to your house. Happily for the trees of this world, Usenet is similar in scope, but it is distributed electronically.

Don't worry that you'll have to wade through hundreds of thousands of messages to find the ones in which you're interested. Usenet is topically divided into thousands of *newsgroups,* each with its own distinctive name and topical coverage. Just about every conceivable subject is represented— and I can guarantee that there are topics you *haven't* conceived of.

Is Usenet a Waste of Time?

Is Usenet just so much fluff, the hue and cry of people with nothing better to do than to try to push their opinions into other people's faces?

Many people conclude this after a brief Usenet session. There's a lot of hot air on Usenet, to be sure, and even worse—the network is susceptible to *spamming,* in which inappropriate messages, including self-serving advertisements, are posted to hundreds or even thousands of newsgroups that have nothing to do with the messages' content.

Usenet is also bedeviled by messages from the maturity-impaired, who think they're being cute by posting *trolls* (obviously false statements that are planted in the hope that people will rise to the bait, making fools of themselves in the trollers' eyes) and *flame bait* (deliberately provocative messages that are posted in the hope of starting a *flame war*). A recent trend: Usenet has become a happy hunting ground for pyramid scammers and con artists of all stripes, including hucksters pushing penny stocks and pornography.

Unfortunately, so many people abuse Usenet that many formerly interesting newsgroups aren't worth reading anymore. Examples include alt.internet.media-coverage, which (at one time) contained intelligent and interesting commentary on the way the media covers the Internet. Other newsgroups that have gone down the tubes recently include alt.folklore .computers, which formerly offered intelligent and humorous discussion of the cultural and social sides of computing. These days, you'll find spams, ads, and a pointless discussion of the relative merits of Macs vs. Microsoft Windows 95, which is as uninformative as it is histrionic. The old regulars have made their way to private, moderated mailing lists.

Spams, scams, and just plain nonsense aside, there are Usenet jewels, too. The trick is to stay away from anything that sounds controversial—today's Usenet just doesn't handle controversy well. If there's a Usenet newsgroup that's topically related to a hobby or professional interest of yours, chances are that you'll find Usenet close to indispensable. In general, the technically oriented newsgroups (especially those in the comp.* hierarchy, discussed later in this chapter) are of the greatest value; there's a real spirit of information exchange and resource sharing. Also of generally high quality are the *moderated newsgroups,* in which every message is submitted to a human moderator, who inspects each message to make sure that it is related to the newsgroup's topic.

NOTE

Please do not post messages to any Usenet newsgroup until you have fully understood the basics of Usenet *netiquette,* discussed later in this chapter. Netiquette isn't mysterious; it's just good manners: Be polite, think of other people's feelings, give credit where credit is due, and don't post anything when you're in the heat of anger. In particular, do not post requests for information that has already been dealt with in the group's Frequently Asked Questions (FAQ) document.

CHAPTER
13

Introducing Newsgroups

With more than 7 million people using Usenet on a regular basis and con-
tributing some 80,000 pages of text, sound, graphics, and computer programs
daily, it's obvious that some kind of organization is needed to make all this
material accessible. The needed organization is provided by the hierarchi-
cal system of newsgroup names.

Here's how this system works. Every newsgroup is part of a *top-level
hierarchy*, such as *sci, soc*, or *talk*. The top-level hierarchy indicates the overall
topic of the newsgroup; for example, *soc* newsgroups cover the social sciences, social issues, and socializing.

Top-level hierarchies fall into three general categories:

🌐 **The standard newsgroups.** Every Usenet site is expected to
carry these newsgroups. (Examples: *comp, misc, news, rec, sci,
soc,* and *talk.*)

🌐 **The alternative newsgroups.** These are optional; Usenet sites
don't have to carry these newsgroups, but most do. (Examples:
alt, bionet, biz, clari, K12, relcom, and more.)

🌐 **Local newsgroups.** These newsgroups are set up to benefit a
local community, a university, or an organization, and they are
sometimes available to outsiders.

A Quick Guide to the Standard and Alternative Newsgroup Hierarchies

Name	Subject Area
alt	Newsgroups that anyone can create, on any subject
biz	Business news, marketing, advertising
comp	Computers and computer applications
misc	Stuff that doesn't fit in the other categories
news	Usenet itself
rec	Hobbies and sports
sci	The sciences
soc	Social issues and socializing
talk	Discussion of social issues

PART
IV

Every newsgroup has at least one other part to its name besides the top-level hierarchy, with the parts separated by dots, as in the following:

```
misc.test
comp.risks
```

Many newsgroups have additional parts to their names, which enable an even finer-grained topical focus:

```
alt.fan.tolkien
alt.fan.woody-allen
```

What's in a Newsgroup?

When you select a newsgroup to read, you'll see a list of the *messages* and *follow-up messages* that people have contributed to that newsgroup. Here's what these terms mean:

- ⊕ **Message.** Also called a *post,* this is a message on a new subject.

- ⊕ **Follow-up message.** Also called a *follow-up post,* this is a message that someone has contributed in response to someone else's message. Some messages never receive any commentary; others receive many follow-up messages. When there are many follow-up messages on a particular subject, a *thread* of discussion emerges, rather like a conversation. A good newsgroup reader program enables you to follow such a conversation. For more information on threads, see "Understanding Threading" on page 225.

- ⊕ **Binaries.** You can find graphics, videos, sounds, and computer programs on Usenet. Because Usenet can handle only ASCII text, these graphics, videos, sounds, and programs are coded in a special way that eliminates all but the standard ASCII characters. Because the resulting files are so large, they're often split into multipart posts. To download and use these files, called *binaries,* your newsreader must decode them. Internet News can decode both single-part and multipart binaries, as you'll learn later in this chapter.

CHAPTER 13

NOTE

Although you'll find computer programs on Usenet, it's not a good idea to download and run one—at least not without checking it thoroughly for viruses. It's safe (for your computer, anyway) to download graphics and videos—your computer can't get a virus from these—but note that more than a few newsgroups contain pornography that might not be legal in your area.

Introducing Internet News

Like Internet Mail, Internet News is a very impressive product that many users will prefer over popular packages, including commercial ones. For an Internet Explorer user, News has the special appeal of conforming closely to the Explorer interface. For information on installing Internet News, see Appendix A.

Running News for the First Time

When you run News for the first time, you'll see the Internet News Configuration wizard. This wizard helps you supply the needed server information.
You'll need to know the following:

🌐 Your e-mail address.

🌐 The Internet address of your news server.

🌐 If your news server requires you to log on, your account and password.

🌐 Your means of connection (LAN, manual connection, or modem). If you connect via modem, I recommend that you choose the manual connection option (unless your Internet service provider bills you for time and you want to work off line).

To begin the wizard, click Next. You'll be asked to supply the preceding information. Please be sure to type everything carefully; one little typo can make it impossible to connect.

When you're finished with the wizard, you're ready to start Internet News.

PART
IV

Connecting to Your News Server

If you chose Manual Connection as your preferred connection mode (this is the recommended option), you must connect to the Internet before starting News. To connect to the Internet, open My Computer, select Dial-Up Networking, and double-click your service provider's icon. (For more information on establishing your Internet connection, see Appendix A.)

To start Internet News, do one of the following:

🌐 From the Windows 95 Start menu, choose Programs Internet News.

🌐 From Internet Explorer, choose Go Read News, or click the Mail icon and choose Read News from the pop-up menu.

🌐 In Internet Explorer, click a newsgroup hyperlink.

The first time you connect to your news server, News will download the list of newsgroup names. This could take a few minutes, so this is a good time to take an exercise break.

NOTE

Internet News can work with more than one news server. For example, you can read the technical support newsgroups available at msnews.microsoft.com. To add this server to News, choose News Options, click the Servers tab, and click Add. In the News Server Name box, type *msnews.microsoft.com* and click OK.

Using the Newsgroups Window

After Internet News has downloaded the complete list of newsgroups, you see the Newsgroups window, shown in Figure 13-1.

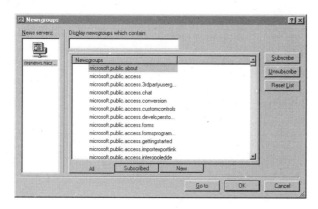

Figure 13-1
The Newsgroups window.

In the News Server panel, select the server you want to access. Using the Newsgroups window, you can do the following:

- **Search for newsgroups of interest to you.** If you type a word in the Display Newsgroups Which Contain box, Internet News reduces the lengthy newsgroup list to just those newsgroups that contain this word.

- **Subscribe to newsgroups.** When you subscribe to a newsgroup, you see the newsgroup's name when you click the Subscribed tab. Subscribing to a newsgroup has no effect beyond your own computer; it's just a way of reducing the huge list of newsgroups to a more manageable size.

- **View a list of new newsgroups.** The next time you log on, there may be new newsgroups. To see a list of new groups, click the New tab.

- **Go to a newsgroup after selecting it from the list.** To read the news in a newsgroup, select it and click Go To.

In the Display Newsgroups box, try typing the first few letters of a word describing a subject that interests you, such as Microsoft, Internet, backpacking, games, or boating. Select a newsgroup that looks interesting, and click Go To.

Looking at Internet News

Internet News (see Figure 13-2) is designed to look and work like Internet Explorer and Internet Mail. In particular, if you've learned how to use Mail, you already know how to use much of this program.

You'll see the following in the Internet News window (see Figure 13-2):

- **Title bar.** To reposition the Internet News window, drag the title bar. To maximize the window quickly, double-click the title bar. Double-click again to restore the previous size.

- **Menu bar.** Here you'll find all the News commands, but the most frequently used commands are found on the toolbar.

- **Toolbar.** The toolbar contains some useful tools. You can choose New Message, Reply To Group, Reply To Author, Forward, Newsgroups, Disconnect, and Stop. You'll find out what these tools do later in the chapter. To display the toolbar, choose View Toolbar.

- **Newsgroup list.** This list box shows the current newsgroup, as well as any others you may have viewed in this session.

🌐 **Message list.** Here you see the current messages in the current newsgroup.

🌐 **Preview pane.** This window shows the text of the message that's currently selected in the message list. By choosing View Preview Pane, you can choose display options for the preview pane. The options are Split Horizontally (the default option), Split Vertically, or None. You can also choose whether to display header information (the message's author, recipient, and subject). The defaults are fine for most people.

🌐 **Status bar.** In this area, News displays messages and information about its status and what it's doing. If you prefer, you can choose View Status Bar to hide the status bar, but you'll miss messages about what News is doing.

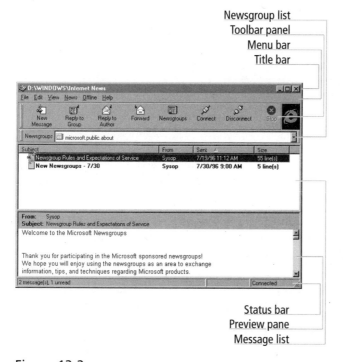

Figure 13-2

Internet News.

NOTE

You can drag and position the toolbar and folder list. Just drag the handles up, down, left, or right.

CHAPTER 13

Netiquette: A Primer

Before you post a message to Usenet, read the following. It sums up the rules that seasoned Usenet users expect everyone, including beginners (called *newbies*), to follow. If you break these rules, you could find yourself on the wrong end of a barrage of irate e-mail—not a pleasant experience.

🌐 Be sure to follow a newsgroup's discussion for at least a couple of days before you post a message. By doing so, you'll learn the types of topics that are appropriate for discussion. You'll also learn what's on people's minds, how you can contribute meaningfully, and how to avoid repeating discussions that have been exhausted.

🌐 If the group has a FAQ (list of answers to frequently asked questions), by all means obtain it and read it. You'll find answers to the questions that newbies typically ask, and you're expected to read them. Newsgroup veterans will be annoyed if you ask the same question by posting a message to the group. One of several excellent Web pointers to Usenet FAQ archives is:

`http://www.sil.org/internet/`

🌐 Before posting a reply message to the newsgroup, consider carefully whether your response is really of interest to everyone. If a person asked a question for specific information, chances are that the reply would interest that person and few others. In such a situation, it's best to reply by e-mail. Your reply goes to the person who posted the original message, not to the group.

🌐 Don't post messages that extensively quote somebody's opinion or request, adding only the words "Me too."

🌐 Do *not* post a "test" message to any newsgroup other than those with the word "test" in their names, such as alt.test or misc.test. If you ignore these suggestions, you could wake up to an electronic mailbox full of very hostile and critical mail the next morning.

PART IV

Understanding Threading

Like all good Usenet newsreaders, News threads messages. This means that messages with the same subject are grouped together. If there's more than one message that pertains to a given subject, you see a plus sign next to the message title. If you click the plus sign, you see all the messages that pertain to this subject. (The word "thread" comes from "following the *thread* of discussion.")

Unlike some newsreaders that simply group messages by subject, News uses true threading. This means that the grouped messages actually refer to each other, and they're listed in the correct order: The third message in a thread is a reply to the second one, and so on.

By default, threads are collapsed. If you would like News to expand threads automatically, choose News Option, click Read, and select Auto Expand Conversation Threads.

Reading the News

Usenet is perhaps the most ephemeral communications system ever invented, next to citizens-band (CB) radio. With very few exceptions, most Usenet newsgroups are not archived. Messages don't persist very long, either: At most servers, they stick around for only a day or two before they're deleted to make room for the avalanche of new postings. That's why they call it "news"—there's very little on Usenet that can be termed "old."

When you log on to Usenet and choose a newsgroup, News downloads the messages it finds on the server. Chances are you'll see anywhere from a few dozen to a few hundred messages.

When you select a message in the message list, you'll see the text of the message in the preview pane, as shown in Figure 13-2 on page 223. At the top of the preview pane, you see basic information about the message (who it's from and the subject).

To view the next message down in the list, just click it, press Alt + left arrow, press Ctrl + >, or choose View Next Message.

To view the previous message in the list, just click it, press Alt + right arrow, press Ctrl + <, or choose View Previous Message.

Hey! I can't read this message!

If you encounter a message that seems to be complete gibberish, it's possible that it has been encrypted using the simple ROT-13 scheme, which rotates all characters 13 letters forward in the alphabet. In a more genteel day (that is, five years ago), Usenet posters would sometimes employ this simple encryption technique to prevent innocent minds from coming face-to-face with something outrageous. Should you encounter a ROT-13-encoded message, you can decode it promptly by choosing Edit Unscramble (ROT 13). Frankly, I haven't seen a ROT-13 message since the early 1990s. If you run across what appears to be a ROT-13 message, chances are that it's a binary graphics file that you've downloaded by mistake. The days are long gone, seemingly, when anyone was concerned about the impact a Usenet post might have on its audience. In unwitting testimony to the times, News drives this point home by providing facilities for *decoding* ROT-13 but— amazingly—none for *encoding* your outgoing messages. Says it all, doesn't it?

Marking Messages and Threads as Read or Unread

Unread messages appear in boldface formatting. When you select a message so that its text appears in the preview pane or if you double-click a message so that its text appears in the message window, News marks the message as read. This means that the message no longer appears in boldface formatting, and the icon changes to show text pinned to a bulletin board.

When News marks a message as read, you won't see the message again the next time you log on to this newsgroup, unless you choose All Messages from the View menu. To increase the time you can look at a message before News marks it as read, choose News Options and click the Read tab. Increase the time interval in the Message Is Read After Being Previewed For 5 Seconds. Click OK to confirm.

You can set up News so that read messages don't appear the next time you log on to this newsgroup. Considering how many messages you'll encounter in many newsgroups, this is a very good thing. To configure News to hide read messages the next time you log on, choose View Unread Messages Only.

Have you set up News to hide read messages? Suppose you run across a really great message that you don't have time to read—but you've looked at it for a few seconds and, as a consequence, News has marked it as read.

Must this message be hidden the next time you log on? No, there's a way to mark the record as unread. Just select the message, and choose Edit Mark As Unread or press Ctrl + Shift + Enter.

> Would you prefer to see only the new messages the next time you log on? You can do so in two ways. To mark just the current session's messages as read (whether you've looked at those messages or not), choose Edit Mark As Read or press Ctrl + Enter. To mark all the messages in the thread as read, choose Edit Mark Thread As Read or press Ctrl + T. To mark the whole worthless bag of messages as read so that they never again vex your monitor (unless you choose View All Messages), choose Mark All As Read or press Ctrl + Shift + A. To mark all messages as read every time you leave any newsgroup, choose News Options, click Read, and click Mark All Messages As Read When Exiting A Newsgroup. With this setting, you see only the new messages the next time you log on, provided that you've also chosen View Unread Messages Only. If you would like to view all the messages at any time, choose View All Messages.

Using the Message Window

A convenient way to read messages is to use the main News window, with its message list and preview pane. You can also read messages in the message window. To view a message in the message window, just double-click the message. You'll see the message in the message window, as shown in Figure 13-3.

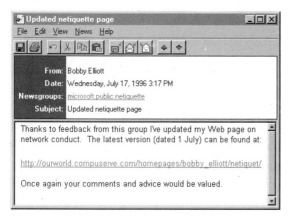

Figure 13-3

The message window in News.

The message window's toolbar includes convenient tools for your reading purposes. Left to right, they include Save, Print, Undo, Cut, Copy, Paste, Reply To Group, Reply To Author, Forward, Previous, and Next. The Previous and Next buttons give you a convenient way of going through the messages in your list.

Using the Pop-Up Menu

Internet News makes full use of pop-up menus, which you can view by clicking the right mouse button on various parts of News. Just what you'll see depends on where you click. If you click in the title bar, for instance, you see options related to minimizing, maximizing, moving, and sizing the window. If you click in the message window, you see options for editing text. In Figure 13-4, you see the pop-up menu that appears when you click in the message list, back in News' main window.

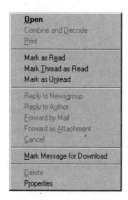

Figure 13-4

The pop-up menu that appears within the message list.

This chapter hasn't covered all these options yet, so don't worry if you don't understand what all of them do. For now, just remember that this is a very convenient way to choose some of the most frequently used options in News.

Reading a Different Newsgroup

If you've finished reading a newsgroup and would like to read a different one, do one of the following:

🌐 To read one of your subscribed newsgroups, click the down arrow on the Newsgroups list and choose a newsgroup to which you've subscribed.

🌐 To read an unsubscribed newsgroup, click Newsgroups. Select a server, and then select a newsgroup. Click Go To.

Joining in the Fray

After reading a Usenet newsgroup for a while, you will doubtless feel the urge to put in your two-cents' worth.

You can send a message in three ways:

🌐 **By replying via e-mail to the message's author.** This is the best way to respond if you have an answer to the author's question and if this answer wouldn't be of interest to many people.

🌐 **By posting a reply to the newsgroup.** Do this *only* if you think that what you have to say would be of interest to many people, not just the author of the message to which you're replying.

🌐 **By posting a new message.** Although valid reasons exist to post messages on a new subject, you should do so only after you fully understand the mission of the newsgroup to which you're posting.

HELP

Everything I've posted is on a search service!

That's right. You need to understand something. When you post a message to Usenet, you're *publishing* your words and whatever else you include in your post— you're making it *public*. Several search services, including Alta Vista and Deja News, enable *anyone* to sit down and put together a portrait of everything you've posted, going back months or even years. It bears repeating: Don't post *anything* to Usenet that you wouldn't want to see on your boss's desk the next morning.

Understanding the Compose Window

No matter whether you're replying, forwarding, or composing a new message, you'll use the compose window to address, write, and edit your message. The compose window is shown in Figure 13-5 on the next page.

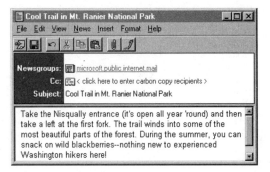

Figure 13-5

The compose window.

The following is a quick guide to the compose window's parts:

🌑 **Title bar.** To reposition the Mail window, drag the title bar. To maximize the window quickly, double-click the title bar. Double-click again to restore the previous size.

🌑 **Menu bar.** Here you'll find all the Mail commands, but the most frequently used commands are found on the toolbar.

🌑 **Toolbar.** The toolbar contains some useful tools. You'll find the following buttons, from left to right: Post Message Save, Undo, Cut, Copy, Paste, Insert File, and Insert Signature. You'll learn more about what these tools do in later sections.

🌑 **Header information.** News automatically supplies the name of the newsgroup. You type a brief subject description.

🌑 **Message body.** Here's where you type your information.

NOTE

Internet News shares its Address Book with Internet Mail. If you're replying by e-mail, as described in the next section, you can capture an e-mail address from the message window and create an Address Book message in exactly the same way you'd do so in Mail. In addition, you can add an address to an outgoing e-mail reply by pasting it from the Address Book . For more information on creating and using the Address Book, see page 202 in the previous chapter.

PART IV

Replying by E-Mail

If your reply would be of interest mainly to the author of the original message, reply by e-mail instead of posting a follow-up message. To reply via e-mail, select the message and click Reply To Author, choose News Reply To Author, or press Ctrl + R. You'll see the compose window.

When the compose window appears, you'll see that News has automatically inserted the author's e-mail address in the To field and added *Re:* to the message's subject. In addition, the text is quoted and the insertion point is positioned at the beginning of the message. You're ready to type!

NOTE

If you've installed Microsoft Word for Windows 95 or Microsoft Office 95, you can check your spelling in any compose window. Choose News Check Spelling, or press F7. If Mail finds a spelling error, the program highlights the error and displays the Spelling dialog box. You can ignore the error, change it by typing it manually or by selecting a suggestion, or by adding the word to the Office dictionary (if it's correctly spelled). When the spelling checker is finished, you see a dialog box that confirms this.

When you've finished typing your message, check the spelling, if you've installed any of the Office 95 products. If not, proofread your message manually (spelling and grammatical errors undermine your credibility on Usenet). If you think your message is ready to send, please read the sidebar "Don't Post in Anger." If you think your message passes muster—that is, it wouldn't shock your mother or anger your boss—click Send.

Don't Post in Anger

You've just finished typing your message. You're ready to click the Send button on the toolbar. Maybe your message is going to just the author. Maybe it's going to the whole newsgroup. Wherever it's going, please hold off just a moment, and do exactly what I say, OK?

If you have composed your message in anger, do the following:

1. Move the pointer to the close box, and click the left mouse button. You'll see a message, "Do you want to save changes to this message?"

2. Click No.

Trust me. Now you're mad at me. Later you'll thank me.

CHAPTER 13

Creating a Follow-Up Message

You can usefully contribute to Usenet by sending a follow-up message *if* the following are *both* true:

- You actually possess some experience or facts or ideas that meaningfully contribute to the topic under discussion.

- What you have to say will prove of interest not just to the original author but to many others who read the newsgroup.

If you're satisfied that you're prospective follow-up post passes muster on both these grounds, have at it. Here's how: Highlight the message, and then choose Reply To Group, choose News Reply To Newsgroup, or press Ctrl + G. You'll see the compose window, with the newsgroup name and with *Re:* conveniently entered in front of the subject.

As you can see, News has conveniently quoted the entire message. Please edit the quoted text down so that you're quoting only the part on which you want to comment. This reduces the cost of Usenet transmission—remember, the Usenet software will make more than 100,000 copies of your message—and lightens the cognitive burden on your poor, beleaguered readers.

An ideal follow-up message zeroes in on the subject by editing out everything in the original post that's not relevant, as shown in Figure 13-6.

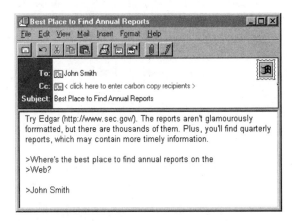

Figure 13-6

A follow-up message.

If you genuinely feel that your message is a positive contribution to the group, by all means send it. To do so, simply click the Send button on the toolbar.

TIP

Are you posting a follow-up message that's of keen interest to the original author as well as of general interest to the group? Send the message by choosing News Reply To Newsgroup And Author, an option available only on the menu.

HELP

I just posted my message, but I don't see it in the newsgroup!

Don't panic, and please, don't post your message again. Here's what's going on. The Usenet software has a fairly low priority in the pecking order of the computer systems where it resides—some things are, after all, more important. Your message will be processed in due time. In fact, it will be flung hither and yon across the globe. Relax.

Posting a Message on a New Subject

As I've advised before, you shouldn't post a new message on a new subject until you've read a newsgroup for a while and grasped the range of acceptable topics.

NOTE

Please don't post a "test—do not read" message to any newsgroup other than one that contains the word "test" in its name. Good candidates include alt.test and misc.test.

If you're sure your post makes sense, click New Message, choose News New Message, or press Ctrl + N. In the compose window, type the name of the newsgroup to which you would like to send the message. You can type more than one newsgroup name, separated by semicolons, but please don't do so unless you honestly feel that your message pertains perfectly to each newsgroup you list.

Forwarding a Message

To forward a message to somebody via e-mail, select the message and click Forward on the toolbar, choose Forward, press Ctrl + F, or click Forward By Mail on the pop-up menu. Type an address. You can add some explanatory text, if you like. Click Send to send your message.

CHAPTER

13

Crossposting: An Unmitigated Evil?

One reason Usenet's in such bad shape is *crossposting,* the sending of a message to more than one newsgroup at a time. Unfortunately, Net abusers try to make money from crossposting messages to dozens or even thousands of newsgroups, without any regard to fitting their message to the topic at hand. For this reason, crossposting is viewed with suspicion, especially in the hands of neophytes who don't understand Usenet's traditions and values.

But there's a good argument for a little modest crossposting now and then. If your message is of genuine interest to more than one newsgroup, crosspost modestly—no one's going to get irritated at you if you post to two or three obviously germane groups. And there's some storage economy in crossposting; it takes less disk space to store a message crossposted to three groups than it does to store three separate messages.

Creating a Signature

A signature—a necessity, or nearabouts, for e-mail—is something of a liability on Usenet. Do you really want your home telephone number to be published in a wide-open public forum where it could be misused? You can see for yourself how risky this is: Just log on to misc.invest. Often, you'll see posts from people who post messages saying, "I just inherited $350,000. Can anyone tell me where I should invest it?" This is a con artist's dream come true.

Still, you might want to include some information in a sig. If you're posting professionally to special-interest groups, such as those in the comp.* or rec.* hierarchy, chances are your message won't be scrutinized by crooks or pranksters (maybe). Maybe you'd want to risk including your full name and institutional affiliation. Too, there's an old Usenet tradition of including a pithy (and preferably enigmatic or caustic) quote in your sig.

To create your sig, choose News Options and click the Signature tab. You'll see the Signature panel, shown in Figure 13-7.

PART

IV

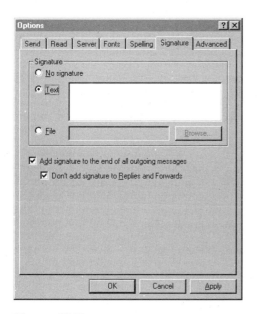

Figure 13-7

The Signature panel.

In the Text box, type a brief signature, or click File and use the Browse button to locate a text file containing your sig, if you want. At the bottom of this panel, you'll find two options:

🌐 **Add Signature To The End Of All Outgoing Messages.**
When you open the compose window to start a new message, Mail adds your sig automatically.

🌐 **Don't Add Signature To Replies And Forwards.** A good choice, since replies and forwards can get overly long.

For both these settings, the defaults—adding to all outgoing messages but omitting for replies and forwards—are fine for most users.

Working Off Line

For anyone who must pay for connect time by the minute, Internet News offers an appealing feature: You can download selected messages or entire newsgroups and read the messages off line (after you've logged off).

Marking Messages for Downloading

To mark messages for downloading, hold down the Ctrl key and select all the messages you want to download. Then choose Offline Mark Message For Download. Alternatively, mark the threads you want to read and then choose Offline Mark Thread For Download. To mark the whole newsgroup for downloading, choose Offline Mark All For Download.

Marking Newsgroups for Downloading

You can also mark entire newsgroups for downloading. To do so, choose Offline Mark Newsgroups. You'll see the Mark Newsgroups dialog box, shown in Figure 13-8.

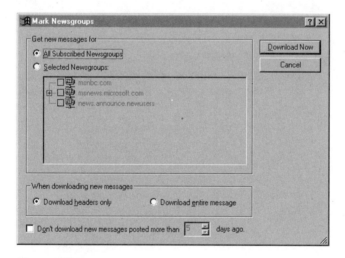

Figure 13-8

The Mark Newsgroups dialog box.

Click All Subscribed Newsgroups, or click Selected Newsgroups and select the newsgroups you want to download, and then choose what you want downloaded: headers only or the entire message. For offline reading, you want the entire message. If you would prefer to read recent messages only, click Don't Download New Messages Posted After and specify the number of days. To download the newsgroups, click Download Now.

Choosing Expiration Options

By default, News deletes downloaded messages five days after you've downloaded them and it deletes read messages. If you would like to change these options, choose News Options and click Advanced. You can select the number of days to wait before deleting messages after they're downloaded. If you deselect this option, Internet News won't delete the items at all. This option is recommended, however, unless you have lots of free disk space! By default, News deletes messages after you've read them. If you would like to keep all messages, including the ones you've read, deselect Don't Keep Read Messages. When you're finished choosing options, click OK.

Cleaning Up Newsgroup Files

If you're downloading entire newsgroups, your newsgroup files might grow very large, even if you use the default expiration options. Happily, News provides options for compacting, reducing, and erasing these files. These options might come in handy if you're low on disk space.

To clean up your newsgroup files, choose News Options and click Advanced. Click the Clean Up Now button. You'll see the dialog box shown in Figure 13-9.

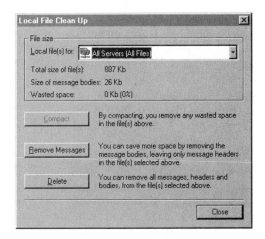

Figure 13-9
The Local File Clean Up dialog box.

In the Local Files For drop-down box, choose the files you want to work with. The default option, All Servers (All Files), works with all your downloaded files. To compact your files, click Compact. To remove message bodies (but leave the headers), click Remove Messages. (This option isn't recommended, because you might not be able to retrieve the message bodies again if they've expired at the server.) If you're sure that you want to get rid of everything you've downloaded, click Delete.

CHAPTER 13

Decoding Binaries

As mentioned earlier in this chapter, with Internet News you can download and decode binary files, including graphics, sounds, videos, and programs. What's more, you can do so even if they're split up into multiple parts, which is necessary given the message-length limitations imposed by some portions of the Usenet network.

To decode a binary that's contained in a single message, just select the message. News will automatically download and decode the message, and it will appear as an attachment. (Look for the paper-clip icon next to the message header in the News window, or look for the shortcut in the message window.) To view or execute the binary, just click the paper-clip icon or double-click the shortcut.

To decode a multiple-part binary, select all the parts of the binary and choose News Combine And Decode. You'll see a dialog box asking you to place all the parts of the file in the correct order. If necessary, select the parts and change the order, and click OK. News downloads and reconstructs the file. As with a single-part binary, you see a paper-clip icon in the News window or a shortcut in the message window; click the paper-clip icon or double-click the shortcut to view or start the binary.

Searching Usenet

There's a lot of information on Usenet—some bogus, some valuable. But one thing's for sure: You're not going to find one particular item by scrolling manually through thousands of newsgroups, unless you're very lucky.

That's why search services are offering searches of Usenet newsgroups, and they're worth exploring. To access Usenet search services, click the Search button on Internet Explorer's toolbar. Currently, Usenet searches are offered by Alta Vista, Excite, and InfoSeek, among others. To access these services from the Internet Searches page, click the links to the search services. If the search service finds a match, you can view the relevant message by clicking the link in the retrieval list.

PART
IV

From Here

🌐 You're just getting started in your tour of the Internet. In the next chapter, learn how to use the fabled and funky Internet Relay Chat, with Comic Chat as your none-too-serious guide.

🌐 Internet Explorer can help you explore the "old" Internet, which is still full of useful resources. In Chapter 15, you explore FTP, Gopher, Telnet, and WAIS.

13 CHAPTER

CHAPTER 14

Using
Comic Chat

Depending on your point of
view, Internet Relay Chat (IRC) is either the coolest thing on
the Net or a time-wasting hangout for the maturity-impaired.

But there's one thing that's certain: It's a very diverting way to spend a few
hours, as you'll quickly discover with Comic Chat. Just make sure you don't
have any appointments!

To use IRC, you need an IRC client. With the exception of Comic Chat,
clients are text-based, so you see the ongoing conversation as a series of typed
lines. In Comic Chat, you engage in real-time conversation with other characters in a comic strip, which is generated on-the-fly as you converse. It might
sound sort of silly, but it's better than the text-based interface of most chat
systems—and after a while, it really grows on you. It's nice to be able to
express a range of emotions while you're conversing on line. I'm not a huge
fan of IRC, but I'm really enjoying Comic Chat—in fact, I've had a heck of
a time pulling myself away from the screen to finish this chapter! I think you'll
enjoy it, too.

Caution: Don't think that the use of comic characters in Comic Chat means that this application is for kids—it isn't. IRC discussion groups, called *channels,* often involve flirting, profanity, sexual situations, and pushy, aggressive behavior. It's strictly an adult playground. On Microsoft's servers, automated watchdogs try to keep the conversation clean, but they can't be everywhere. I wouldn't turn the kids loose, even on Microsoft's server, without supervision.

What Is Internet Relay Chat (IRC)?

In brief, IRC is a real-time chat system of global dimensions that's made possible by the Internet. With IRC, you can engage in conversations with people from all over the world. On a given IRC server—at any given time, there are dozens of hundreds in operation worldwide—you can join a conversation channel and get involved in a text-based give-and-take session with as many as a dozen or two people.

IRC can be fun, but it has a deservedly poor reputation. It's a hangout, for one thing, of some of the most malicious and antisocial hackers you'll ever run across, and they have one aim in common: to ruin everyone's fun. If you can manage to steer clear of the maturity-impaired, however, IRC provides an interesting diversion to the everyday grind. It's a fun way to spend a lunch break, for one thing. If you're lucky enough to find a channel visited by like-minded people, and you return regularly, you can form lasting relationships that could migrate to other media, including e-mail and Real Life.

In a text-based IRC client, the conversation runs something like this:

```
[Joe-Bob] Where are you from?
[Nikkie] Belgium.
[Joe-Bob] What part?
```

You can describe actions as well as type text:

```
[Joe-Bob opens the bar and pours everyone a longneck]
```

What Is Comic Chat?

Comic Chat is a graphics-based IRC client that links the give-and-take of IRC chat with a real-time comic strip. You can choose one of several characters, and you see your character on screen, interacting with others, as if you were living out a cartoon (see Figure 14-1). The words you type appear in your character's word balloons in the frames of a comic strip. Comic Chat auto-matically inserts other characters in each cartoon panel and creates new panels as needed. Before long (if others on line at the time are fun and social companions) you find yourself in a story. You can even choose emotions for your character by choosing them from an emotion wheel.

Figure 14-1
Comic Chat in action.

Installing and Starting Comic Chat

To start Comic Chat, choose Programs Microsoft Comic Chat from the Start menu. You'll see the Connect dialog box, shown in Figure 14-2.

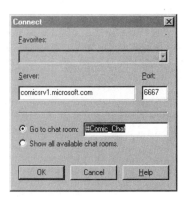

Figure 14-2
The Connect dialog box.

There are many IRC servers in existence, although they tend to come and go. By default, Comic Chat hooks you up to Microsoft's chat server, and that's a good thing: It's policed against antisocial behavior, which is rampant on IRC. Before proceeding, however, you need to choose information about yourself, so click the Cancel button.

Choosing a Persona

To choose a character for yourself, choose View Options and click Personal Info. You'll see a dialog box that prompts you for your real name, a nickname, and a profile.

Caution: Don't type your real name in the Real Name box—it just isn't a good idea. There are plenty of antisocial types on IRC. Don't ever disclose any personal information, such as your e-mail address, your phone number, or your login name or password, to anyone you meet on IRC—or chances are, you'll be sorry.

Choose a nickname for yourself that doesn't disclose too much. If you'd like, type a brief description of yourself, but bear in mind that this is accessible to everyone. (You'll find out how to access other people's profiles later in this chapter.)

Now click the Character tab to choose a character for yourself. You can also choose an emotion from the emotion wheel, as shown in Figure 14-3.

Next, click Settings. The important option here is Page Layout. Choose a panel width (1, 2, or 4 panels) that doesn't cause your screen to scroll horizontally. (If you later find that the screen scrolls, choose this command again and reduce the number of displayed panels.) Try 2 to start.

If you're connecting to an IRC server that's not set up to handle Comic Chat, click Don't Send Graphic Information. You can still see comic characters on your end of the conversation.

Finally, click the Background tab and choose the background you prefer. Click OK to confirm your choices.

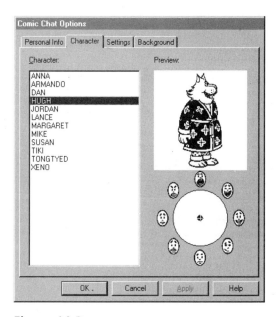

Figure 14-3
The Character page of the Comic Chat Options dialog box.

Connecting to the Server

To connect to a server, choose File New Connection or press Ctrl + N. You'll see the Connect dialog box. Click Show All Available Chat Rooms so that you'll be able to choose the chat room you want. Click OK to connect to Microsoft's default IRC server.

When you've made the connection to the server, you'll see the Chat Room List, shown in Figure 14-4 on the next page.

If the list is lengthy, you can type a word in the Display Chat Rooms That Contain text box; click Also Search Descriptions to help you locate a chat room of interest. Otherwise, look for #newbies, a good place to start. (You might find some reasonably friendly people there.)

If you've previously met someone on this server you like, you can search for that person's nickname by typing the name in the Containing User Nickname text box.

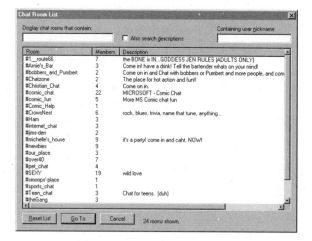

Figure 14-4

The Chat Room List.

TIP

Note the number of members in each chat group. More than seven or eight active members might make the conversation complex and difficult to follow, but a room with only one or two participants might be moribund. (Participants sometimes go away from their computers temporarily without logging off.)

When you've found a room that looks good, click Go To. You'll see the main Chat window, shown in Figure 14-1 on page 243. You'll probably want to jump into the swing of things, but take a moment to learn what the various parts of the window are for.

Understanding the Chat Window

The Chat window (Figure 14-1) has four panes:

🌐 **Self-view pane.** Here's where you can choose an emotion for your character. To choose emotions, drag the black dot (shown in Figure 14-1) around. At the edges, you find the eight extreme emotions: shouting, angry, happy, bored, sad, laughing, scared, and coy. As you drag the dot from the edge toward the center, the emotion is less extreme. Take some time to experiment with the emotion wheel. To adopt a neutral pose, drag the dot to the center.

- **Member list pane.** This pane lists the other characters currently on line. You can view the member list as a list of text names or icons. To select one of these options, choose View Member List or View Member List Icon. You can also click the right mouse button in the member list pane and choose GetProfile or Ignore.

- **Viewing pane.** Here, you see the underlying IRC conversation as a comic strip. If you'd like to see just the text, choose View Plain Text. To restore the comic strip, choose View Comic Strip.

- **Compose pane.** In this pane, you type the words that you want to appear in your character's word balloon. You can choose Say (words everyone can read), Think (thoughts everyone can read), Whisper (words only one person can read), and Action (words, prefaced by your nickname, that appear in a box at the top of the cartoon panel).

Jumping into the Conversation

You can talk, show a thought balloon, whisper privately to someone, or describe an action you are taking, as the following sections explain.

Talking to Someone

To say something, do the following:

1. Click the person to whom you want to talk.

2. On the emotion wheel, choose an emotion.

3. Type the text you want to appear. Don't worry about capitalization, since the text appears in all capital letters, but do watch your spelling. If you include the word "you," your character will point to the person you're talking to. If you include "I," your character will point to itself.

4. Click Say, or use the Ctrl + Y keyboard shortcut.

TIP

Somebody bugging you? Ignore them. Right-click their icon or nickname in the members list, and click Ignore. You won't see this person's character or messages, although the other participants will (unless they choose to ignore this person too).

CHAPTER

14

Thinking a Thought

A thought shows others what you're thinking and can add a fun dimension to your conversation.

To think something, do the following:

1. On the emotion wheel, choose an emotion.

2. Type the text.

3. Click Think, or press Ctrl + T.

Whispering to Someone

When you whisper to someone, only that person can see what you said.

To whisper to someone:

1. Click the person to whom you want to whisper.

2. On the emotion wheel, choose an emotion.

3. Type the text you want to appear in the balloon.

4. Click Whisper, or use the Ctrl + W keyboard shortcut.

Performing an Action

You can describe an action for your character to perform. The action begins with your name. It appears in a box at the top of the cartoon panel.

To perform an action:

1. Type the text that describes your action. Remember that Comic Chat will automatically insert your name at the beginning of the action, so plan your text accordingly ("*Ryouga* sidles up to the bar and orders a tall, cool one").

2. Click Action, or use the Ctrl + I keyboard shortcut.

Viewing a Character's Profile

Did you fill out your profile? No? Maybe somebody else did. To find out, click a character's name or icon in the member list pane, and click the right mouse button. Choose Profile from the pop-up menu. You'll see the character's profile, if any, in a special frame inserted within the comic. (Only you see this frame.)

Comic Chat Tips and Tricks

Once you've learned how to join in the give-and-take of a Comic Chat conversation, you're ready to have fun. You can read this section after you've explored a chat channel for a while.

Adding Favorites

Found a great chat room? Add it to your Favorites by choosing Favorites Add To Favorites. To return to your favorite chat rooms later, choose Favorites Open Favorites, choose the favorite from the dialog box, and click Open.

Changing Channels

Often you'll find that a conversation degenerates, sometimes because there are just too many participants and at other times because of the juvenile behavior of some participants. To bid them farewell and choose a new channel, choose View Chat Room List. From the Chat Room List dialog box, choose a new chat room and click Go To.

Creating a New Channel

If you don't find a channel on a subject you like, you can create a new one by following these instructions:

1. Choose File New Connection. When the Connect dialog box appears, type a new channel name (begin the name with a pound sign, as in #over40).

2. Click OK to create the new channel.

3. Choose Member Administrator Topic, and type a brief, descriptive topic for your channel. Click OK to confirm.

If somebody disrupts your channel by flooding (typing a single character and pressing Enter repeatedly) or by other means, you can kick them off the channel. To do so, choose Member Administrator Kick and choose the offender's name.

Saving and Printing

If you've had a great session, you might want to save it and print it. By default, Comic Chat automatically prompts you to save the chat session when you exit the channel. To print a conversation, choose File Print, choose the settings you want from the Print dialog box, and click Print.

From Here

🌐 There's one chapter remaining on your tour of the Internet, and it's important. In Chapter 15, you learn how to harvest the riches of the "old" (pre-Web) Internet, including FTP, Gopher, WAIS, and Telnet.

🌐 Part V of this book covers the cutting edge of Internet technology, including three-dimensional virtual worlds (VRML), secure shopping, and NetMeeting.

PART

15

CHAPTER

More
Internet
Resources

Microsoft Internet Explorer is appropriately named—it isn't just a Web browser. The program enables you to access the riches of the broader Internet, including services such as File Transfer Protocol (FTP) and Wide Area Information Server (WAIS), which you might have heard about already. FTP provides a full suite of tools for exchanging computer files (including program and data files) via the Internet and for making sure that they arrive in bit-perfect condition. WAIS is the search software that lies behind some of the Web search engines you've been using.

You don't need any additional software in order to gain access to these information-packed resources. What's more, you can use the Internet Explorer skills you've already learned.

What can you access with Internet Explorer?

- Without any help, Internet Explorer can navigate Gopher menus and FTP file archives.

- With the assistance of the Telnet helper program included with Microsoft Windows 95, Internet Explorer can access the wealth of information stored on mainframe computers.

- By accessing World Wide Web pages called *gateways,* Internet Explorer can access just about every other Internet resource in existence, including WAIS databases and Archie file searches.

This chapter shows you how to use Internet Explorer to make full use of these varied Internet resources. You'll also find concise, plain-English introductions to these resources as well as to the useful information you'll tap into when you access them.

Using Gopher

Gopher is a menu-based information system that enables you to browse the information resources of a variety of organizations, including universities, government agencies, nonprofit organizations, and corporations.

What's Available on Gopher?

Gopher menus include two kinds of items:

- **Directories.** When you click one of these, you see another Gopher menu. Gopher has lots of menus within menus.

- **Resources.** When you dig down far enough in a series of Gopher directories, you get to the goodies, including plain-text documents, GIF graphics, sounds that you can download and play, searchable databases of names and telephone numbers, and programs that you can download to your computer.

Where Did Gopher Come From?

University of Minnesota campus computing officials wanted to find a way to make all kinds of computer-based resources available—course listings, general information about the university, the telephone numbers of faculty and staff, and so on. But there was a problem. This information was stored on a variety of computers and in a variety of data storage formats. Their solution? They created a new Internet standard that would let people browse all these varied types of information by using a single easy-to-use interface, based on menus. Where did the name Gopher come from? It's the university's mascot (and a play on words, because Gophers can "go fer" information).

Since Gopher's development, Gopher servers have appeared at universities, corporations, and other organizations throughout the world—for the same purpose as at the University of Minnesota—making lots of different kinds of information available. As with most Internet tools, you access Gopher servers using a client. But you don't need a separate program to browse Gopher menus; Internet Explorer, like most Web browsers, works as a full-fledged Gopher client.

Accessing a Gopher Site

You can access a Gopher site in two ways:

- **Click a Gopher hyperlink.** Hyperlinks to Gopher sites appear exactly the same as hyperlinks to other Web sites. It's considered good manners, however, for Web authors to warn people when a hyperlink points to a Gopher site.

- **Type a Gopher address directly.** A Gopher address closely resembles other Web addresses, with one exception—it starts with "gopher" instead of "http," as in the following example:

```
gopher://gopher.well.sf.ca.us/
```

TIP

Remember, you can always tell what's "under" a hyperlink by moving the pointer over the hyperlink and looking at the status line. The status line displays the address of the site you're accessing. Remember, however, that you don't see the full address unless you change one of Internet Explorer's default settings. To change this setting, choose the View Options command. If necessary, select the Appearance tab. In the Addresses area, turn on the Show Full Addresses (URLs) option. Click the OK button to close the Options dialog box.

Digging into Gopher Menus

When you access a Gopher resource using Internet Explorer, the program opens the Gopher document as if it were a Web page. But don't expect fancy graphics—Gopher menus are strictly text-only.

CHAPTER 15

The name Gopher has yet another shade of meaning: you can think of Gopher navigation as something like digging down into a real gopher hole. As you select items from menus, you will sooner or later reach the bottom level, where you'll find a resource, such as a text file or graphic.

The items on Gopher menus automatically appear as if they were hyperlinks, as you can see in Figure 15-1. When you click an item, you see a new Gopher menu, which may contain one or more resources, such as a text document like the one shown in Figure 15-2. If you access a graphic, Internet Explorer displays it. If you access a sound, the Internet Explorer plays it (assuming you've installed the corresponding sound player). If you access a program file, Internet Explorer asks you whether you want to open and run the program or download and save it on disk.

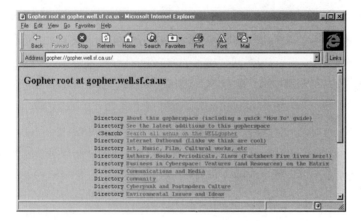

Figure 15-1

A Gopher menu displayed by Internet Explorer.

HELP

Where are the navigation buttons?

There aren't any navigation buttons on a Gopher page. In a well-designed Web page, you'll find navigation buttons, which let you navigate among the related pages. For example, there's usually a button that enables you to display the site's welcome page. But Gopher menus lack such amenities. Just remember: to go back up one level in a Gopher menu, click Internet Explorer's Back button.

PART
IV

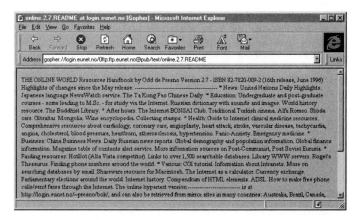

Figure 15-2

A text document at the "bottom" of a Gopher "hole."

Finding the Good Stuff on Gopher

Where's the good stuff on Gopher? You can find out in two ways:

- **Gopher Jewels.** This is a subject tree of Gopher goodies, categorized in dozens of subject areas.

- **Veronica.** This is a search service that searches all the directory titles and resource names in GopherSpace.

Gopher Jewels

Take a look at Gopher Jewels, a list of more than 2000 hyperlinks to cool Gopher sites. You can access Gopher Jewels, shown in Figure 15-3 on the next page, at the following address:

```
http://galaxy.einet.net/GJ/
```

You'll find goodies in just about every conceivable area, including the arts, education, genealogy, history, journalism, law, museums, religion, technology, and travel.

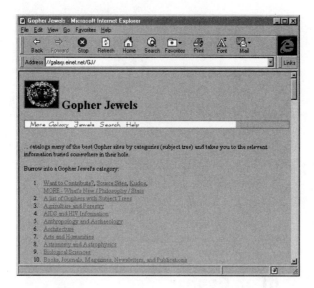

Figure 15-3

Gopher Jewels.

Veronica

A search engine that's designed to find directory titles and resources in Gopher servers worldwide, Veronica isn't as sophisticated as Web search engines such as WebCrawler or Lycos. It doesn't index the *content* of Gopher documents. It simply looks at directory titles and resource names. As a result, Veronica searches aren't very accurate, and what's worse, Veronica servers always seem to be busy. Still, anyone who wants to get the most out of the Internet should try searching for interesting resources with Veronica— but be prepared to get up at 2 a.m., when the servers aren't as busy as they are during daylight hours.

To access a Veronica server, try the following address, which accesses a Web gateway to Veronica:

```
http://www.scs.unr.edu/veronica.html
```

You see the page shown in Figure 15-4. This page lists lots of Veronica servers. Note that there are two kinds: the kind that lets you search directory titles only and the kind that lets you search all of GopherSpace (translation: directory titles plus resource names). Try the directory titles search first; search all of GopherSpace only if the directory titles method doesn't yield anything of interest.

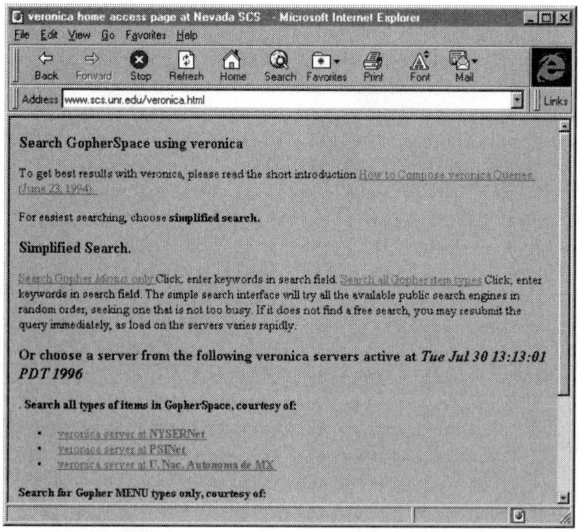

Figure 15-4
A Veronica menu.

To search Veronica, click a hyperlink to one of the servers. You see a page that lets you type one or more search words, as shown in Figure 15-5 on the following page. Veronica won't retrieve an item unless it contains *all* of the search terms you type.

Assuming Veronica was able to find something matching your search words, you see a new, custom-made Gopher menu, which contains hyperlinks to matching documents. As usual, you can access any of these items by clicking one of them.

HELP

My Veronica search didn't find anything!

Did you type two or three search words? Try typing just one. If that still doesn't work, try some synonyms ("social science" instead of "sociology") or a simpler form of the word ("forest" instead of "forestry").

Perhaps the most common problem with Gopher searches is that the server finds too many items rather than too few. By default, the server displays a few hundred retrieved items (called *hits*), but who knows what goodies lie in the hundreds or thousands more that weren't displayed? If you see a message at the bottom of the page indicating that Veronica didn't display all the hits, consider doing the search again with more specific search words.

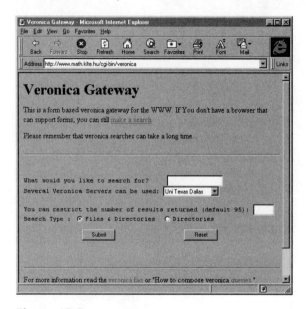

Figure 15-5
A Veronica search page.

Using FTP

Like most Web browsers, Internet Explorer doesn't fully implement FTP. For example, you can't use Internet Explorer to *send* files to somebody else's computer. For that, you'll need an *FTP client,* a program that's fully designed to utilize FTP in a two-way exchange. Internet Explorer can only *receive* files via FTP. This may not be the Christmas spirit, exactly, but that shouldn't stop you from making full use of it.

What's Available via FTP?

Via FTP, you can access anything that's stored on the file system of an FTP-accessible computer. In fact, full FTP access lets you get *into* the file system of another computer and actually *control* the computer remotely. Yes, it's true—with full FTP access, you can delete files, overwrite them, open and modify them, and in general wreak havoc. I'm sure you can appreciate why most FTP-accessible computers demand a login name and password before such access is granted.

But there's another type of FTP service that isn't so persnickety about access. It's called *anonymous FTP*—"anonymous" because you don't need to supply a username and password when you access the server. To be sure, the access you get is read-only—you can't erase or modify the files you find—but you can download them, and that's good enough to make anonymous FTP a valuable resource. Organizations make anonymous FTP services available to provide public access to shareware programs, public documents, and freebies of all kinds.

Accessing an Anonymous FTP Server

You can access an FTP server in two ways:

🌐 **Click an FTP hyperlink in a Web page.** Like Gopher hyperlinks, hyperlinks to FTP look exactly the same on screen as hyperlinks to other Web sites do. If you've enabled the full display of addresses by turning on the Show Full Addresses (URLs) option in the Options dialog box, you can see what kind of site you're about to access by moving the pointer over the hyperlink and looking at the status bar. If it's an FTP site, you see an address that begins with "ftp" instead of "http."

🌐 **Type the address to an FTP site directly.** You can do this by choosing the File Open command or, even better, by typing the address in the Address box.

Navigating FTP File Directories

The best thing about FTP is that it lets you directly navigate the file directories of a distant computer. That's also the bad thing. Navigating the directory structure will seem like a step backward into yesteryear's computer interfaces. It will help enormously if you're familiar with the concepts of directories and subdirectories—hey, remember MS-DOS? Actually, most of the computers you'll access with anonymous FTP are UNIX machines. UNIX is a very powerful and a not very user-friendly operating system. But don't let that throw you—UNIX's directory structure is much like that of MS-DOS for the simple reason that MS-DOS (beginning with version 2.0) incorporated UNIX-like directories and subdirectories.

15 CHAPTER

Here's a terminology refresher course, in case Windows 95 has dimmed your recollection of MS-DOS's oddities. A *directory* is a list of files (usually in alphabetical order). A *subdirectory* is a directory within a directory. If you select the subdirectory, you see a new directory—a new list of files. But you might want to get back to the *parent directory,* the directory that's one level "above" the subdirectory you're in right now. (With Windows 95, we now speak of "folders" and "folders within folders"—and isn't it easier to understand?)

When you first access an anonymous FTP server, you might find yourself at the top level of the directory tree—the *root directory,* as shown in Figure 15-6. If so, you will want to look for a directory called /pub, as shown in Figure 15-7. That's where the goodies are. A really good FTP hyperlink will land you at the top of the /pub directory.

Figure 15-6

The root directory of an anonymous FTP server.

To open a subdirectory, just click it. It's a lot easier to navigate directories with Internet Explorer than it is with MS-DOS or UNIX. Internet Explorer turns the items in directory lists into hyperlinks, so all you need to do is click the item you want and—Presto! You see a new page, with yet another directory—unless the item you clicked is a resource, such as a program, graphic, or sound. As with Gopher resources, clicking a hyperlink to a resource produces the appropriate action: programs download, graphics display, and sounds play (assuming you have the correct helper program installed).

To get back to a parent directory, scroll to the top of the page—you'll find a hyperlink called something like "up to the parent directory" or perhaps "up to higher level directory." Click this hyperlink to go up to the parent directory.

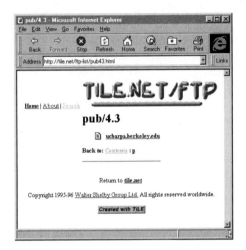

Figure 15-7
The /pub directory of an anonymous FTP server.

Finding the Good Stuff via FTP

Normally you'll access FTP file archives through innocent-looking hyperlinks on Web pages—hyperlinks that, without prior warning, land you in the midst of a UNIX directory structure. But now you know what to do.

How do you go hunting for FTP resources? In the past, the best way was to use the Archie service, which is described in this section, but it was the best way because it was the only way. Now you'll be well advised to use a wonderful Web service called shareware.com (http://www.shareware .com), which enables you to choose from more than 190,000 downloadable freeware and shareware programs. If you know the name of the file you're trying to locate or if you're interested in finding out what life was like on the Internet before the Web came along, try Archie.

15
CHAPTER

Like most Internet tools, Archie consists of server programs and client programs. The server has a database of programs and other resources that are available at thousands of publicly accessible FTP file archives worldwide. The client is a program that can contact the Archie server.

Still in use by UNIX addicts, Archie is probably the clunkiest Internet tool. To search for a file with Archie, you must know all or part of the name of the file you're looking for—there's no subject index. What you get in return is a list of publicly accessible FTP archives that contain copies of the file. You have to switch to FTP to obtain the files—Archie tells you only where they are.

Internet Explorer can't function as an Archie client—but you can access a Web page, called an *Archie gateway,* that knows how to talk to Archie servers. This service, shown in Figure 15-8, is known as ArchiePlex, and it's available from a variety of locations:

Location	Address
NASA	http://www.lerc.nasa.gov/archieplex.html
Amdahl Corp.	http://www.amdahl.com/internet/archieplex/
Imperial College	http://src.doc.ic.ac.uk/archieplexform.html

Figure 15-8
ArchiePlex.

ArchiePlex is much better than garden-variety Archie. It not only gives you a (relatively) user-friendly way of typing the file name or part of the file name you're searching for but also returns a Web page containing hyperlinks that you can click to access the file (assuming ArchiePlex found anything matching what you typed).

When should you use ArchiePlex? Only when you know the name or part of the name—the *exact* name—of the file you're looking for. If you're hunting for cool software, shareware.com is much better.

Using Telnet

It's a sad fact, but it's true: some computers can connect to the Internet, but they can't talk the Internet talk. Included in this category are legions of mainframe computers as well as thousands of MS-DOS–based bulletin board systems. To access the resources stored on these computers, Internet Explorer starts Telnet, a utility that's included with Windows 95.

In Figure 15-9, you see what a typical Telnet session looks like. Not much to write home about, is it? But think of the content. This figure displays the online library of the University of Virginia (http://www.virginia.edu/lib-itc.html), called VIRGO. Once you figure out how to use the commands—there's plenty of help available from on-screen menus—you can perform keyword searches of one of the world's finest online research libraries.

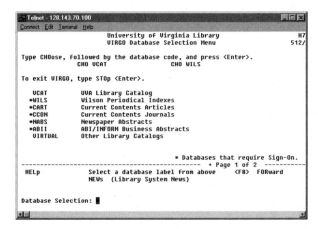

Figure 15-9

A Telnet session with the University of Virginia Library.

15
CHAPTER

Accessing Telnet

From Internet Explorer, you can start a Telnet session in two ways:

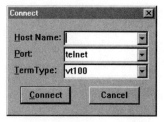 **Click a hyperlink to a Telnet site.** These hyperlinks have a distinctive address, one that begins with "telnet" instead of "ftp."

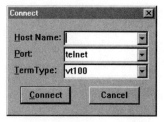 **Type a Telnet address directly.** You can use the File Open command or type the address in the Address box.

You can also access a Telnet session by starting the Telnet application and opening a session directly, without Internet Explorer being involved. To do so, follow these instructions:

1. From the Start menu, choose Run. You see the Run dialog box.

2. In the Run dialog box, type *telnet* and click the OK button. Windows 95 starts the Telnet application.

3. In the Telnet window, choose the Connect Remote System command. You see the Connect dialog box, shown in Figure 15-10.

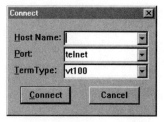

Figure 15-10

The Connect dialog box.

4. In the Host Name box, type the Internet domain name (the "dot address") of the Telnet site you want to access. The settings in the other boxes (Port and TermType) ought to be fine, but change these if you've been instructed to do so.

5. Click the Connect button. Telnet tries to access the computer you've specified. If you don't see anything in the Telnet window, try pressing Enter a couple of times.

6. Follow the logon instructions to access the Telnet resource, paying special attention to any messages about how to log off at the end of your session.

PART IV

266

Surviving Telnet Sessions

From the Web user's perspective, a Telnet session is a blast from the past—it's strictly text-only, no mice allowed. To communicate with the computer on the other end of the connection, you'll need to type commands—like *help* and *back* (or *prev*) and *top*. If you make a typing mistake, you can usually correct it by pressing the Backspace key—but you may have to press the Del key instead. To send a command, press Enter. Should you make an error typing the command, you'll know it—you'll see a friendly message, such as "command not recognized." Simply try again.

HELP

I want to save some of this neat stuff I found!

With the Telnet application, you can save the contents of your Telnet session to a *log*, which is nothing more than a text file. The drawback to saving a session this way is that the file may contain all sorts of extraneous stuff, like the commands you type and send to the Telnet computer itself. To eliminate this, you should activate the log *just before* you access some useful text and turn it *off* when the useful text stops coming. To activate the log, choose the Terminal Start Logging command; you see the Open Log File dialog box that asks you where to save the log file and what to call it. To turn the log off, choose the Terminal Stop Logging command.

Where Are the Telnet Goodies?

Telnet may be a retrograde technology, but you'd be wrong to write it off. Available through Telnet are thousands of useful resources, including the computerized card catalogs of some of the world's most famous research libraries. Telnet resources can be found through links scattered here and there in Web pages, but there's a more direct way: HyTelnet. The name is short for "Hypertext Telnet," and it's a good name: it's a Web-based gateway to the wonders of Telnet.

HyTelnet is a Web-accessible service that enables you to search a database of Telnet resources. To access HyTelnet, use the following address:

```
http://galaxy.einet.net/hytelnet/HYTELNET.html
```

CHAPTER 15

Don't forget to capitalize "HYTELNET." Assuming all goes well with accessing the site (never a sure thing on the Web), you see the HyTelnet search form, as shown in Figure 15-11.

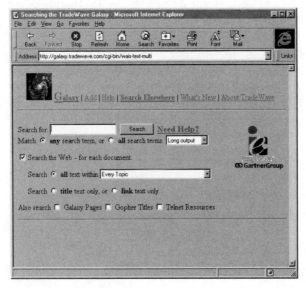

Figure 15-11

HyTelnet.

To search HyTelnet, type one or more keywords in the search box, which you'll find at the bottom of the HyTelnet page. Assuming HyTelnet finds any matching resources, you see a new Web page that lists hyperlinks to Telnet sites matching your search words. To access one of these sessions, click the hyperlink—Internet Explorer starts the Telnet application and connects you to the site.

Using WAIS

WAIS software enables service providers to create huge databases and to enable ordinary folks like you and me to search them. That's why it's called "wide area"; ideally, WAIS databases are available from far and wide.

As mentioned at the beginning of the chapter, you may have already used WAIS software without knowing it. WAIS pops up almost anytime you see a search box in a Web page. But when people ask, "Have you searched WAIS?" they're usually referring to something different—specifically, the WAIS Directory of Servers, which is a database of WAIS databases. Think of the Directory of Servers as a kind of clearinghouse for publicly accessible WAIS-based information. People who develop WAIS databases can add their database descriptions to the Directory of Servers.

Using Internet Explorer and a WAIS gateway, you can access the Directory of Servers and search for databases containing information pertinent to your interests. To access the Directory of Servers, use the following address:

`http://www.wais.com/directory-of-servers.html`

You see the directory's search page shown in Figure 15-12. In the Find box, type one or more search terms that describe the *general topic* in which you're interested, such as "child psychology" or "Bill Clinton." Then click the Search button. The result of this search is a new Web page listing the databases, if any, whose descriptions match the search terms you've typed. (If WAIS doesn't find anything, click the Back button and try again.)

Figure 15-12
The WAIS Directory of Servers search page.

Figure 15-13 shows a list of the databases retrieved by a Directory of Servers search. Note that the items are ranked using a numeric score; a score of 1000 means that the item is most likely to conform to your interests. (But some of the other top-scoring items might be just as good, or better—the search software isn't perfect.) To access one of the databases, click its hyperlink.

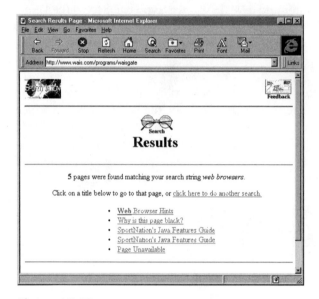

Figure 15-13
The results of a WAIS Directory of Servers search.

When you access a specific database, you are presented with another search screen that lets you type more specific search terms. After you click the Search button, you see a new page listing items that match your description—and again, these are ranked in numeric order, with the top-ranking documents placed at the top of the list.

From Here

You've learned how to explore Internet with Internet Explorer, including electronic mail, Usenet, Internet Relay Chat (IRC), and the additional Internet resources covered in this chapter (Gopher, Telnet, FTP, and WAIS). It's time to look at the cutting edge of Internet technology!

🌐 In Chapter 16, learn how explore three-dimensional worlds with Internet Explorer's VRML support.

🌐 In Chapter 17, learn why Web ordering with credit cards may soon become the safest way of doing credit card business anywhere.

🌐 In Chapter 18, explore Microsoft's new Internet telephony and online collaboration tool, NetMeeting. In the future, we'll be working together using tools like this one—and saving lots of money on travel bills.

15
CHAPTER

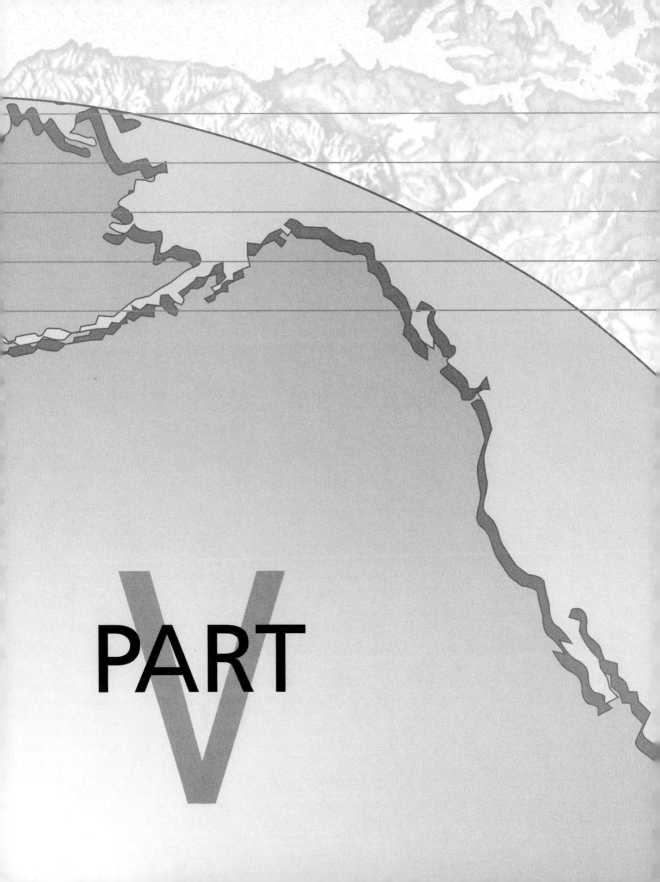

PART V

The Cutting
Edge

16

Exploring Virtual Worlds (VRML)

When you look at Web pages, you're seeing two dimensions. If you've ever played the computer game Doom, though, you'll know how interesting and exciting a three-dimensional computer display can be. Using your mouse or a joystick to navigate, you move *into* the screen, exploring rooms and passages as you please. The presentation of three-dimensional worlds in this way is often called *virtual reality,* because it really seems as though you're entering an almost-real world that exists entirely within the computer. It's great fun, and thanks to a new computer programming language called VRML, you can navigate three-dimensional worlds on the Web.

VRML stands for Virtual Reality Modeling Language. It's designed to enable Web authors to embed information about three-dimensional worlds in Web pages. If you're using a VRML-capable Web browser, the three-dimensional world appears in line (that is, within the Web page you're viewing). You can enter this world and explore! In Figure 16-1 on the next page, you see a VRML representation viewed in line.

Figure 16-1

A three-dimensional world viewed in line.

Internet Explorer can't view three-dimensional worlds without help—specifically, Microsoft VRML Support for Internet Explorer 3.0. After installing this program, your copy of Internet Explorer takes on new navigation capabilities, which don't become evident until you access a page containing a VRML world. At that time, a new toolbar appears.

In this chapter, you learn how to install and use the VRML toolbar and to navigate within virtual worlds. You'll also learn how to find the hottest VRML sites on the Web.

Accessing a VRML Site

To get started with the Internet Explorer VRML Add-In, you need to access a Web site that includes a three-dimensional world. Try the Using VRML Support site:

`http://www.microsoft.com/ie/most/howto/vrml.htm`

When you access this site, you'll notice that Internet Explorer takes a little longer to download the page than it would normally. That's because it's downloading the virtual world file. When the downloading is complete, you see the VRML toolbar, as shown in Figure 16-2.

PART

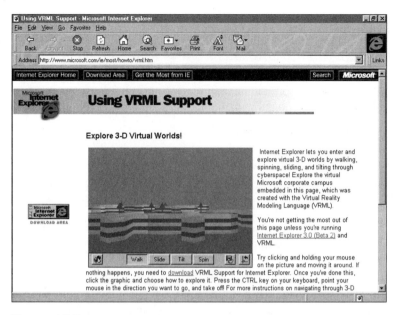

Figure 16-2

A three-dimensional view of the Microsoft campus.

You'll learn about the toolbar in the next section, but you can start navigating this world right away. Just hold down the mouse button, and advance the pointer in the direction you want to travel.

NOTE

Virtual worlds can contain Web addresses (URLs). You'll know when you're over one because the pointer changes shape to a hand. To access a shortcut, click the mouse button. To return to the virtual world, click the Back button.

If you'd like to see a list of the shortcuts contained in the world you're viewing, click the right mouse button and choose Shortcuts. If the world contains shortcuts, you'll see a list of them on the pop-up menu. To go to a shortcut, choose it from the menu.

CHAPTER 16

Using the VRML Toolbar

The VRML toolbar appears when you access a page containing a virtual world. You'll see the buttons shown in Figure 16-3.

Figure 16-3

The VRML toolbar.

Click This	To Do This
Menu button	Displays the VRML Add-In menu. You can also display this menu by right-clicking anywhere in the virtual scene or on the VRML Add-In toolbar.
Walk button	Move forward or backward through the scene, or turn to the left or to the right.
Slide button	Shift your viewpoint horizontally or vertically, without moving forward, backward, turning, or spinning.
Tilt button	Tilt your viewpoint without changing your current location. You can tilt up, down, left, or right.
Spin button	Spin the virtual world around its center.
Reset button	Return to the starting scene.
Straighten button	Cancel the tilt and straighten your viewpoint with respect to the scene.

HELP

I don't see the toolbar!

Wait until the virtual world completes downloading. If the toolbar still doesn't appear, enlarge the virtual window. Still don't see the toolbar? Right-click the virtual world, and make sure that Show Toolbar is checked.

Maneuvering with the Mouse

The best way to learn how to navigate a virtual world is to try it. If you get lost, just click the Reset button.

I can't move anywhere!

Some virtual worlds do not support collision detection (the ability to detect the surfaces of walls and other objects). To move in such worlds, you must disable collision detection. To do so, click the right mouse button, and make sure that the Walk Through Walls option is selected.

Walking

Walking is the way you'll normally move through a virtual world. As you walk, the scene will rotate to accommodate your turns. To walk, click the Walk button, press and hold the left mouse button, and move the mouse in the direction you want to go.

To move to an object quickly, double-click it.

Sliding

When you slide the scene, it pans past you as if you had just moved laterally or vertically without changing the direction you're facing. To slide, click the Slide button, press and hold the left mouse button, and move the mouse in the direction you want to go.

When should you slide? In many cases, it's easier to get to something if you slide left or right (or up or down) to get the best angle of attack.

Tilting

You can tilt the virtual world any way you like. If you're looking at a landscape—a scene that's meant to be navigated untilted—the effect might not be very desirable, though.

If you've just tried a tilt and you're not too happy with the results, you can de-tilt the scene by clicking the Straighten button.

16 CHAPTER

Maneuvering with the Keyboard

If you would prefer to use the keyboard to maneuver through virtual worlds, you can do so.

Use These Keys	To Do This
Arrow keys	Walk forward, backward, left, or right
Ctrl + arrow keys	Slide laterally or vertically
Shift + arrow keys	Tilt the scene

Maneuvering with the Joystick

You can also move through virtual worlds by using the joystick—but you'll have need of your mouse, too. To start exploring a virtual world with your joystick, use the mouse to click the virtual scene. Then you can use the joystick to walk in any direction.

I can't control this scene with the joystick!

Your joystick might need calibration. To calibrate your joystick, access the Microsoft Windows 95 Control Panel and choose the Joystick controls.

To slide, hold down the Ctrl key and move the joystick in the direction you want to go.

To tilt the scene, hold down the Shift key and move the joystick in the direction you want the scene to tilt.

1. Use the mouse to click the virtual scene.

2. Move the joystick in the direction you want to go.

Does your joystick have a POV (point of view) hat? If so, you can use the hat as a slide control. Move the hat forward or backward to slide your viewpoint up or down. Move the hat left or right to slide your viewpoint laterally.

PART

V

Spinning Objects

If you're viewing an object that's suspended in space in front of you, try spinning it. Because this command spins the entire virtual world, it doesn't work very well when you're inside a complex building or landscape—unless, that is, you're a fan of total spatial disorientation.

To spin an object:

1. Click the Spin button on the VRML Add-In toolbar.

2. Hold down the left mouse button, and move the pointer in the direction that you want the object to spin. After you release the mouse button, the world continues to spin.

3. To stop spinning the object, click the object.

TIP
To start spinning an object quickly, hold down the right mouse button and drag in the direction you want to spin.

If You Get Lost

You can return to the virtual world's starting point by clicking the reset button on the toolbar.

Is the scene tilted at a crazy angle? Straighten up and fly right by clicking the Straighten button.

Improving Performance

If the world you're viewing seems to perform sluggishly, you can improve performance by deselecting the Load Textures and Load Inlines options. To do so, click the right mouse button and choose Options.

From Here

 Continue your exploration of the cutting edge in Chapter 17, which discusses secure shopping on the Web.

🌐 In Chapter 18, you'll learn how to use NetMeeting, which enables you to engage in audio conversations and conferences using shared applications.

CHAPTER 16

CHAPTER 17

Security
and Privacy

These aren't fun issues to think about. But it's increasingly clear that every Internet user should be concerned about security and privacy while using the Net.

Security and privacy are two different things.

🌐 **Security** refers to the protection of computer and networking systems against unauthorized intrusion by computer criminals. Although there are security issues in using a PC connected to the Internet, such as computer viruses, security is mainly a concern of Internet service providers and companies trying to do business on the Internet.

🌐 **Privacy** refers to your ability to keep information about yourself hidden from prying eyes. Ideally, you should be able to prevent anyone from obtaining information about you, your computer system, and your Web site viewing tastes, and other personal data.

CHAPTER
17

Companies and individuals sometimes have common interests when it comes to security and privacy, and sometimes they don't. For example, you would like a high degree of security and privacy of credit card information when you order stuff on the Web and so would everyone trying to sell stuff on the Web—that's mutual self-interest. However, more than a few firms would love to invade your privacy while you're using the Web, compiling information about your browsing, searching, and shopping choices—that's conflicting interests.

This chapter explains why security and privacy protection is needed and walks you through the many options Internet Explorer offers to protect your security and privacy while you use the Internet. You'll also learn why this protection isn't perfect; much more needs to be done to assure the security and privacy of people using the Internet.

New In Version 3: You'll find improved security and brand-new privacy protection features in Internet Explorer version 3. Once you understand what these features can do, you will probably feel much more secure about using the Internet for shopping and personal purposes.

TIP

Many people don't upgrade to new versions of Internet Explorer, which is understandable—it's somewhat time-consuming and tedious to download and install software. However, wise Internet users know that they should always use the latest version of a browser. Newer versions solve problems that earlier ones couldn't. What's more, Internet security and privacy protection is a fast-evolving area. For the highest level of protection, always upgrade to the latest available version of Internet Explorer.

Why Is Security and Privacy Protection Needed?

It's paranoia time. Here's what could happen to you while using Internet Explorer:

 Criminal Hackers. A *sniffer* is a program that runs on a computer connected to the Internet. The program scans all the messages that are routed through the network to which the computer is connected, looking for information that conforms to a certain pattern (such as a Visa card number). Because Internet messages are normally sent in plain text, finding these patterns is easy to do—and a criminal computer hacker doesn't even need to monitor the program manually. When the pattern is found, the information is displayed on-screen, enabling the criminal to read it.

🌐 **Imposters.** Suppose you've decided to order something on line. You've accessed a Web site that appears to be the official Web site of a famous West coast winery. It's a glamorous production. However, you don't notice that the URL indicates that the site you've accessed is actually located outside the U.S. You upload your credit card data, and somebody goes on a shopping spree with it!

🌐 **Saboteurs.** If you're not careful about where you obtain computer programs on the Internet, you could infect your system with a computer virus.

🌐 **Snoops.** Some servers—mainly commercial ones—write data to your hard drive in files called *cookies*. In most cases, this is quite legitimate and in your own interest. The cookie files contain information about your preferences, customization choices, and previous page selections. Cookies give Web sites much more functionality and make them easier to use. However, there is a major push underway to use cookies to collect marketing data. At some sites, cookies can be used to compile a dossier about your searching, browsing, and on-line ordering preferences.

🌐 **Pilferers.** Suppose you manage to upload your credit card information to a commercial service operating on the Web. Nobody caught it with a sniffer, and the site isn't an imposter. But can you trust the site's personnel? Credit card companies complain that hundreds of millions of dollars are lost annually due to pilfering at the company's end of the transaction.

Internet Explorer offers many solutions to security and privacy protection on the Internet—but as you'll see, there are some remaining problems. The following sections indicate how the program gives you some measure of protection against criminal hackers, imposters, saboteurs, and snoops. New measures now underway will give you protection against pilferers, too, so that the Web will eventually become the safest way by far to use your credit card.

CHAPTER 17

Safeguarding Online Transactions (Dealing with the Criminal Hacker Problem)

The key to safeguarding your data from criminal hackers is to *encrypt* it. To encrypt data means to scramble it so that it can't be read on any computer while en route. When the data arrives at its correct destination, the receiving computer *decrypts* it.

On the World Wide Web, encryption becomes possible with *secure browsers* and *secure servers*. A secure browser, such as Internet Explorer, can encrypt the data that you send, and a secure server can decrypt the data at the other end. All this is done automatically, and almost instantly. Along the way, it is virtually impossible to decode and read the encrypted data.

Caution: Internet Explorer's ability to contact secure commercial servers provides protection for your credit card data, but it does nothing for the text you upload to search services or for your e-mail messages. These can be intercepted and read while en route by anyone with the technical means to do so, including dishonest system administrators. A complete privacy solution for Internet users would involve encrypted e-mail and search service uploads as well as Usenet and commercial ordering security. Such a solution might be right around the corner, thanks to operating-system level encryption support that is currently under development at Microsoft. This support is slated to provide encryption/decryption support for any Windows application that is designed to take advantage of it.

Public Key Cryptography: How It Works—and How It Will Affect You

Some call it a technical revolution. Almost certainly, it's going to affect your life. It's called *public key cryptography*. Basically, public key cryptography is a new method of sending super-secret messages between two parties who have never communicated before.

Encryption—scrambling a message so that nobody can read it except its intended recipient—has been around since the time of Julius Caesar, but it's always had an Achilles' heel: Somehow or other, you had to convey the *key* to the recipient. (The key tells how to decode the message.) This could be done by means of a courier. However, as you can imagine, conveying the key is fraught with peril. What if the courier is disloyal?

(continued)

PART
V

Public Key Cryptography:
How It Works—and How It Will Affect You *continued*

Public-key cryptography solves this problem by using two keys, a public key and a private key. To engage in a secure transaction, you send your public key to somebody, and that person uses your public key to encrypt the message. En route, nobody can decode the message. Only you can decode it, using your private key. As long as the public key is carefully designed, it's practically impossible to break the code by deriving the private key from the public key.

When you use Internet Explorer to contact a secure server, the program and server exchange public keys, and a secure channel of communication is established. Both the data sent by you and by the server are sent in encrypted form so that nobody—not even a criminal armed with a sniffer—can intercept it en route.

How will public key encryption affect you? By making on-line commerce possible, although—as you'll learn elsewhere in this chapter—there's still a key piece that needs to come into the picture (protection against pilferers). But that's solvable. What's troubling about public-key encryption is the perfect cover it provides for illegal activity, such as drug dealing, money laundering, and terrorism. The U.S. Federal Bureau of Investigation (FBI) is deeply concerned that, in an encryption-driven future, the electronic equivalent of wiretapping will become impossible, creating unparalleled opportunities for organized crime. But it's far from clear how these concerns will pan out, and how they're going to be balanced against the legitimate privacy concerns of citizens and Internet users.

Understanding Security Protocols

For Internet browsers and servers to exchange encrypted data, both must be able to work with the same *security protocol*. A security protocol is a set of standards that specify how two computers can communicate by means of a secure (encrypted) channel. To let you order securely from most of the secure sites on the Web, Internet Explorer recognizes and works with the following security protocols:

🌐 **Secure Sockets Layer (SSL).** This protocol, originally developed by Netscape, is the one used in most secure Web sites.

🌐 **Private Communication Technology (PCT).** This Microsoft-developed protocol builds on SSL and introduces additional features that can help give a greater margin of security.

CHAPTER 17

You don't have to choose a protocol when you access a secure site—it's all automatic.

Accessing a Secure Site

Accessing a secure Web site is no different from accessing any other site on the Web—you click a hyperlink or type the URL directly.

Often, the site's welcome page isn't secure. After all, lots of people are still using browsers that lack security features. Look for a link that enables you to access the secure version of the service.

After you've logged on to the secure service, look for a lock icon on the status bar. The lock icon tells you that you have accessed a secure server, and that the information you upload is safe from prying eyes. It's that simple.

Viewing Security Information

Once you've logged on to a secure Web page, you can view the security information. It's not really necessary to do this unless you want to satisfy yourself that the transaction really is secure.

To view security information, do the following:

1. Choose the File Properties command. You'll see the Properties dialog box as shown in Figure 17-1.

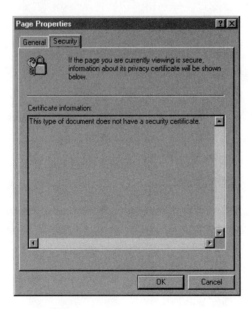

Figure 17-1

The Properties dialog box.

2. Click the Security tab. You'll see the Security page with the security certificate information in view.

3. Click OK to exit the Properties dialog box.

Choosing Warning Options

If you would like to adjust Internet Explorer's warning settings, choose View Options, and click the Advanced tab. When you do, you'll see the page shown in Figure 17-2.

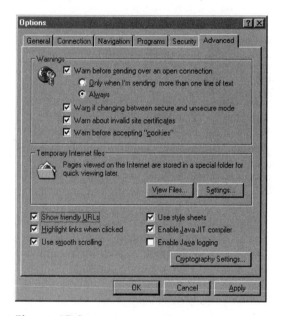

Figure 17-2

The View Options Advanced page.

Options that affect on-line transactions include the following:

- **Warn Me Before Sending Over An Open Connection.** If you select this option, you can choose Only When I'm Sending More Than One Line Of Text, or Always. Frankly, I find all these warnings to be intrusive. You should be aware that any text you send is insecure, but this isn't a concern when you're using a search service to find an innocuous subject. I recommend deselecting all open connection warnings, but please remember that the Internet isn't secure and you shouldn't send personal information (and especially your credit card numbers) unless a secure channel of communication has been established.

- 🌐 **Warn If Changing Between Secure And Insecure Mode.** With this option, you'll see a warning when you leave a secure Web connection and return to an open (unsecured) connection. This warning is useful when you've been looking at pages in a secure site, and you hyperlink out of it; without the warning, you might not realize that your communications are no longer secure. I recommend that you enable this option.

- 🌐 **Warn Me About Invalid Site Certificates.** With this option, Internet Explorer will display a warning if the program detects a discrepancy between the security certificate and the particulars (such as the Internet address or e-mail address) of the site you've accessed. This could be a minor error on the server's part, but it could also mean that somebody has tried to set up a bogus site to collect credit card numbers. If you're sure the site is what it says it is, click OK. If you have any doubts or you're not sure, click Cancel. I recommend that you enable this option.

- 🌐 **Warn Me Before Accepting Cookies.** This option lets you confirm cookies before they're downloaded. For more information, see "Approving Cookie Downloading (Dealing with the Snooper Problem)," later in this chapter.

Validating Sites and Users with Certificates (Dealing with the Imposter Problem)

Is encryption really safe? It does nothing to protect you (or merchants, for that matter) from imposters. Suppose you access a (fictitious) company called Sailing Wares, Inc. You see a message informing you that this site offers security. But how do you know you've really reached Sailing Wares, Inc., and not some criminal who's set up a computer to pose as a legitimate business? The answer lies in *security certificates*. A security certificate is an encrypted document, verified and signed by an independent third party, that proves that the person or organization you're dealing with is authentic.

Internet Explorer version 3 uses two kinds of certificates:

- 🌐 A *site certificate* is issued and validated by an independent, third-party agency. When your browser accesses a secure Web site, your browser examines the security certificate. If the security certificate is valid, you know that the server you've accessed is really located at the company you want to do business with. If the security certificate isn't valid, it means that something in the certificate doesn't match up—for example, the site's name or e-mail address isn't what it's supposed to be. This might be due to sloppy record-keeping, or it might be due to criminal activity. In either case, you'd be well advised to skip ordering from this site.

🌐 Companies selling goods on the Web have their own concerns about imposters. What if someone has stolen your credit card and is trying to use it to order goods illegally? *Personal certificates* identify you as the person you say you are. A personal certificate is like showing your identification when you use your credit card. It's in your interest as well as the interests of merchants and banks to make sure that no one is using your card illegally.

A complete solution to the imposter problem requires both types of certificates.

NOTE Personal certificates are still in development. In the future, you will be able to obtain personal certificates from a certificate-issuing agency, but only after you show some type of personal identification. For now, some secure sites will download personal certificates for you; secure sites use these to make sure that, when you access the site again, you're doing so from the same computer. But that's not an adequate level of protection. For more information, see "Unsolved: The Pilfering Problem," later in this chapter.

If you would like to view your personal and site certificates, choose View Options, click the Security tab, and click Personal or Site in the Certificates area. Within the dialog boxes that appear, you can view the certificates and delete them, if you want. For more information about publisher certificates, see the next section of this chapter.

Verifying Software Publishers (Dealing with the Saboteur Problem)

To deal with the sabotage problem, Internet Explorer warns you about the virus peril when you're about to download a file from the Internet. But version 3 of Internet Explorer goes even further by providing *publisher certificates*. Publisher certificates attest that the software you're downloading is coming

CHAPTER 17

from a trusted source, such as a well-known computer software publishing company.

To choose software downloading options, choose View Options and click the Security tab. You'll see the following options in the View Content area:

- **Allow Downloading Of Active Content.** This option allows you to prevent the downloading of any active content, if you're fearful of viruses.

- **Enable ActiveX Controls And Plug-Ins.** This option allows you to selectively turn off the downloading of ActiveX controls and plug-ins.

- **Run ActiveX Scripts.** This option allows you to selectively turn off ActiveX scripts that you may encounter on Web pages.

- **Enable Java Programs.** This option allows you to selectively turn off Java programs.

- **Safety Level.** When you click this button, you see a dialog box offering three options: High, Medium, and None. With the High option, the program avoids unsafe content and displays a warning message. With the Medium option, you see a warning, but you can choose to proceed. With None, you have no warnings and no protection.

TIP

I recommend that you use the High option in the Safety Level dialog box. Using this option will prevent Internet Explorer from downloading any active content that doesn't have a valid certificate. You will still be able to view Java applets, however.

Approving Cookie Downloading (Dealing with the Snooper Problem)

Many Web users are under the impression that you can browse the Internet in perfect anonymity, without anyone knowing which sites you've visited. This impression is false.

PART

V

Every time you visit a Web site, you potentially leave a great deal of information about yourself, including:

- The organization or company with which you're affiliated
- Your geographical location
- The type of computer and operating system you're running
- The browser you're using
- The Internet address of the computer you're using
- The exact time and date of your visit
- The pages you've looked at and how long you looked at them

The means to collect, store, and analyze this information is your own computer, used without your consent or knowledge. Many servers write files to your hard disk, called *cookies*, that compile additional information about you.

At many sites, the use of cookies is innocent enough; the goal is simply to tailor the site to your benefit. Cookies were introduced by Netscape Communications to get around a problem in Web access—namely, that it's difficult for one page to pass information to another page without adding lots of incomprehensible codes to the URL. Cookies provide a way for a page to leave information for another page. At many sites, this information is used to record your preferences, and in most cases, cookies are quite innocent: Microsoft's default start page, for example, uses cookies to record your preferences for customized home and MSNBC pages. (See Chapter 9.)

However, a New York-based advertising firm has figured out how to use cookies to track your movements though the several dozen commercial sites with which the company contracts. This advertising firm builds a database about you that monitors your browsing behavior. The purpose of the database is to assist Web advertisers target the market more effectively. If you've visited any of the sites that contract with this firm, there is a cookie on your hard drive that gives you a unique identification number. This number is used to create a profile about your browsing habits and interests. When you access a site that has contracted with this firm to provide ads, the site sends your ID number to the marketing firm, which sends back ads tailored to your interests.

Is this in your best interest? After all, you'll see ads tailored to your preferences. On the other hand, privacy advocates worry that this monitoring activity goes far beyond the transaction monitoring common in the retail world; it amounts to surveillance concerning which store windows you've

CHAPTER 17

looked into. Worse, they say, it's done without the user's knowledge or consent—and to add insult to injury, it employs your own hard drive. Cookies files, incidentally, can consume up to 1.2 MB of your disk space!

Like to see your cookies? Using Windows Explorer, display the directory C:\windows\cookies. There they are! Don't think that you prevent new ones from being written by deleting the entire \cookies directory; Internet Explorer will simply write a new one. As described later in this chapter, you can choose an Internet Explorer option that lets you selectively decide whether to download a specific cookie.

TIP

If you're concerned about your privacy while you're surfing the Web, start your surfing sessions at The Anonymizer (http://www.anonymizer.com). When you use The Anonymizer as your starting point, subsequent sites cannot determine the sites you've previously browsed in the current session. You can still make use of virtually all of the Web's features, including Java programs and password-based authentication.

New In Version 3: If you want, Internet Explorer version 3 will warn you every time a server attempts to write a cookie to your hard drive. You can inspect the cookie and prevent the server from sending it. To turn on cookie approval, choose View Options and click the Security tab. Click Warn Me Before Accepting "Cookies," and click OK.

After choosing this option, you'll see a dialog box (such as the one in Figure 17-3) whenever a server tries to send you a cookie.

Figure 17-3
The cookie dialog box.

You'll be able to see the cookie's contents, or at least the first dozen or so characters, as well as the cookie's expiration date. Cookies are coded, so it's hard to tell what's intended. You can also look at the cookie's expiration date; in general, it's a good sign if the cookie expires in a few days or weeks, a bad one if it's semi-permanent. To accept the cookie, click Yes; to reject it, click No.

If you reject the cookie, you can still access the site. But you might find that you're being besieged by cookie after cookie, requiring you to go through a whole series of these dialog boxes. Check to see whether the server is trying to send you the same cookie over and over, the intent being (presumably) to wear you down until you give in and click Yes. Another option (the preferred one): leave the site and don't come back.

Unsolved: The Pilfering Problem

Is Web commerce poised to explode? The jury's still out. To be sure, the Web is already big business—millions of dollars worth of on-line orders have already been received. But that's a pittance compared to the amount we spend on telephone orders. For this reason, some experts believe that the Web just isn't going to mature into a major shopping channel. Others attribute the slow growth of Web commerce to the fact that secure browsers and servers are just now becoming available.

But there's another reason. When you place a credit-card order via a secure Web server, somebody has to *manually* read your number, contact a credit-card verification service, and get an authorization code for your card. This is ridiculously low-tech for such a high-tech area, isn't it? What's more, it creates opportunities for employees to pilfer credit card numbers. Of course, you take the same risk when you use your credit card to order by mail or by phone.

Recent proposals by both Visa and MasterCard would solve this problem by combining personal certificates and automatic authorization programs. There's a real benefit to this technology: Your credit card number won't be seen by *anyone*, including the people at the company from which you're ordering. Once this technology is in place, credit card ordering via the Web will become much safer than ordering by mail or by telephone.

Look for this technology in the next version of Internet Explorer.

CHAPTER 17

Let's Go Shopping!

For now, you'll find that roughly several thousand companies have opened up shop on the Net. It's a mixed bag, selling everything from hot-sauce to lingerie, but some patterns seem to be emerging. In general, the businesses that succeed on the Web are those that offer products Web users like or that take special advantage of the Internet's potential as a shopping medium. An example: Amazon.com Books (http:/www.amazon.com), which offers over one million book titles on line. Here, database and Web technology are joined to offer something you can't get in just any neighborhood bookstore.

After you've shopped around a bit, you'll see that certain types of products and services seem to be doing better than others on-line. Here's a snapshot of the current scene (subject to change, of course, like everything on the Web):

- **Books and compact discs.** These are naturals for on-line ordering. A store can put its entire catalog (perhaps containing as many as 150,000 items) on line with a searchable interface.

- **Clothing.** You won't find everyday items on the Web; the action here is strictly in specialty items, such as lingerie, bizarre T-shirts, funny ties, hats, and specialty shoes.

- **Computer equipment.** It makes sense that computer people would feel comfortable ordering computer equipment on line. Several excellent on-line vendors offer great prices on selected equipment.

- **Gifts.** Flowers and specialty gift shops are prevalent on the Web, indicating that this is another popular area for on-line orders.

- **Specialty foods and wine.** Hot sauces, Zinfandels, designer beers, spices, and sweets. All that surfing makes you hungry!

- **Sports and recreation gear.** You'll find plenty of on-line stores that sell specialty gear for golfers, sailors, backpackers, and other sports enthusiasts.

TIP

To keep on top of the Web's fast-breaking commercial developments, check out The All-Internet Shopping Directory (http://www.webcom.com/~tbrown/). This site lists Web vendors whose sites meet stringent guidelines for quality and service. You'll find lists, currently updated bi-weekly, of the Web's top shopping sites, and plenty of links to the newest and hottest credit-card burners on the Web.

PART
V

Selected Secure Shopping Sites

🌐 **CDWorld**   One of the best CD stores on the Internet, this offers a convenient search engine that lets you scan more than 100,000 discs by artist's name, title, or recording label.

http://cdworld.com/

🌐 **iMALL**   Here's an Internet shopping mall that's beautifully organized with a familiar plan—a real shopping mall! The opening graphic shows a big mall seen from the outside. You click on the graphic to go "in," and then you see a "floor plan"—and again, it's clickable. Very nicely organized! Among the wares you find for sale are housewares, arts and collectibles, specialty items, electronics, gourmet foods, computer stuff, gifts, books, and more.

http://www.imall.com/homepage.html

🌐 **Internet Shopping Network**   If you're skeptical about Internet shopping, this is the place to start. You'll find hot deals on computer and electronics equipment—some of the best deals around. You can see a picture of what you're buying and full technical information (much more, generally, than you'd find in a print-based catalog).

http://www.internet.net/

🌐 **MarketplaceMCI**   Accessing this site is like stepping into a gigantic, big-city shopping mall. You'll find dozens of on-line "stores" here, selling a huge variety of goods. Every store accepts secure on-line credit-card ordering, too. Like a real mall, this one has a Borders bookstore, a T-shirt store, Nordstrom, Hammacher Schlemmer, and much more.

http://www2.pcy.mci.net/marketplace/index.html

🌐 **Travel Now**   This secure site offers hotel and airline reservations, tours and packages, and cruises. An excellent feature is the hotel search page, which enables you to search for the best rate.

http://www.travelnow.com/

CHAPTER 17

From Here

🌐 There's one stop left on your tour of the Internet's cutting edge: NetMeeting. Take a look at the way people will work together in the future!

CHAPTER 18

Using
NetMeeting

The Internet's going to change the way we work—that's certain. Already, e-mail is close to being indispensable, both for internal communication within companies and with coworkers and colleagues the world over. With Microsoft NetMeeting, you can use the Internet to collaborate.

New In Version 3: In brief, Microsoft NetMeeting—currently available for Windows 95 and soon for Windows NT—is a real-time Internet communication tool that enables you to converse with other Internet users as if you were using a telephone. (You'll need a sound card, speakers, and a microphone to use NetMeeting for real-time audio communication.) But it's far more than an Internet telephone. NetMeeting includes the following advanced features:

🌐 **Point-to-point audio communication via the Internet.** Think of it as a free long-distance phone call. The audio quality isn't fantastic, and often there's a delay of a second or two—but hey, it's free!

- 🌐 **A shared "whiteboard" space.** Everyone participating in the conference, whether it's just 2 of you or 25, can collaborate within this graphical space. Everyone can draw and type, and everyone sees the results, even as they're created.

- 🌐 **A chat area.** Users can type and send text-based messages, which everyone else who's connected can see.

- 🌐 **File transfer.** While you're in a meeting with one or more other people, you can send a file—and everyone will receive a copy. Others can send files to you, too.

- 🌐 **Application sharing.** You can start any Windows application on your system, and others can see what you're doing. For example, you can start Excel and show everyone your worksheet. You can even select an option that enables collaborators to make changes to your document.

- 🌐 **Multipoint communication.** Most other Internet telephone standards support only point-to-point communications for their white board features. With NetMeeting, you can involve three or more people in the shared white board space, the chat area, and application sharing.

- 🌐 **Standards-based.** Unlike many Internet telephony programs, NetMeeting is based on open standards that are currently supported by more than two dozen companies. This is very important, since the reason Internet telephony hasn't taken off is that the various programs won't work with each other. With Net-Meeting, you'll be able to talk to people who use other standards-based programs, including a recent offering from Intel.

Whether or not you've ever tried an Internet telephony application, you'll be yakking away happily—and collaborating over the Internet—with this chapter as your guide.

Understanding Internet Telephony

Let's start off with an important point: the Internet just wasn't designed for the real-time delivery of voice, let alone audio or video. It has taken some very clever programming—and some industrial-strength compression technology—to make Internet telephony possible. Even so, you'll find that voices often sound garbled, and sometimes there are interruptions and delays.

PART

V

Another drawback of Internet telephony is that it's somewhat inconvenient to use—you have to be near your computer, and you have to be logged on to the Net. You might meet both of those conditions when you're working in your office or if you have some other kind of unlimited Internet access, but it's not so convenient when you're at home logging on intermittently and paying per-hour charges. (However, if you are a home user, you can arrange via e-mail to call the other party at a prearranged time.)

On balance, the MCIs and AT&Ts of this world don't have much to be concerned about, at least at this point; long-distance telephones aren't going away any time soon. Still, if you're the type of person who sits in front of a computer all day (like me), you'll find NetMeeting of great value for calling other computer shut-ins.

It's a mistake, however, to think of Internet telephony as merely a substitute for the telephone, *sans* long-distance charges. Rather, it's an opportunity for *collaboration*. Think of NetMeeting as a telephone *plus* the tools you need to work with others, even if they're located halfway around the world. Here's an example of what you can do with NetMeeting:

- **Go over a proposal with a client.** As you work on the figures and agree on the terms, you can make the changes. When you're done, you can send your client the completed file for further review and printing.

- **Write a document collaboratively.** You and your collaborators can jointly compose a Microsoft Word document on-screen.

- **Make a presentation.** Using NetMeeting's application-sharing capabilities, you can share a Microsoft PowerPoint presentation in a conference involving two or more participants—even if they're scattered all over the world. You can even give them control of the application so that they can navigate through the slides as they please.

- **Develop a Web page design.** Work interactively with your Webmaster to develop your home page. As you express your preferences, your Webmaster can compose the code. With a click of the mouse, you can see the results in Internet Explorer.

These are only some of the potential applications of NetMeeting. Because you can share any Windows application using NetMeeting, the possibilities truly are limitless.

CHAPTER 18

Understanding the ULS Server

A problem for Internet telephony is that so many people connect to the Internet using modems. With most modem connections, your computer is assigned a temporary Internet address. The next time you log on, you will probably be assigned a different Internet address. That's no problem when you're browsing the Web, but it is a problem if people are trying to call you. It's as if your telephone number changed every time you made a call.

To solve this problem, NetMeeting's designers created a User Location Server (ULS). When you start NetMeeting, the program sends your e-mail address and your current Internet address to the server. By accessing your name through the User Location Server, people can call you even though your address has changed.

TIP

If you would rather not make your number public, start NetMeeting, choose Tools Options, and click My Information. Remove the check mark next to Publish This Information On The User Location Service.

NOTE

If you're using a modem and you're not on the User Location Server, you need to give callers your Internet address. To find out what your current Internet address is, access http://www.anonymizer.com/cgi-bin/snoop.pl and check the list of personal data that this page (called I Can See You) has found out. Check next to the words *You Are Calling From...* to find out your exact, current Internet address. You can then e-mail this to people who would like to call you, but bear in mind that this address will remain in effect only as long as you're connected in this session. For more information on this page and what it's all about, see Chapter 17, page 292.

Not all User Location Servers are public. If you're using NetMeeting in an organization, you might be given the address of an organizational ULS. (An organization will be able to set up a ULS using the Microsoft Information Server and Microsoft Windows NT.) To specify a default User Location Service other than Microsoft's, start NetMeeting, choose Tools Options, click My Information, and type a new address in the User Location Service box.

PART

V

Getting Started with NetMeeting

This section introduces NetMeeting. You'll find step-by-step instructions on running the program for the first time and understanding NetMeeting's window.

Running NetMeeting for the First Time

The first time you run Microsoft NetMeeting, the Audio Test Wizard will appear and you'll be asked to test your microphone. Be sure it's connected and ready to go.

You'll also be asked to provide this information:

- Your e-mail address
- Your name
- Your city
- Your country
- Any comments you would like to make visible on the public server
- Whether you'd like your name published on the User Location Server
- The User Location Server you would like to use (the default is uls.microsoft.com)

To start NetMeeting, choose Start Programs Microsoft NetMeeting and follow the on-screen instructions.

CHAPTER

18

The Audio Test Wizard will tell you whether your sound system is capable of *full duplex audio* (you and the person with whom you're talking can speak at the same time) or *half duplex audio* (you will have to take turns talking). If the test shows that your system is capable of full duplex audio, be sure to verify this setting after the wizard finishes. To do so, choose Tools Options, click the Audio tab, and select Enable Full-Duplex Audio. Click OK to confirm your choice.

Looking at NetMeeting

After you've finished running the NetMeeting configuration wizard, you'll see NetMeeting on-screen, as shown in Figure 18-1. In addition, you'll see the NetMeeting icon on the taskbar.

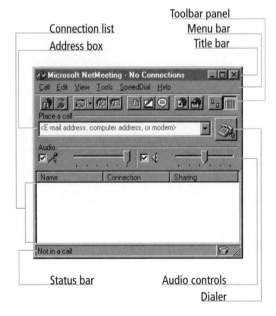

Figure 18-1
Microsoft NetMeeting.

You'll see the following in NetMeeting's window:

🌐 **Title bar.** To reposition the NetMeeting window, drag the title bar. To maximize the window quickly, double-click the title bar. Double-click again to restore the previous size.

- ⊕ **Menu bar.** Here you'll find all the NetMeeting commands, but the most frequently used commands are found on the toolbar.

- ⊕ **Toolbar.** The toolbar contains some useful tools. You'll find the following buttons: Directory, Hang Up, Share Application, Collaborate, Work Alone, Send File, Whiteboard, Chat, Web Directory, NetMeeting Home Page, Large Icons, and Details. You'll learn what these tools do later in this chapter. To display or hide the toolbar, choose View Toolbar.

- ⊕ **Address box.** Use this box to type the number you want to call. Click the down arrow to choose recently dialed numbers.

- ⊕ **Dialer (Call button).** Click here to dial the number you've entered into the address box. To display or hide the dialer, choose View Dialer.

- ⊕ **Audio Controls.** Here you can adjust the microphone and speaker volume. To display or hide the audio controls, choose View Audio.

- ⊕ **Connection list.** In this area, you see the people with whom you're connected.

- ⊕ **Status bar.** In this area, NetMeeting displays messages and information about its status and what it's doing. You can hide the status bar by choosing View Status Bar, but it's worth keeping it visible because some of the messages are useful or important.

TIP

With the connection list, you can view information about the people who are connected. If you choose View Large Icons, you see a large icon with the person's name; to see information about this connection, right-click the icon and choose Properties. You'll see the person's name, information about whether sharing is enabled, information about the type of connection that's been achieved (voice or no voice), and any other information that the person has elected to make public by means of the User Location Service. It's better to choose View Details; this option shows you the all-important connection information without your having to display Properties. When you first make your connection, you'll want to know whether audio is enabled, so it's nice to see this information without having to do anything.

CHAPTER 18

Making a Call

After you've installed NetMeeting, you'll probably want to try to place a call right away. To get the most out of this experience, spend a few moments reviewing your long-distance phone bills. This will help enormously when it comes to overlooking the audio deficiencies of Internet telephony.

Placing a Call via the Internet

You can call someone on the Internet by doing one of the following:

 Placing a call using a User Listing Service (ULS). You choose a name from the User Location Service.

 Placing a call by typing an Internet address directly. If someone has given you an Internet address (and is running NetMeeting or a compatible program), you can place the call by typing the address.

To place a call using the User Listing Service, follow these steps:

1. Click Directory, choose Call Directory, or press Ctrl + D. You'll see the Directory dialog box.

2. To search for a user, click the column in which you would like to search and then scroll through the list.

3. When you've found the user you want to call, select the user's information and click Call. (If you want to cancel the call, choose Call Cancel Placing Call.)

To place a call using someone's Internet address, do this:

1. In the address box, type the person's Internet address. The address will consist of four numbers separated by dots, with no spaces.

2. Click the Call button.

TIP

After you place calls, you can see a list of the most recently used numbers by clicking the down arrow next to the address box. You can place a call to one of these numbers by choosing a number and clicking the Call button. You can also make calls by choosing a SpeedDial shortcut. For more information on SpeedDial shortcuts, see "Using SpeedDial Shortcuts" later in this chapter.

It says, "The person you called is not able to accept Microsoft Net-Meeting calls!"

This message could be caused by any of several problems. You might have typed the number incorrectly (check your typing and try again). A network error might have prevented the call from getting through (try again). Finally, the other person might have quit NetMeeting and closed the NetMeeting icon on the taskbar. Send e-mail or, as a last-ditch act of desperation, place a real telephone call to find out whether you have the right address—and, while you're at it, ask the person to start NetMeeting. To configure NetMeeting to accept calls even when the NetMeeting window is closed, choose Tools Options, click the General tab, and select Show Microsoft NetMeeting On The Taskbar and Notify Me Of Calls Even If The Microsoft NetMeeting Window Is Closed.

Establishing the Call and Carrying on a Conversation

If you've successfully made contact with the person you're calling, you'll hear a chiming sound and you'll see two names in the connections list, as shown in Figure 18-2.

Figure 18-2
A call in progress.

Don't be surprised if you can't say "Hello" right away. NetMeeting needs a little time to determine what type of connection is possible. If audio is possible, you'll see *Audio Enabled* under Connection in the connection window. If audio isn't possible, you'll see *No Voice*.

CHAPTER 18

If you're calling a system that isn't capable of full duplex sound, you won't be able to talk and listen at the same time, even if your system is capable of full duplex. The connection uses the least common denominator when it comes to full duplex or half duplex capabilities.

TIP To see information about the person you're talking to, right-click the person's name and choose Properties. You'll see a Properties dialog box, which lists the information that this person has made available to the User Location Service.

While you're talking to someone, you have a good opportunity to create a SpeedDial shortcut for this person. In the connections window, right-click the person's name and choose Add SpeedDial. After adding this shortcut, you'll see it in the SpeedDial menu. For more information, see "Using Speed-Dial ShortCuts" later in this chapter.

If the person you're talking to can't hear you very well, try increasing the microphone volume by moving the slider control. Also, try speaking more directly into the microphone. To adjust the speaker volume, move the slider control next to the speaker icon.

TIP If you install or upgrade a sound card after installing NetMeeting, choose Tools Audio Tuning Wizard to run this wizard again. (It's the same one that appears when you run NetMeeting for the first time.)

Placing a Call via a Local Area Network (LAN)

If your organization has a local area network to which your computer is connected, you can use NetMeeting for internal communication and collaboration. To call someone on your local area network (LAN), you need to use Advanced Calling in the Call menu.

To place a call on a LAN, follow these instructions:

1. Choose Place Advanced Call. You'll see the Advanced Calling dialog box, shown in Figure 18-3.

2. In Call Using, choose the network protocol that has been installed for your LAN. (If you're not sure which protocol to choose, contact your network administrator.)

3. In the Address box, type the user's numerical LAN address. (Again, if you're not sure what the number is, contact your network administrator).

4. In the Call With area, choose the type of call you want to make (Both Audio And Data, Audio Only, or Data Only).

5. Choose OK. (If you want to cancel the call, choose Cancel.)

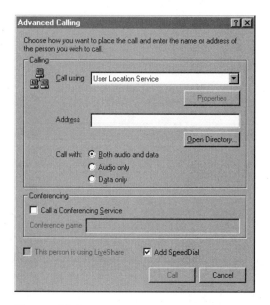

Figure 18-3
The Advanced Calling dialog box.

Calling a Conferencing Service

If your organization has set up a NetMeeting server, you might be able to join named conferences. To join a named conference, do the following:

1. Choose Place Advanced Call.

2. In Call Using, choose the network protocol that has been installed for your LAN. (If you're not sure which protocol to choose, contact your network administrator.)

3. In the Address box, type the conference computer's address. (Again, if you're not sure of the address, contact your network administrator.)

4. In the Call With area, choose Data Only.

5. In the Conferencing area, click Call A Conferencing Service and type the name of the conference.

6. Choose OK. (If you want to cancel the call, choose Cancel.)

18
CHAPTER

Receiving a Call

When a call comes in, you'll hear a ringing sound and you'll see a dialog box asking whether you want to accept the call. Click Accept to accept the call, or click Reject to decline.

You might want to change the default call receiving options. By default, NetMeeting answers calls even when the program isn't running and automatically starts the NetMeeting window.

To choose call receiving options, choose Tools Options and click the General tab. You can choose the following options for call receiving:

🌐 **Show Microsoft NetMeeting Icon On The Taskbar.** This icon enables you to choose call receiving options quickly. If you do not want to be disturbed, you can right-click this icon and choose Do Not Disturb, even if NetMeeting isn't running. (This is the same as choosing Call Do Not Disturb Within NetMeeting.) If you choose this option and later want to receive calls, be sure to choose it again so that the check mark disappears next to Do Not Disturb.

🌐 **Restore The Microsoft NetMeeting Window After Accepting A Call.** With this option enabled, Windows automatically starts NetMeeting when you accept a call.

🌐 **Notify Me Of Calls Even If The Microsoft NetMeeting Window Is Closed.** This option lets you receive calls when NetMeeting isn't running.

🌐 **Automatically Accept Calls When I'm Not In A Conference.** With this option, NetMeeting automatically accepts calls, except when you're in a conference. If you receive a call while you're in a conference, you'll see an alert box asking whether you want to accept the call.

🌐 **Automatically Accept Calls When I'm Participating In A Conference.** With this option, NetMeeting automatically accepts calls when you're in a conference. This is a convenient option, since you might not want to interrupt your conference to manually accept calls.

Starting a Conference

When you start a conference, you don't need to actually place a call. Rather, the people who call you can join or leave, very much as they would in a chat room on Microsoft Comic Chat. You can choose to accept callers automatically or to screen them.

To choose options for accepting calls while in a conference, choose Tools Options and click General. You'll see the General page of the Options dialog box. In the Incoming Calls area, select the automatic call accepting option you want. You can choose to accept calls automatically only when you're not in a conference, or you can choose to accept them automatically when you're in a conference. If you choose neither of these options, NetMeeting will ask you whether you want to accept the call.

To start a conference, choose Call Host Conference. You'll see an information box explaining how conferences work. Click OK to continue. You'll see your personal icon in the connections list. As others call in, you'll see their names on the list, too.

Since conferences do not use audio, you will use the Chat window to communicate with the people in your conference. For more information on the Chat window, see "Using Chat" in the next section.

If you're the host of the conference, you can disconnect someone, if you want. To disconnect a person, right-click the person's name and click Disconnect.

To stop the conference, click Hang Up or choose Call Hang Up. If you're the host of the conference, everyone who's connected will lose their connection.

Using Chat

If you're placing a nonaudio call or if network performance degrades so that you can't understand the audio, you will need to communicate using the Chat window. To open the Chat window, click Chat, choose Tools Chat, or use the Ctrl + T shortcut. You'll see the Chat window, shown in Figure 18-4 on the next page.

CHAPTER 18

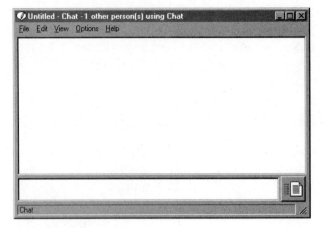

Figure 18-4

The Chat window.

When you open the Chat window in a conference, other participants' Chat windows open too.

The following sections explain what you can do when you're using the Chat window.

Conversing with Chat

Chat works exactly like a text-based Internet Relay Chat (IRC) client: You type a line of text and press Enter. The program then sends what you've typed to other conference participants. In the window, you see a running record of what everyone has typed, as shown in Figure 18-5.

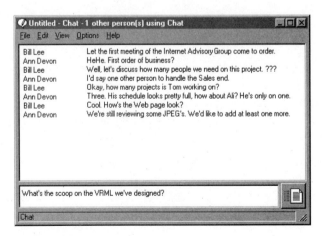

Figure 18-5

A Chat window in action.

As you type a line of text, you'll hear a typewriter sound when you press Enter. You also hear this sound when others type, which is convenient because it lets you know that somebody has contributed another comment.

Choosing the Chat Format

By default, NetMeeting places a person's name at the beginning of each line the person types and wraps lengthy lines so that the line starts next to the person's information. If you choose Options Chat Format, you can change the default display. You can display or hide the person's name, and you can display or hide the time and date in the information automatically inserted with each line of text. You can also choose formatting options: you can put the entire message on one line instead of wrapping the text. If you've selected all the information display options (Name, Date, and Time), you can choose a formatting option that places the information display on the line preceding the text the person types.

Saving, Retrieving, and Printing Chat Files

If you want, you can save a Chat conversation. To save the conversation, choose File Save, type a filename, and click Save.

You can open previously saved conversation for review, or you can open it at the beginning of a conversation you've resumed so that you can continue a running record of what everyone has said. To open the previously saved conversation, choose File Open, locate and select the conversation, and click Open.

To print a conversation, choose File Print, select the print options you want, and click Print.

Exiting Chat

To exit Chat, choose File Exit or just click the close box.

NOTE

If you haven't saved a conversation, you'll see an alert box when you exit the conversation. This alert box asks you whether you want to save the conversation. To save it, click Yes. To abandon the conversation, click No. To return to Chat, click Cancel.

18
CHAPTER

Using the Whiteboard

The Whiteboard provides a shared graphical workspace for generating and sharing ideas. Despite the fact that the Whiteboard appears to resemble the simple Paint accessory, it's surprisingly full-featured, offering multiple pages, a yellow highlighter that you can use to highlight text or graphics, and screen capture capabilities that enable you to take a "snapshot" of a window and show it to others in the conference.

Starting the Whiteboard

To start the Whiteboard, choose Tools Whiteboard or use the Ctrl + W shortcut. You'll see the Whiteboard window, shown in Figure 18-6. After you start the Whiteboard, all other conference participants will also see the Whiteboard on their screens. Collaboration is automatically enabled, so a change made by any participant will be seen by everyone. (To prevent others from making changes, choose Tools Lock Contents or click Lock Contents on the toolbar.)

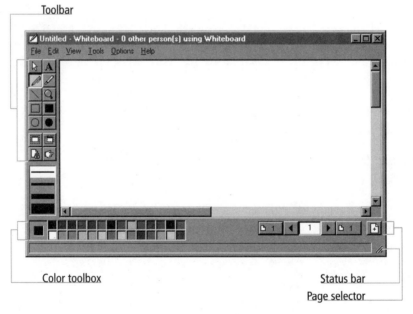

Toolbar

Color toolbox

Status bar

Page selector

Figure 18-6

The Whiteboard window.

Understanding the Whiteboard Window

The Whiteboard window has the usual window features, including the title bar and menu bar. In addition, you'll find the following:

🌐 **Toolbar.** Click here to use the various tools, which are discussed in the following section. To hide or display the toolbar, choose View Toolbar.

🌐 **Color toolbar.** Click here to select a color when you're typing or drawing.

🌐 **Page selector.** These tools are useful when the Whiteboard contains more than one page. For more information on these tools, see "Paging Through the Whiteboard" later in this chapter.

🌐 **Status bar.** The status bar displays the Whiteboard's messages. To hide or display the status bar, choose View Status Bar.

When you're working in the Whiteboard window, you can zoom in for a closer look. To zoom in, choose View Zoom or just click the Zoom tool. To restore the window to the default magnification, choose View Zoom or click Zoom again.

Normally, you see your own pointer in the window. If you would like to enable someone to use a remote pointer in your window, choose Tools Remote Pointer or just click the Remote Pointer on the toolbar.

Using the Tools

On the toolbar, you'll find the tools that enable you to create text and drawings, highlight text or graphics on-screen, and paste windows into the Whiteboard. Here's a quick overview of the tools you can use to add content to the window:

🌐 **Text.** Click here to add text to the Whiteboard. After clicking the tool, click the pointer where you want to start entering text. To change the font, font size, or font effects (strikeout or underline), click Font Options (next to the Color toolbox) or choose Options Font. Make the choices you want in the Font dialog box, and click OK. To change the text color, choose a color from the Color toolbox, or choose Options Colors, click a color in the Color dialog box, and click OK.

🌐 **Draw.** Click here to draw a freehand line. After clicking the tool, drag within the window to draw freehand shapes.

CHAPTER 18

- **Line.** Click here to draw a straight line. After clicking the tool, just drag within the window to draw a straight line and release the mouse button where you want the line to end.

- **Unfilled Rectangle.** Click here to create a rectangle that doesn't have a background color.

- **Filled Rectangle.** Click here to create a rectangle that's automatically filled with the background color currently selected in the color selector.

- **Unfilled Circle.** Click here to create an ellipse that doesn't have a background color.

- **Filled Circle.** Click here to create an ellipse that's automatically filled with the background color currently selected in the color selector.

For each drawing object you create, you can choose a color and line width:

- To change the object's color, choose a color from the color selector, or choose Options Colors, click a color in the Color dialog box, and click OK.

- To change the object's line width, click a line width in the toolbar, or choose Options Line Width and choose a line thickness from the submenu.

Editing Objects

After you enter an object using the text or drawing tools, you can do the following by selecting the object with the Selector tool:

- **Move the object.** Click on the object and drag it to its new position.

- **Delete the object.** Press the Delete key. (To reverse this action, choose Edit Undelete or press Ctrl + Z.)

- **Send the object to the background layer.** Choose Edit Send Back.

- **Bring the object to the foreground layer.** Choose Edit Bring To Front.

Highlighting Objects

A nifty feature of the Whiteboard is the Highlighter. To highlight something within the Whiteboard window, click the Highlighter tool. If necessary, click the yellow color in the color selector.

Pasting a Window into the Whiteboard

You can show conference participants a selected part of your screen or all of another window. You do this by pasting a graphic "snapshot" of the selected screen area or window into the Whiteboard.

NOTE

Unlike a shared application, a window pasted into the Whiteboard isn't live. Conferees won't see any changes you subsequently make in the original window. However, pasting a window into the Whiteboard consumes much less Internet bandwidth. If there is no need to show conferees a running application, use the Whiteboard. For more information on sharing applications, see "Sharing Applications" later in this chapter.

When you paste a window into the Whiteboard, you can select a portion of the screen or you can paste the entire window.

To prepare for pasting the screen area or window, minimize the Whiteboard and arrange the screen so that the material you want to paste is visible. Then restore the Whiteboard.

To paste a portion of the screen into the Whiteboard, click Select Area (or choose Tools Select Area). The Whiteboard disappears, enabling you to select a screen area by dragging. When you release the mouse button, you see your selection within the Whiteboard. To position the selection, click the Selector tool and drag the selection.

To paste a window into the Whiteboard, click Select Window (or choose Tools Select Window). The Whiteboard disappears, enabling you to click the window you want to paste into the Whiteboard. After you click this window, the Whiteboard reappears and you see the window within the Whiteboard. To position the window, click the Selector tool and drag the window.

Paging Through the Whiteboard

You can add more than one page to the Whiteboard using the tools shown in Figure 18-7.

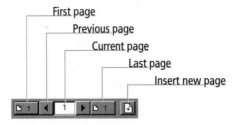

Figure 18-7

The page selector tools of the Whiteboard.

To add a page to the Whiteboard, click Insert New Page. The number in the Last Page box increases to show the total number of pages.

To move to a page, click the Next Page or Previous Page button or type a page number in the Page box. You can go to the beginning page by clicking First Page or to the end page by clicking Last Page.

Sharing Applications

The most advanced feature of NetMeeting is the program's ability to display a shared application on the screens of everyone participating in a conference. Optionally, others in a conference can control the program and work with the data you're displaying.

To share an application, begin by starting it and displaying the information you want to share. If you don't want to permit others to take control of the application, choose Tools Work Alone. To give others the ability to choose commands and alter data, choose Tools Collaborate.

NOTE If you've shared an application, clicking in its window will bring it to the foreground, not only on your computer but on the computers of everyone in your conference.

PART

V

If someone else is sharing a program with you, you can see the program by choosing Tools Collaborate. To take control of the program, double-click the program window. (You can do this only if the person sharing the program has enabled collaboration.)

TIP If the window someone is sharing with you is too large to fit on your screen, Windows will scroll your entire screen to accommodate it. If you prefer to scroll only the window in which the application is displayed, choose Tools Options, click General, and click Scroll Shared Windows Only. To turn off scrolling, click Don't Scroll.

Sending and Receiving Files

One of NetMeeting's most useful features is file transfer, which enables you to send and receive files while you're connected with others. (If more than one person is in a meeting with you, you can send the file to everyone in the meeting or choose the person to whom you'd like to send the file.) The file transfer is efficient (and relatively speedy, depending on the quality of your Net connection). Best of all, the person receiving the file can verify whether it arrived intact and confirm this via audio or the Chat window. For this reason, NetMeeting provides a better way to send files than e-mail attachments (see Chapter 12), which require an exchange of e-mail to verify.

To send a file when you're chatting with one person or to send a file to everyone in the current conference, you can choose Tools Send File or press Ctrl + F. To send a file to just one person in a conference, right-click the person's name and click Send File. You'll see an Open dialog box. Choose the file you want to send, and click Send. NetMeeting then displays a progress indicator that shows how much of the file has been sent. When the file has been received successfully, you'll see a message confirming this.

If you want to receive files from others in a conference, choose Tools Options, click General, and select Receive Files Sent To Me In A Conference. When a file begins to arrive, you'll see a dialog box that enables you to accept or reject the file. If you accept the file, you can save it or open it.

If you would like to change the directory to the one in which NetMeeting saves files, choose Tools Options, click the General tab, and select the directory by clicking the Browse button in the File Transfer area.

CHAPTER 18

Using SpeedDial Shortcuts

You can create a SpeedDial to yourself and give this shortcut to others so that they can call you easily. However, you can do this only if your computer always uses the same Internet address.

The easiest way to create a SpeedDial shortcut is to do so while you're in a conference with someone. To create the SpeedDial shortcut, right-click the person's name in the connections window and choose Add SpeedDial.

To create a SpeedDial when you're not connected with someone, choose Call Create SpeedDial. You'll see the Create SpeedDial dialog box, shown in Figure 18-8.

Figure 18-8
The SpeedDial dialog box.

In the Calling Information area, choose the connection method and type your Internet address, if necessary. In the SpeedDial area, choose Save On The Desktop to save the shortcut on your computer's desktop or choose Send To Mail Recipient to e-mail the shortcut to someone. Choose OK to confirm your choices. If you choose Send To Mail Recipient, Windows will start your e-mail program and place the shortcut in a new, blank message. Otherwise, you'll find the shortcut on your desktop. You can paste this shortcut into a mail message, if you want.

To keep the SpeedDial menu from becoming overloaded with numerous SpeedDial shortcuts, you might want to organize your SpeedDial folder, an operation that closely resembles organizing favorites in Internet Explorer. You can add new folders to the SpeedDial folders and add shortcuts to them.

The folders will appear as menu items on the SpeedDial menu, and the shortcuts will be contained in submenus. In this way, you can conveniently organize your shortcuts so that the menu is easy to use.

To display the SpeedDial folder, choose SpeedDial Open SpeedDial Folder. You'll see the SpeedDial folder, shown in Figure 18-9.

Figure 18-9
The SpeedDial folder.

Before you get started, take a moment to decide how you want to organize your SpeedDial shortcuts. For example, you might want to organize all your shortcuts into two folders called Work Contacts and Friends.

Creating a New SpeedDial Folder

After you decide how to organize your SpeedDial list, you can create any of the needed folders by following these instructions:

1. Open the SpeedDial Folder, if necessary, by choosing SpeedDial Open SpeedDial Folder.

2. Click the New Folder button on the toolbar. You'll see a new folder in the window.

3. Type a name for your new folder.

Organizing Shortcuts Within the SpeedDial Folder

The SpeedDial folder is a standard My Computer folder, so you can use familiar Windows techniques to move shortcuts into folders, rename files, and delete files and folders.

CHAPTER 18

From Here

With this chapter, you've come to the end of the Official Microsoft Internet Explorer Book. If you've learned to use all the tools discussed in this book, you have gone very far beyond the beginner's stage. In fact, you're now familiar with the most advanced Internet toolkit in existence.

What's next for you? Consider becoming an information provider as well as an information consumer. That's the beauty of the Internet: You can give as well as receive. With the knowledge you possess right now, you can contribute to mailing lists, Usenet, chat groups, and NetMeeting conferences. But the next step is learning how to publish your information on the World Wide Web. Thanks to powerful new tools from Microsoft, every bit as impressive as the ones you've already learned, anyone can learn how to create and publish Web documents. And if you'd like to go the distance, you can learn how to use the Microsoft Information Server to transform a Microsoft NT Workstation into a powerful tool for Internet publishing.

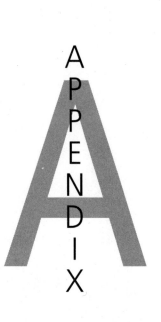

APPENDIX

Installing Internet Explorer and Getting Connected

To use Microsoft Internet Explorer, you need to install the software. If you don't already have an Internet connection, you'll need to get connected to the Internet. You should first install Internet Explorer and the additional programs contained on the companion disc for this book.

This appendix focuses on the Microsoft Windows 95 and Microsoft Windows NT versions of Internet Explorer 3. The companion disc for this book also contains the latest version of Internet Explorer for Windows 3.1 and the Apple Macintosh. For more information on those versions of the program, see Appendix B.

Installing Internet Explorer

To install Internet Explorer, do the following:

1. Insert the companion disc for this book.

2. Choose Start Run. You'll see the Run dialog box.

3. In the Open box, type your CD-ROM's drive letter, followed by a colon and SETUP.EXE. If your CD-ROM is drive D, you type d:setup.exe.

4. Click OK. You'll see a setup wizard that will guide you through the installation process.

Installing VRML Support

To install VRML support, choose Start Run from the Program menu, and locate the file VRMLOCX.EXE on the companion disc for this book. Click OK to install VRML support.

Connecting to the Internet

After you install Internet Explorer, your copy of Windows will include the latest versions of Microsoft's Internet connection utilities. To connect to the Internet, you first must decide which kind of connection method to use (automatic or manual). After you've made this decision, you then run Get On The Internet, which you'll find by choosing Start Programs Accessories Internet Tools. The following sections tell you how to get connected.

NOTE If you already have an Internet connection, you still need to run Get On The Internet in order to configure Internet Explorer properly. Choose Start Programs Accessories Internet Tools, and choose Get On The Internet from the submenu. In the wizard's Setup Options page, choose Current, and click Next until the setup wizard is finished.

Deciding Which Connection Method to Use

You can connect to the Internet via a modem or a local area network (LAN).

🌐 **Connecting via a modem.** If you connect to the Internet via a modem, you'll tie up a telephone line during the time you're connected. If you plan to access the Internet frequently, you might want to have a second telephone line installed so that your original line is available for calls.

🌐 **Connecting via a LAN.** If you're using a computer that's connected to a local area network (LAN), ask your network administrator if it's possible for you to connect to the Internet via the LAN. Connecting via a LAN is much better than connecting via a modem. You're permanently connected to the Internet, and your connection is much faster.

A Quick Guide to Modems

To connect to the Internet via a modem, you must equip your computer with this accessory, which isn't always included as standard equipment. Modems differ according to how they're installed and how fast they can send and receive information.

Some modems, called *internal modems,* are installed by putting a circuit board in one of your computer's expansion slots. The other type of modem is called an *external modem.* An external modem has its own power supply and a case. External modems are less convenient and more costly than internal modems, but they enable you to use the modem with more than one computer.

For Internet use, speed is important. A modem's transmission speed is rated according to the number of bits per second (bps) the modem can transmit or receive. At the minimum, you'll need a 14,400-bps modem. You'll be much happier with a 28,800-bps modem.

Choose a Plug-and-Play modem and let Windows automatically detect, install, and configure the modem. When you're ready to install your modem under Windows 95 or Windows NT, choose Start Settings Control Panel, and double-click Add New Hardware. Use the Add New Hardware wizard to search for new hardware.

329

Choosing a Service Provider

If you connect to the Internet via a modem, you will need a subscription with a service provider or an online service, such as The Microsoft Network (MSN). Each has advantages and disadvantages.

- **Connecting via an online service.** Online services present you with a "home base" that features well-organized, rich content that might not be available on the Internet. Such services include chat rooms on various subjects, the full text of major national newspapers with archive searches, and much more. You can also access the Internet, including the Web, Usenet, e-mail, and all the other services discussed in this book. However, the convenience of an online service comes at a price. Your subscription might give you only a few hours of free use per week. In addition, you can run up additional charges by using premium services. Many people find that they run up bills of $50, $100, or more when they make heavy use of online services. If you want to connect to the Internet by means of MSN, you don't need to read any further: just click the Microsoft Network icon on the desktop, and follow the instructions to sign up. (Note that MSN might not offer Internet access in your area.)

- **Connecting via an Internet service provider.** An Internet service provider (ISP) doesn't give you a "home base" in the way that online services do. They simply enable you to access the Internet, where you can use all the tools discussed in this book. A big advantage of an ISP is low cost. In most areas, you can find an ISP that charges $19.95 per month for unlimited Internet access.

If you decide to connect to the Internet by means of an ISP, you can choose an ISP in two ways:

- **Let Microsoft choose an ISP for you.** This is the easiest way to hook up to the Internet. The only information you need to supply is your telephone and credit card numbers; Microsoft's server does the rest. For more information, see "Getting on the Internet with an Automatic Connection."

⊕ **Choose your own ISP.** To find an ISP in your area, check the yellow pages of your phone book under Computers—Networks. For details on connecting to the Internet with an ISP of your choice, see "Getting on the Internet with a Manual Connection."

Getting on the Internet with an Automatic Connection

The easiest way to connect to the Internet is to let Microsoft's server choose one for you. Keep your credit card handy so that you can supply the number when requested. To get on the Internet with an automatic connection, choose Programs Accessories Internet Tools, and select Get On The Internet from the submenu. When you see the Internet Connection Wizard, click Next and choose Automatic. Windows will connect with a server by means of an 800 number, at no charge to you, and guide you through the process of selecting an Internet service provider for your area.

After you've finished, you can click the icon labeled The Internet on your desktop to connect to the Internet. The connection's automatic.

Getting on the Internet with a Manual Connection

If no automatic connection is available for your area or if you prefer to choose your own Internet service provider, you'll need to call the ISP on the phone and make arrangements for your subscription. Be sure to obtain the following information:

⊕ **Type of connection.** Your ISP must support the PPP protocol.

⊕ **The phone number.** This is the phone number you dial to access your ISP's computer.

⊕ **Your user name.** This is also called *login name*. It's what you type to gain access to your ISP's comptuer.

⊕ **Your password.** You must supply this after your user name to gain access to your ISP's computer.

⊕ **Method of supplying your Internet Protocol (IP) address.** Some ISPs assign this automatically when you log on. Others give you a permanent IP address. Find out which method your ISP uses. If you're assigned a permanent IP address, be sure to write it down.

⊕ **DNS server address.** You need to supply the Internet address of the DNS server and the alternate DNS server. DNS servers translate numerical Internet addresses into the domain names you're familiar with (such as www.microsoft.com).

What you should type to initiate the connection. Usually, this is "ppp," but check with your service provider to make sure.

After you've obtained this information, choose Start Programs Accessories Internet Tools, and select Get On The Internet. Click Next, and then choose Manual. You'll see the Internet Setup Wizard, which will guide you through the process of supplying the needed information.

After Internet Setup Wizard has finished and you've restarted your computer, you can double-click The Internet on your desktop to connect to your Internet service provider. You'll see a connection window. If nothing happens, press Enter. You'll be prompted to supply your user name and password. In addition, you might need to type something to initiate the connection, such as "ppp," and then press Enter. Click the Continue button to complete the connection.

HELP

I can't connect!

Lots can go wrong with a manual connection. Here are some things to check:

Is your modem turned on? If you're using an external modem, make sure you've turned on the power switch.

Is your modem properly installed? If not, make sure you've installed your modem properly. Click Start Programs Settings Control Panel, double-click Add New Hardware, and run the wizard to detect new hardware.

No dial tone? Make sure your modem is properly connected to your telephone line.

Did your ISP reject your logon attempt? You might have typed your user name or password incorrectly. Check with your ISP to make sure.

Getting on the Internet
via a Local Area Network (LAN)

If you're using a computer at work and it's connected to a LAN, ask your network administrator whether you can use the LAN to access the Internet. Not all LANs are connected to the Internet. If your LAN is connected to the Internet, you're in luck. Generally, LAN connections are much faster than modem connections.

To connect to the Internet via a LAN, you need to know whether your organization uses a *proxy server*. A proxy server is a computer program that guards your organization against unauthorized computer access from the outside via the Internet. If your organization has a proxy server, you need to know the proxy server's Internet address.

Choose Start Programs Accessories Internet Tools, and choose Get On The Internet from the submenu. Click Next, and then choose Manual. You'll see the Internet Setup Wizard. In the How To Connect page, click Connect Using My Local Area Network. Click Next and supply your proxy server's address, if needed. When the Internet Setup Wizard is finished, you can double-click The Internet on your desktop to connect to the Internet via your LAN.

APPENDIX B

The Internet
Explorer Family

Microsoft is committed to providing versions of Internet Explorer for all types of computers in common use. Currently, Internet Explorer 3.0 for Microsoft Windows 95 and Internet Explorer for Microsoft Windows NT 3.0 are the most advanced versions of the program; the versions for Macintosh and Microsoft Windows 3.1 systems currently have fewer features. However, Microsoft plans to upgrade both programs to version 3.0 by the end of 1996. At that time, both programs will match the features of the current Windows 95/Windows NT version (3.0). In addition, the company plans a version of Internet Explorer for UNIX systems; this program will also match the features of the Windows 95/Windows NT version. By the end of 1996, users of virtually all popular computers will be able to run a full-featured version of Internet Explorer that is optimized for their computer systems.

	Internet Explorer 3.0 for Microsoft Windows 95 and Microsoft Windows NT	Internet Explorer 2.01 for Macintosh	Internet Explorer 2.01 for Microsoft Windows 3.1
User Interface Features			
Cascading style sheets	Yes	No	No
Content Advisor (Parent's ratings)	Yes	No	No
Customizable home pages	Yes	Yes	Yes
Customizable toolbar	Yes	No	Yes
Drag-and-drop capability	Yes	Yes	No
Frames	Yes	No	Yes
Internet shortcuts	Yes	Yes	Yes
Multilingual support	23 languages	9 languages	20 languages
Tables	Yes	Yes	Yes
TrueType fonts	Yes	Yes	No
Active Content Support			
ActiveX control support	Yes	No	No
Java applet support	Yes	No	No
JavaScript support	Yes	No	No
Java support with Just-In-Time (JIT) compiler	Yes	No	No
Netscape-plug-in compatibility	Yes	Yes	No
Multimedia Support			
GIF animation	Yes	Yes	Yes
Inline AIFF, AU, MIDI, and WAV audio formats	Yes	Yes	Yes
Inline AVI (Windows), QuickTime, and MPEG movies in-line	Yes	QuickTime and AVI	AVI and MPEG
Navigates three-dimensional VRML worlds	Yes	Yes (Power Macintosh only, with QuickDraw 3D add-in)	No

PART

V

Progressive playback of audio/video files	Yes	No	No
Progressive rendering of graphics	Yes	Yes	Yes
Support for native document formats (such as Microsoft Word and Microsoft Excel) within browser	Yes	No	No
Security			
Client authentication with digital certificates	Yes	No	Yes
Code signing with Authenticode (software certificates)	Yes	No	No
Secure connection with SSL and PCT	Yes	SSL only	SSL only
Access to Additional Internet Tools			
Access Internet e-mail through browser	Yes, with Internet Mail or any other e-mail client	Yes (Eudora Light mail program is included with IE2.01)	Yes (with add-on kit)
Access Usenet News through browser	Yes, with Internet News or any other newsreader	Yes	Yes (with add-on kit)
Application sharing	Yes	No	No
Full HTML support in Mail and News	Yes	No	No
Graphical Internet Relay Chat (IRC) client	Yes	No	No
Internet telephony	Yes	No	No
Multipoint communication with shared whiteboard space	Yes	No	No

APPENDIX B

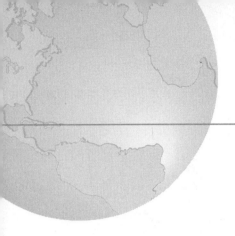

Index

Y

Z

Bryan Pfaffenberger is a leading authority on the World Wide Web and is the author of several bestselling books on the Web, including *Netscape Navigator: Surfing the Web and Exploring the Internet* (AP Professional) and *Mosaic User's Guide* (MIS Press). His books have collectively sold more than half a million copies and have been translated into 10 foreign languages. When he's not explaining how to use the Web, he's a professor in the Division of Technology, Culture, and Communication at the University of Virginia, teaching the history and sociology of technology. His hobbies include backpacking, playing folk guitar, and collecting California wines.

The manuscript for this book was prepared and submitted to Microsoft Press in electronic form. Text files were prepared using Microsoft Word 7.0 for Windows. Pages were composed by Microsoft Press using Adobe PageMaker 6.01 for Windows, with text in Garamond Light and display type in Frutiger Bold. Composed pages were delivered to the printer as electronic prepress files.

Cover Graphic Designer
Greg Erickson

Interior Graphic Designer
Kim Eggleston

Interior Graphic Artists
Travis Beaven, Wen-Jin Ko

Principal Compositors
Barbara Remmele, Barbara Runyan

Indexer
Lynn Armstrong

IMPORTANT—READ CAREFULLY BEFORE OPENING SOFTWARE PACKET(S). By opening the sealed packet(s) containing the software, you indicate your acceptance of the following Microsoft License Agreement.

MICROSOFT LICENSE AGREEMENT
(Book Companion Disks)

This is a legal agreement between you (either an individual or an entity) and Microsoft Corporation. By opening the sealed software packet(s) you are agreeing to be bound by the terms of this agreement. If you do not agree to the terms of this agreement, promptly return the un-opened software packet(s) and any accompanying written materials to the place you obtained them for a full refund.

MICROSOFT SOFTWARE LICENSE

1. GRANT OF LICENSE. Microsoft grants to you the right to use one copy of the Microsoft software program included with this book (the "SOFTWARE") on a single terminal connected to a single computer. The SOFTWARE is in "use" on a computer when it is loaded into the temporary memory (i.e., RAM) or installed into the permanent memory (e.g., hard disk, CD-ROM, or other storage device) of that computer. You may not network the SOFTWARE or otherwise use it on more than one computer or computer terminal at the same time.

2. COPYRIGHT. The SOFTWARE is owned by Microsoft or its suppliers and is protected by United States copyright laws and international treaty provisions. Therefore, you must treat the SOFTWARE like any other copyrighted material (e.g., a book or musical recording) except that you may either (a) make one copy of the SOFTWARE solely for backup or archival purposes, or (b) transfer the SOFTWARE to a single hard disk provided you keep the original solely for backup or archival purposes. You may not copy the written materials accompanying the SOFTWARE.

3. OTHER RESTRICTIONS. You may not rent or lease the SOFTWARE, but you may transfer the SOFTWARE and accompanying written materials on a permanent basis provided you retain no copies and the recipient agrees to the terms of this Agreement. You may not reverse engineer, decompile, or disassemble the SOFTWARE. If the SOFTWARE is an update or has been updated, any transfer must include the most recent update and all prior versions.

4. DUAL MEDIA SOFTWARE. If the SOFTWARE package contains both 3.5" and 5.25" disks, then you may use only the disks appropriate for your single-user computer. You may not use the other disks on another computer or loan, rent, lease, or transfer them to another user except as part of the permanent transfer (as provided above) of all SOFTWARE and written materials.

5. SAMPLE CODE. If the SOFTWARE includes Sample Code, then Microsoft grants you a royalty-free right to reproduce and distribute the sample code of the SOFTWARE provided that you: (a) distribute the sample code only in conjunction with and as a part of your software product; (b) do not use Microsoft's or its authors' names, logos, or trademarks to market your software product; (c) include the copyright notice that appears on the SOFTWARE on your product label and as a part of the sign-on message for your software product; and (d) agree to indemnify, hold harmless, and defend Microsoft and its authors from and against any claims or lawsuits, including attorneys' fees, that arise or result from the use or distribution of your software product.

DISCLAIMER OF WARRANTY

The SOFTWARE (including instructions for its use) is provided "AS IS" WITHOUT WARRANTY OF ANY KIND. MICROSOFT FURTHER DISCLAIMS ALL IMPLIED WARRANTIES INCLUDING WITHOUT LIMITATION ANY IMPLIED WARRANTIES OF MERCHANTABILITY OR OF FITNESS FOR A PARTICULAR PURPOSE. THE ENTIRE RISK ARISING OUT OF THE USE OR PERFORMANCE OF THE SOFTWARE AND DOCUMENTATION REMAINS WITH YOU.

IN NO EVENT SHALL MICROSOFT, ITS AUTHORS, OR ANYONE ELSE INVOLVED IN THE CREATION, PRODUCTION, OR DELIVERY OF THE SOFTWARE BE LIABLE FOR ANY DAMAGES WHATSOEVER (INCLUDING, WITHOUT LIMITATION, DAMAGES FOR LOSS OF BUSINESS PROFITS, BUSINESS INTERRUPTION, LOSS OF BUSINESS INFORMATION, OR OTHER PECUNIARY LOSS) ARISING OUT OF THE USE OF OR INABILITY TO USE THE SOFTWARE OR DOCUMEN-TATION, EVEN IF MICROSOFT HAS BEEN ADVISED OF THE POSSIBILITY OF SUCH DAMAGES. BECAUSE SOME STATES/COUNTRIES DO NOT ALLOW THE EXCLUSION OR LIMITATION OF LIABILITY FOR CONSEQUENTIAL OR INCIDENTAL DAMAGES, THE ABOVE LIMITATION MAY NOT APPLY TO YOU.

U.S. GOVERNMENT RESTRICTED RIGHTS

The SOFTWARE and documentation are provided with RESTRICTED RIGHTS. Use, duplication, or disclosure by the Government is subject to restrictions as set forth in subparagraph (c)(1)(ii) of The Rights in Technical Data and Computer Software clause at DFARS 252.227-7013 or subparagraphs (c)(1) and (2) of the Commercial Computer Software — Restricted Rights 48 CFR 52.227-19, as applicable. Manu-facturer is Microsoft Corporation, One Microsoft Way, Redmond, WA 98052-6399.

If you acquired this product in the United States, this Agreement is governed by the laws of the State of Washington. Should you have any questions concerning this Agreement, or if you desire to contact Microsoft Press for any reason, please write: Microsoft Press, One Microsoft Way, Redmond, WA 98052-6399.

What's on the Companion CD

For Microsoft Windows 95 and Microsoft Windows NT

- Microsoft Internet Explorer version 3.0
- Internet Assistants for:
  - Microsoft Access 95
  - Microsoft Word 95
  - Microsoft Excel 95
  - Microsoft PowerPoint 95
  - Microsoft Schedule+
- Internet Viewers for:
  - Microsoft Word 95
  - Microsoft Excel 95
  - Microsoft PowerPoint 95
- NetMeeting (Windows 95)
- Comic Chat
- Internet Mail and News
- ActiveX Controls
- ActiveX Control Pad
- HTML Layout Control
- Hellbender
- Surfwatch Trail
- TrueType Fonts
- ActiveMovie
- Microsoft Bookshelf Internet Directory

For the Apple Macintosh

- Microsoft Internet Explorer version 2.0.1
- Internet Assistant for Microsoft Word
- Internet Viewer for Microsoft PowerPoint
- Surfwatch Trail
- TrueType Fonts

For Microsoft Windows 3.1

- Microsoft Internet Explorer version 2.1
- Internet Assistant for Microsoft Word 6.0
- Internet Viewer for Microsoft Word 6.0
- Surfwatch Trail
- TrueType Fonts